A
Stroke
of Luck

My Life In The Music Business

William D. (Smitty) Smith

Published by Rick Wilson, Pasadena, California

ISBN: 978-0-6152-3565-3

Forward

William "Smitty" Smith passed away November 28, 1997.
He was born August 30, 1944 in Belleville Virginia. As a
teen he learned to play the piano in Norfolk VA. From
there he migrated to Toronto, Ontario Canada. There he
performed with three bands that were major players in the
Canadian music scene, The Soul Searchers, Grant Smith &
The Power, and Motherlode with whom he shared in a top
ten hit "When I Die".

Next his career took him to Los Angeles where he became
a world renowned studio player and recording artist. He
recorded and performed with Etta James, Bob Dylan,
David Clayton Thomas, Ry Cooder, Bozz Scaggs, The
Pointer Sisters, David Lindley, Brenda Russell, Larry
Carlton, Rita Coolidge, Bill Withers, Linda Ronstadt,
David Foster, Nell Carter and many other world class
artists.

In January 1992 Smitty had a stroke that ended his music
career. The following is an un-edited transcription of a
small mountain of hand written pages that he started
about a year and a half later.

<u>A Stroke of Luck</u>   <u>By William D. Smith</u>

Los Angeles Times
February 1, 1992

<u>POP MUSIC REVIEW</u>

Lending a
Helping Hand
to a Friend

By STEVE HOCHMAN
SPECIAL TO THE TIMES

We're quite used to seeing Jackson Browne, Bonnie Raitt and Graham Nash performing in support of some political or environmental cause. So though the circumstances were unfortunate, it was a nice twist to see them Thursday at the Palace singing to benefit an ailing friend, keyboardist/songwriter William (Smitty) Smith, who is recovering from a stroke he suffered on New Year's Day. A friend in need just seems to be a better inspiration than an issue.

As a musician, Smith, 47, is known both for his conviviality and his command of rock, soul and gospel styles, and has long been a favorite musical partner of such notables as Bob Dylan, Nash, Ry Cooder and David Lindley. As a songwriter he's known for smooth gospel-rooted soul. Both facets were represented Thursday, the former in casual acoustic sets by Lindley, Cooder, Browne and Nash, the latter by more formal turns by pop-soul stalwarts Boz Scaggs, Brenda Russell and Michael McDonald.

Thoughout the show there was a warm feeling of family – literally in such moments as Cooder's 13 year-old son Joachim joining his dad on percussion in the early show's opening set and Lindley's 21 year-old daughter Roseanne impressively belting a blues number with her dad in the second show. Unscheduled guest Raitt joined Browne for two gorgeous songs in the second show.

The warmth extended to the soul portions as well. In a particularly fitting case of what goes around comes around, drummer Dallas Taylor, himself the honoree of a concert two years ago after he had a liver transplant, backed singer Bonnie Sheridan (formerly Bramlett) on a show stopping blues.

Scaggs (looking fit and trim and comeback ready), Russell and McDonald all turned in powerful short sets of their own, backed effectively by a versatile crew, including Toto guitarist Steve Lukather and noted drummers Jeff Porcaro and Jim Keltner.

The only slightly sour note was the absence of Dylan who, though unavailable for this date, had been included in some press releases and advertisments due to a miscommunication.

But that hardly dampened the spirit of the event, which hit it's peak at the end of the first show when Smith was brought on stage in a wheelchair as singer Phil Perry raised the roof with a gospel–fired version of "I Need You", a song Smith co-wrote. Choked with emotion, Smith waved his hand across the musician–strewn stage and said simply, "My friends – give them a hand."

PREFACE

This Book is a compendium of my life (well all of it but
four years) in the Music Business. It tells you the ups and
downs of this business. It shows you how people treat
you differently when you have a disaster. I'm glad I wrote
this book. I wish a book like this was around when I first
started playing music. Maybe my life would have turned
out a little differently. This book is about me, a multi
talented minority person living in North America, and a
lunatic when it came to the business of music. Being that I
was a lunatic about business, it made me a placater and in
the business of music, which made me all the time a
impecunious person. This is not a hate book. On the
contrary, it's done with my own brand of humor that I got
through osmosis from meeting, working and knowing
people like Bob Dylan, Bette Midler, B.B. King,
Bobby King, Carol Dennis, Bill Wyman, Nell Carter, John
Lennon, Bill Elkins, Phil Kaufman, David Lindley, Ry
Cooder, Ringo Starr, Sam and Dave, Jimmy
Weatherspoon, Willie Weeks, Reggie McBride, Richie
Havens, Chuck Berry, Chubby Checker, George Coleman,
Jimmy Smith, Bonnie Raitt, Jackson Browne, Linda
Ronstadt, George Lucas, Chuck Rainey, JoAnn Albert,
Tony Braunagel, Mary Unobsky, Jim Keltner, Lou
Diamond Phillips, Renee Armand, Eddie Beatty, Kenny
Cleveland, Larry Williams, John Lee Hooker, Etta James,
Ricky Lee Jones, U.S. Bonds, Jimmy Soul, Rod Stewart.
My dream one day is to get all these people in one room.
They are some of the sickest people that I've met in this
business. These people look at life with their own kind of
humor. As they go through life I get the feeling they're
saying to themselves, Oh well, I've got to live life anyway,

what the heck, I might as well do it with a smile on my face, and with a sense of humor, that way I can make it through life better. In no way did I write this book out of being bitter. I have too much God in my heart for that. The stuff I wrote about in this book, I've been carrying around with me for about 30 years. I just thought I should put it into words. If this book can get to just one person who is multi talented, who was or is a placater and malcable, I'll be a happy person. Like the guy said in my book, "Talented musicians are a dime a dozen," I hope this book will change that. I wrote this book after putting God in my heart, so there is no malice in my heart. As a matter of fact I'm looking for a solution, that's why I wrote this book, (A peaceful solution that is) If you the reader have any suggestions after reading this book, please write and tell me, your suggestions will be printed in my next book. So please print carefully. My mailing address is P.O. Box 298, North Hollywood California, Zip Code 91603. Thank you very much, God Bless you.

(1)
7/6/93
PREFACE PRAYER by WILLIAM SMITH
Dear God, Bless this book so the readers may understand it even though you're in heaven look down upon me and anoint me with the knowledge that I may see my short comings. Bless me with felicity that I might be amicable. God I don't want to appear acate but please make me a soft person especially in the heart. I mean no disrespect to no one I only want to express my feeling I don't want to adulate on anybody just to try and show you how I feel about living in North America and coming up here. Thank you God for allowing me to do that, Oh and by the

way thank you for letting me live another day. All I can say is I hope you like this book. If you don't, Oh well what can I say but thank you God. Amen.

(2)

7/6/93

Oh well let's see where shall I start. Toronto, January 17, 1964. I arrived in Toronto with a guitar player named Gene Evans and Eric Johnson a drummer. I played organ we were an organ trio. We had just left a lady by the name of Jewell Bryner, a female singer who had a bald head. At that time she was considered different. That was my first road job. I made all of $125 a week that was a lot of money then. Her husband ran numbers, that's something like the lottery. You play it mostly in the black section of town. Gene and Eric had previously played with a group called the Del Nights up in Canada and they had met some women there, the guitar player Gene fell in love with a pretty young girl named Rosie.

(3)

7/6/93

Now Rosie had a girl friend named Helen, they both taught school. Like I previously said before, Gene had fallen in love with her. So he was always trying to convince me to leave Jewell to start a group in Canada. He would tell me that there was no prejudice in Canada, black and white could live together you could walk down the street holding a white girls hand. That it was so different there. So we gave Jewell our 2 week notice. She didn't like it (meaning Jewell), but we went our separate ways. I remember the three of us taking a Greyhound bus from Harrisburg, P.A. to Toronto.

(4)   Going to Toronto
7/6/93

So off we went, the Greyhound's heater broke so we had to ride all the way there without a heater. Boy was I excited. I had talked to Helen on the phone, couldn't wait to meet her, I felt it was apropos to meet her. I met Helen after I had arrived. We were met at the bus station by the club owner of the place in which we were to play. The club owner's name was Norm Pushell, he said that we would be playing from Wednesday to Saturday that we'd be making $125 a week. All we would have to do is play after hours. I said, Oh boy easy job. When we got there none of us had no money to speak of I think Eric had about 10 cents, so we stayed at the singer of the band's house.

(5)

7/6/93

Jack Hardin was his name, he's dead now, God Bless his soul. So when I got there he had a one bedroom Apt. the three of us slept in the bedroom in his bed. He and his wife Florence slept in the living room. I woke about 1:00pm that Wednesday. Me and Gene had a process. I had to get mine fixed so I asked Jack did they have a black barber shop up here, he said, yeah man, so I went to the barber shop. The owner of the barber shop his name was the late Jay Trotman, the other barbers name was Roland Williams and the other barbers name was No Dough.

(6)   Living in Toronto
7/6/93

Now if I wanted my hair to look like a white boy I had to wait my turn. In the barber shop was a guy named Jay Jackson and Eric Mercury we became good friends. We hung out together. Jay was or is a singer, I don't know what he's doing now. Eric's doing a lot of commercials, such as Michael Jordan, Coors, etc. I'm proud of him. They took me under their wing. I went to Jay's house to play cards, met his mother and father. His father and him had a fight, it was just like home.

(7)

7/6/93

Even though Jay's father might have been a little bibulous he was a kind man. He's had a great influence on me. He had an incredible picture collection of all of us at that time. Almost everyday I was there with him, I played cards and listened to music. He told me about the times when he was in the service. Damn it was just as bad for blacks in Canada as it was for blacks in the States. He's dead now, what a man. Then I met Eric's mother, father, sister and brothers. His sister's name is Dorothy, she's a nice lady. His brother, the one I know, knew. His name is Albert, both of them treated me like family.

(8)

7/6/93

Anyway back to the club after I got my hair fixed I came home. There I met Helen, a pretty girl. She talked liked she looked. We spent a long time talking until it was time to go to rehearsal. We went to rehearsal that night the place was the Flamingo Club, the first thing I noticed was they didn't serve alcohol there. I said to Gene how's he going to pay us that kind of money if he doesn't serve alcohol. I said to myself, oh well, so we rehearsed. So that Friday we started to play and we finished at 3:00 in the morning.

(9)
7/6/93

So we all went to Norm, the club owner to get paid (collect our money owed). Then he told us that he didn't do to well at the door. I was so fractious, that I fulminated. I walked out of his office and went to my hotel room, by then we all had got rooms. We told the hotel owner that we had got jobs and we'd pay him when we got paid. Norm told us that he couldn't pay us $125 a week. He could pay us $70 a week. You could take that or you could go home. It's the only place we could stay is in Canada. So we had to stay there. It didn't take much to convince us to stay. Gene was with Rosie, I was with Helen.

(10)
7/6/93

I said to her what else could go wrong. She told me that she had a rheumatic heart condition that she could not have children. I said, oh well we didn't have to worry about having a baby. In those days they didn't have birth control. So we made love, guess what, she got pregnant. We got married. What did I know, a pretty white girl hears a talented black boy from Virginia, the only thing is we never got to know each other as people. We got a divorce. We both started to see other people. Its been some 30 years she's never had another baby. We had a beautiful little girl named Jeanenne.

(11)

7/6/93

Oh well I guess it wasn't meant for us to be together. We stayed together about 2 years. Boy we had a pretty little girl. I traveled a lot, she told me that she didn't like to be alone she had to be with somebody. I guess I didn't like to be alone either. Even though we did that I think she is a smart women. Even then she was never a capricious person, she was right on even then. Today my daughter from her she's a singer, producer, writer, piano player. That is called, it was meant for at the time to get together. Oh what was I saying, the Flamingo Club, to supplement our income for the $70 a week we did other jobs like, High School dances and weddings.

(12)

7/6/93

I did that and got prescriptions filled for Helen and Jeneanne. It was a crazy time then. I was young, messed around, drank, smoked dope. Could nobody tell me nothing, I knew everything. If you did why didn't you ask Norm for money. Why? because I was black and was lucky to be working. It was just as bad in Toronto as it was in the States the only difference in Canada they didn't have no ghetto's. Sometimes I was so tired that I fell asleep on the stage. As far as the Flamingo Club? I worked there for about 6 months. Gene the guitar player had to get a day job to make money. Eric the drummer got married in 1964 and moved to New York City.

(13)

7/6/93

So that left me. I ended up staying there I had no place else to go but back to Virginia, that place was worse than Canada. In spite of the environment I met and played with some great musicians there at the Flamingo Club. Such as Doug Richardson sax, the late great Ronnie Pauks, Billy Blackburn, Carlena Williams singer, etc. Whenever I would walk down the street with Helen, because she was white and I was black, people would stare at us. Not only was I looked at on stage, but off stage too!

(14)

7/6/93

I remember Helen's father was a engineer of some kind, a nice man, he's dead now. He had a bunch of blacks working under him, so I said, he's cool. When we got married, Helen and I thought he would understand, but when we did he got upset. I immediately thought he was prejudice, but he wasn't. He was trying to show us what it would be like for a mixed couple to live in Canada at that time. Sure at the time Helen and I was into each other, but the people in Canada wasn't, you see people don't like anything that is different. We were going against the norm.

(15)

7/6/93

So I played the Flamingo Club until it closed, so I worked around town. Jack Hardin the singer that I used to work with at the Flaming Club had a day job driving a truck and delivering auto parts. He got me a job doing that I was driving a truck, delivering parts during the day and playing music at night. Damn I was tired, then the Billy Martin orchestra came into town. I don't know why he

called it that, it was only 4 pieces. The organist he had, Joe
Johnson, had to leave in a month, so he wanted me to
practice with him. I had to do it with him every night,
except Sundays. A place called the Concord I remember
playing and sleeping at the same time, because I had a day
job. Only in North America can you be talented an be out
of work.

(16)

7/6/93

We just have very little respect for our artists in North
America the only stipulation is that I had to travel. So
with the Billy Martin band which consisted of Johnny
Scott saxophone, and Chris Waller drums, I have to give a
special thanks to Johnny Scott. He taught me a lot about
standards, such as 'I'll Take Romance", the french song
"Ma Vie" and etc. Johnny was a little older than me. He
was in the service in the 50's. He was stationed in
Germany, for I don't know how many years he protected
the U.S. So when it was time for him to come home, he
arrived in Maryland, he walked in a bar an ordered a
drink, they wouldn't serve him.

(17)

7/7/93

The very people he tried to protect in the U.S. wouldn't
serve him. He was so hurt, so he moved to Canada as if
that was any better. When I met him, he drank a lot, but
boy could he play. I guess he was trying to forget about
that incident that happened in the service. He was from
Buffalo. Chris was a drummer with the group. He was
the first black guy that I met who had a savings account.
Then I thought he was crazy, he would save some money

out of his pay every week. Even though it was little money then if you were black you didn't get paid a lot whether you were in the U.S. or Canada. We used to gamble a lot and run women to supplement our income.

(18)

7/7/93

If you could make it in those days, you could make it anywhere. Billy Martin was the leader. I remember he would always wear a suit even when he was driving on the road. He would change his shoes every day. He would always want to rehearse trying to learn the latest songs. Even though it was a lounge act we never made anymore money. We would play a club 2 weeks at a time and when he did make more money he would hire a guitar player by the name of Terry Logan. We gambled a lot, we got to be good buddies, boy could he solo.

(19)

7/7/93

Then when it really got good he would hire a go-go girl, she was white. At first she never spoke to us, then she later told us the reason. Billy the leader was coming on to her, he would tell her she shouldn't talk to us we were prejudice, later her and all of us became good buddies. Then from time to time, he would hire an all black singing trio name the Charmains. The leader of the group was named G.G. She was the first vegetarian that I've ever met. She never wanted to learn how to drive. She said that she would always have somebody to drive her around. She was going to be a star. I wonder did she make it. Good luck. This is a piss poor business for a black person.

(20)

7/7/93

My first wife would visit me from time to time on the road
with our little girl Jeneanne. It was bad for both of us she
didn't like to be alone, I didn't either. I would tell my girls
my wife was coming. It was a bore for her to travel, she
had fallen out of love with me. You see at the time I was
unstable, unreliable, but full of talent. I wasn't ready to
have a baby, I thought I was in love. Helen wasn't in love,
but we had a baby. Soon she would leave I would go back
to what I was doing, my cocky life. She would go back to
doing what she was doing. A crazy time then.

(21)

7/7/93

Finally we got a divorce, that really hurt me. I tried so
hard even though I had a bunch of women and she was
dating a lot of men we tried, but it didn't work. Now
being that the band worked out of Montreal Que. Canada,
we worked a lot in around the Que. Province. I met a lot
of French people they where nice. They were nice people.
I was even invited into some of there homes. Jack, where
are you now. Hello man. I met one girl up there she is
half Black and half Jewish. She lived in Montreal so that
made her French. She spoke it.

(22)

7/7/93

She would work during the day and I would work to 3am
in the morning. We would go for walks in the mornings
after I would get off work. We would go to restaurants
and she'd be singing in the streets. We would go to the

after hours club to hear the great Nelson Simons Trio, he's
a guitar player. What a player. Then we would go back to
my room that is if I didn't have nobody there, you see I
told you I was cocky then. We would arrive at the Esquire
show bar. In the midday on a Monday to setup our
equipment being that it was basically black musicians
playing there. Girls would hang around even when we
where setting up, so I would grab one and go into the
dressing room. Here I go again, I guess that came with the
territory.

(23)

7/7/93

Sex, music, and gambling that's all I knew, as a matter of
fact, I thought that's the only way a person should live.
Especially if you was black, hell that's all you had, then we
would have a week off or play in the Province of Ontario.
Then I would go home. The second thing I would do is to
call Jay Jackson my partner and say Jay! Where can I find
Merc, that's Eric Mercury my other partner. So Jay would
give me his numbers all five or 6 or 7 of them. The three
of us would get together smoke, drink, play cards, no
women. Just at that time have fun, boy we were close. I
did nothing without telling them. Merc and Jay was with
a singing group.

(24)

7/7/93

Jay and his sister Shawn had their own TV show up there
called Music Hop. They were the token blacks up there,
they were a good looking couple, so he and her worked a
lot. Just like me he spent a lot of money he didn't have.
He ended up broke he had to get a day job. Once again if

he was a white boy he wouldn't have to struggle the way he did, because his parents had to struggle and work hard to keep food on the table all that I didn't eat. None of his white colleagues would give him a hand like I said that's the way it is in North America. Eric Mercury got a job working on the train up in Canada. You see you couldn't get anything else at the time. From what I understand somebody busted him he was under age they wanted the job.

(25)

7/7/93

By this time the quitar player that came up to Toronto with me, Gene Evans, started a band. He needed a lead singer, so Merc started singing with him. It was a nice band. I don't know anything else about them except they played a lot. Hell who didn't, that's the only way you could make a little bit of money at the time, for example Billy Martin an all black band, would gross about $600 a week for us. An all white band for that same job would gross about $2000 a week. You see no justice. I don't care where you're at in North America.

(26)

7/7/93

But we would play anyway, we would be glad to get the work. Even though the three of us had to work so hard. We were sociable, and peaceful people. Because that's the only way you could be, if you wasn't you would become misleading. We were determined, nothing I mean nothing was going to bring us down. So, in spite of the way we were humiliated we were going to do it. I don't know what it is North Americans have a way (especially if you're black) of trying to abuse your dignity. Don't they know that that only makes you stronger? Anyway back to Billy Martin. Jay, Merc, and I was so close that we decided to get a group together. So, I gave my two weeks notice with Billy Martin.

(27)

7/7/93

So, I played organ, Bruce Yates played guitar, Eric Johnson played drums, Steve Kennedy played sax, Eric Mercury singer, Jay Jackson singer, Dianne Brooks singer. We knew a lot of gangsters in Toronto (I won't name no names) we played our first job at a club called the Memory Lane off of Younge Street in Toronto. I'll never forget the bouncer was a gangster. I had to get Jeanenne's prescription filled (that's my little girl). I told him I had to do that and he said he could fill it for me. I said my God what are they into. We played there for about a couple of months. Jay left the group to pursue TV shows, Steve Kennedy had a day job, so we didn't travel. Steve was living with Dianne.

(28)

7/7/93

He was the only white guy in the band. I remember we didn't have no work so, I went to an agent and he booked us out of town for a week. Steve got mad at me cause I did that. He said that would interfere with his day job, so I told him we would get another player. Somehow he went, you see he didn't know what it was like to struggle. I met him at a club called The Blue Note. That was a club in Toronto that opened on the weekends. I think he played in the house band there for about 3 years, so he could do that and keep his day job too.

(29)

7/7/93

At the time of me playing at home in Toronto I found out that my first wife was seeing other guys. She found out that I was seeing other women. Like I said before we went our separate ways. Till today we remain associates. Bruce Yates lives in Montreal, he missed it, he wanted to go back there, so he did. So we became a trio for awhile. Even though we played pop music we where considered a R & B band cause we were basically black and we got paid like a black band. Boy did I do some messing around then while I was still married. I met a girl named Stephanie Taylor, a white singer. She did a lot of commercials, she also went to college, she majored in psychology.

(30)

7/7/93

She was a pretty girl, soft spoken. She always ate healthy foods. She would always tell me to dry between my toes, because of her I met her roommate John Peter Bradford, smart guy. He later would become president of a college there I think it was called Rochdale. He convinced the Canadian Government to give him the money to open it. By that time I had met another girl by the name of Carol Shannon, he needed a secretary, I got her work there. John and I was good buddies, Carol had a little boy named Michael he was about five years old. When we wasn't fighting we got along fine, she always thought I ran around. Who me? Eventually we drifted apart. Carol and I (once again personally) had sort of a forlorn life.

(31)

7/7/93

You know I felt like a black buck. A sex machine with talent, from one girl to another. From one band to another, whoever was working. If they could only see the talent and the person, but instead they see the color. The name of the group was called The Soul Searchers. We worked around town. Dianne Brookes did a lot of back up on records, she did commercials, she did her own records, she's so talented. We would hear a commercial and say, "That's Dianne." You could tell her voice, she could sing anything. Now that's another lady that had it rough coming up even though she's shy, quiet, withdrawn.

(32)

7/7/93

Now Toronto in those days, people where able to see through that and hired her. She was not an aggressive person. A pretty lady, I don't know, I think she was the first or one of the first black women to sing backgrounds in Canada. She really is distinctive in her singing. I learned a lot about Jazz and other music from her. She would eventually leave The Soul Searchers because she had so much work and her own records at the time. I didn't play well enough to play on her records, but anyway thanks Dianne for the things I learned from you.

(33)

7/8/93

These are some of Dianne Brooks' credits, Count Basie Band lead singer. Rob McConnellis Boss Brass lead singer. Ann Murray backgrounds on Snowbird, Boz Skags and numerous commercials. Man, she can sing anything. I'm proud to say I recommended her for the Boz Skags job. After she left the group a girl by the name of Maty Gavin replaced her, she could sing but Dianne could sing anything. We worked around town. After about a year, Terry Logan joined us, he was the guitar player that I used to play with in the Billy Martin band. He added depth to the band. We played around Ontario and in New York. We played with people like Tiny Tim, The Doors, The Chambers Bros. This is while Dianne and Terry was with us.

(34)

7/8/93

As you can see when it came down to supporting Dianne Brooks I was no neophyte. Steve Kennedy was and is a talented saxophone player, song writer, and singer. We wrote a lot of songs. The rhythm section ended up playing on Sunday nights at a place called The Penny Farthing. It was in Toronto's Village, we played jazz there. It was there I played long hours into the night. High on LSD, backing up saxophone players learning about jazz. It was there I met Glen McDonnell. He eventually replaced Steve Kennedy with the Soul Searchers. He didn't come in the band till after I separated from Helen. Glen's a good player too. Wherever you're at now Glen I hope you're kicking ass.

(35)

7/8/93

Now lets see, Steve Kennedy, I think he's from a town called Stoville Ont. You see I'm doing this book off of the top of my head. He used to play in a band called the

21

Silhouettes. He use to play in a club called The Blue Note that's where I met him. We went down stairs to the parking lot of The Blue Note to talk. He had a pint of booze with him, you see then he was bibulous. After we talked, we made up our minds that we would play together. I'm glad cause I learned a lot about music from him not only could he play sax, but he could write music and sing. It was a learning experience playing with him even though we argued sometimes. He was another guy that had a lot of girls. Boy what a group.

(36)

7/8/93

Then there was Terry Logan, I think he's from New Orleans, like I said before I met him with The Billy Martin Band. Terry lived in Montreal for awhile, so he spoke good french. That's what I liked about him, he could pick up things fast like one time we get into an argument. He said to me, you think you can play don't you, I said, Yeah. He said I'll show you I'll learn to play that thing, not only did he learn, he started to work as an organ player. He was very quiet but, very smart, he could play, he was very funny, what a character. Then there was Eric Johnson, he's from Norfolk, Virginia USA. We came to Canada together. He was the drummer in the band. Also the leader. You had to be nice to him or you couldn't use the band car. I don't know why they gave the car to me, I didn't have a license.

(37)

7/8/93

He ran that band with an iron hand, if only he could have figured out a way to get us some more money. I use to

enjoy playing with him. We both learned jazz together.
Then there was Eric Mercury he was the singer in the
band. I don't know where he was born. I know he was
from Toronto. He went to school there. He's Canadian,
he's a bright person. Like when I would get into a
argument back then I was a fractious person. I would
fulminate at the turn of a hat. Get mad walk off stage go
home. I would never compromise with no one. Now if
that was Eric Mercury he would reason, compromise. Not
only was he talented, he could reason and compromise
too! I didn't have those qualities then. A great guy, we
were good buddies on and off stage.

(38)

7/8/93

Then there was me, I know where I was born. Belleville,
Virginia. August 30, 1944. I was raised by my mother of
eight kids she did the best she could. Boy was I head
strong did not value money, we had none. We were on
welfare until I left home. I had a lot of talent, but no value.
I would mesmerize people with my talent, but with my
thinking? I was capricious, I was very short tempered, but
I could think fast. I was quick to put others down if they
wasn't like me. That was a stupid way to be. I wasn't
completely developed. The talent part was right on. I
guess that's why I was in the Soul Searchers and knew
such great people as them.

(39)

7/8/93

There you have The Soul Searchers. I remember one time
in November of 1966, we played a club called the Sapphire
club there one night I met a 21 year old girl named

Delores Murry, now here I was this 21 year old cocky
black musician who dated a lot of women, met Delores I
remember cause it was her birthday she was in College at
the time. A country girl from London Ontario. A very
quiet country girl, her girlfriend was taking her out to
celebrate her birthday. So they sent the band each a glass
of champagne up to the stage on my intermission I went to
her table and introduced myself to her. She quietly said
hello. She had been drinking she didn't drink. I noticed
that she had nice legs nice tits she was built just I like
them. But boy was she slow, a country virgin.

(40)

7/8/93

Boy I wanted her bad even though she liked the music I
know I couldn't get to her not only was she slow, and a
virgin she couldn't understand what I was talking about
cause at that time I was a slicker, fast and bull headed.
Bull headed enough to know that if I wanted her I would
have to slow and down take it easy. I tried for a year, we
would go out to her dormitory. I would sit and talk to her
for hours in the band car. After about three months she
would let me kiss her I had never experience nothing ever
like that the more she refused the more I wanted her so
bad, so bad I wanted her that I would stutter.

(41)

7/8/93

I remember we were in a restaurant and I ordered dinner.
The waitress brought the roll and the butter first so
Delores with her nice self was trying to butter my roll for
me the butter went one way the roll the other way she
tried she didn't know what she was doing, boy I laughed I

was high on marijuana I said to my self, "slow girl looks good I'll just get the sex," but did she fool me with her so called slow self. It took me a year to get to her. It's a reason why I'm telling you this story you'll find out later. The Sapphire. I learned a lot about R&B there the first time I took LSD I was working there I met and hung out with a lot of pimps I won't mention their names for I'm not trying to incriminate anybody in this book.

(42)

7/8/93

Boy did I mess with a lot of girls then, all these years I never wanted to admit it to myself I always justified it. It's a wonder I didn't get AIDS I've been checked thank God I don't. So back to The Soul Searchers we played around Ontario Canada, New York, Halifax Nova Scotia by the time we went to Halifax Steve had left the band. Glen McDonald replaced him on sax, Glen was a serious player he loved John Coltrane he would always try and turn me on to him. Me? I didn't understand that kind of stuff it was too progressive mumbo jumbo music I would always say. Then one night in Halifax Glen was playing some John Coltrane music "Giant Steps", that was the name of the song. It hit me all a sudden what he was doing, when I realized what he was doing, Coltrane that is, I cried like a baby.

(43)

7/8/93

I said to myself that's impossible nobody could play like that, that's got to be a machine. Glen assured me that that was Coltrane, every since then 1968 I've been trying to play that song "Giant Steps". I met a great piano player

by the name of David Garfield. Every time I see him I ask
him to play that song for me, to this day July 1993 that
song haunts me. Now because of that song and Coltrane
and Glen McDonald, I listen to people like Art Tatum,
Dizzy Gilipsie, Winton Marsalis, Charlie Parker, Herbie
Hancock, Nelson Simon, Miles Davis, Billy Childs, Ray
Brown, Buddy Rich and etc. Glen thank you so much for
your patience.

(44)

7/8/93

When the Soul Searchers played a club called the Mercury
Club, the band members had a difference in opinion and
went there separate ways. I won't say what, it was so long
ago I don't remember. Lets see Dianne had been long
gone. I think she was with the late great Count Basie. Eric
Mercury left and went to New York, and I got a part time
job backing up go-go girls at a place called the Zanzibar.
Eric Johnson went with another trio, I don't know their
name or I don't remember. Now Steve was already with
Grant Smith after the Soul Searchers broke up and I
couldn't sub no more for Bobby Blackburn at the Zanzibar
because I had ran out of reasons why he should take off
work and let me take his place. So I went to Montreal.
There I met a guy by the name of Willie Love, a French
saxophone player he had a band and they would back up
some female impersonators at a club called the Hawaiian
Lounge.

(45)

7/8/93

It got so crazy in that club that when I saw a girl and guy
walking down the street holding hands that seemed funny

to me because I was so used to seeing guys with guys, girls with girls. I shared a dressing room with a female impersonator don't get me wrong I'm not prejudice against gays a nothing like that but when Delores came to visit me in Montreal I was glad to see her. I remember one the impersonators was the MC. He would ask the audience where are you from, the person would say New York he would say welcome to Canada then he would ask some other person where are you from? They would say I'm from Toronto he or she would say welcome to Canada. The French and the English fought up there like the blacks and the whites in the U.S. fights.

(46)   Living in Montreal
7/8/93

I remember one time I was playing in a little town called Joliett Que. we had just got finished setting up our equipment in the hotel where we were playing so me and the drummer went to the bar to get a drink. I was drinking then. I said hello to the french guy standing next to me he didn't say nothing to me, he looked fractious. I tried to start a conversation with him. Then with him I became worried the more I was worried the more he was capricious. Then he finally left, when he did I ask the bartender what's wrong with him? The bartender told me that he played the same thing that I did. He couldn't get a job at that hotel because he couldn't speak English. Now he was born speaking French, that's a French speaking town. I told the bartender there's going to be some hell up here. It was.

(47)

7/8/93

Not only was I catching hell in the US but in Canada too. Back to the Hawaiian Lounge like I said the only thing that saved my sanity was Delores. While I was living in Montreal we had Mondays off. Glen and another saxophone player pooled their money together and came up with the idea of doing a record on me, good idea. I flew back to Toronto on my day off from that Hawaiian Lounge to record. I thought that was great I got Dianne Brooks to sing backgrounds for me. Everything was going great at my recording session. Steve Kennedy brought with him the drummer from Grant Smith and the Power, Wayne Stone. And also Kenny Marco, the guitar player with Grant Smith and the Power. That was about Sept. of 68.

(48)

7/8/93

Not a bad sounding record you see in those days the recording industry where a little behind the times there where about 5 studios in town then they didn't even have a funky Bass player then such as the great Chuck Rainey, Jamie Jamison the Motown great then so I did ballads. The late Ronnie Parks played on my record he was a jazz saxophone player who played jazz bass. Boy could he play saxophone. He died in '71 I still have his cufflinks. While I was on my break Steve ask me if I wanted to join Grant Smith's band with him I said Hey man I got a record coming out and besides I live in Montreal now how can I do that? He said move back here. So with the help of this organ playing lady (I can't remember her name) I moved back. I don't know why I did that I had a record coming out so I moved to Toronto into a flat with Kenny Marco, Wayne Stones and his girlfriend Pip.

(49)   Living Back in Toronto
7/8/93

Even though I had finished my record, I joined Grant
Smith's band they didn't have no keyboard they had
trumpet Ralph, sax Steve, bari-sax Brian, guitar Kenny,
drum Wayne and me on organ bass. Brian doubled on
bass but when I joined the band he played sax all the time.
He was the co-leader, Grant Smith was the other leader.
Both of them Grant and Brian would stand in front of
Stony the drummer and scream at him and tell him to play
harder that would make him more uptight I would say to
Brian don't holler at him that's wrong. He would say to
me that's the only way he'll learn. On a dare I told him I
could take that same drummer and make a hit record. He
said to me you're crazy Stony can't play that good I told
him that he could play anything if you'll just leave him
alone.

(50)
7/8/93

So myself Kenny Marco the guitar player, Wayne Stone
the drummer, Steve Kennedy sax player got together and
called it the Bang Gang. We sounded good we just had to
get some original material we were playing other groups
songs in other words cover songs. Steve's a good writer I
wasn't good at writing lyrics Steve was and is, it was the
melody I used to fool around with all the time on the
organ then I said Steve can you put some lyrics to it. Steve
said yes, so he did that. So he took that song to Doug
Riley he was the keyboard player he worked with a long
time ago in 64. Doug had moved on to do commercials,
TV shows, Radio shows etc. Dougie was so big at the time

he had a management co. with a guy by the name of Mort
Ross.

(51)

7/8/93

Oh let me put this down before I forget. The girl I was
dating when I was with Billy Martin, she had a roommate
a very bright girl she was very militant, rightly so the way
things where in those days. I admired her so much at 19
she had her own boutique I remember I use to go every
day and tell her about this buddy of mine Eric Mercury. I
use to tell her you've got to meet him you and him are just
alike you are both bright people you'll get along great I
said. I left Billy's band and got the Soul Searchers
together. I got my girlfriend at the time to bring her up as
a result they married they're divorced now, but they are
the best of friends she's the godmother of Eric's baby to his
second marriage.

(52)

7/8/93

Now I'm not saying if it wasn't for me they wouldn't be
friends now that's something he had to work hard at (their
friendship I mean), but if it wasn't for me they would have
never met. You see I believed in the both of them there's a
reason why I mentioned this you'll find out later. Now
where was I, we were talking about the Gang Bang, oh
yeah. Dougie and Mort listened to the song they liked it
before they heard the song they heard the group first they
liked what they heard, so Mort said you guys sound good
I would like to make a record with you guys I heard a
song today by Santana called "You've got to change your

evil ways". I said Mort that's already a hit can I try to write a song? He said can you write?

(53)

7/8/93

I said no but I can try, so the group and I went to a little town in the Province of Ontario called London. Kenny Marco knew a club owner named Nick Peniceko he had a attic over top of his club it had a shower no kitchen it was there I kept playing this melody on the organ then I said Steve can you put some lyrics to this? He said yeah he did the name of the song was When I Die. We stayed in that club (The Image) for one month. I wrote with Steve about 10 songs Nick let us have 70% of the door that worked out to about 60 dollars a week. Whew, glad I was doing a little light amateur pimping. We went back to Toronto and played what we had done for Mort & Doug. They liked it, they put out "When I Die" on Revolver Records that was their label.

(54)

7/8/93

Mort said if we put the record out we would have to change the name Bang Gang to something serious. He said change the name to Motherlode. I said what does that mean. He said a vain of ore. He put out the record, Glen said what about the record that we put out on you. I said I don't know this records better, then I called Brian of Grant Smith and I told him I told you so. Motherlode had a meeting with the late Neil Bogart of Buddah Records. He listened to our record he said "When I Die" is a hit I can put it on my label and play it across the States and make it a hit. Sure enough it was a hit. We never saw a royalty statement from that record. In other words we never got paid.

(55)

7/8/93

That song jumped up the charts about 20 points a week. Mort got real crazy he wanted to take a million dollars insurance on the group. He ask me what do you want to do about the publishing? I said you take care of it. Boy did he ever. I didn't know how to even spell publishing then. Let him take care of it. Dougie wasn't like that. He's an accomplished piano player. I use to sit up at the office and listen to Dougie play all the time. Dougie's very subtle and quiet when he found out what Mort was doing he had the moving company move his furniture out of the office.

(56)

7/8/93

Now Buddha had already paid Mort money for a second record . We went in the studio and made some demos. That record was awful. We had a hit record we would open the show for people like The Association, Janis Joplin, Chicago, and Paul Butterfield. We never had the proper equipment. I remember we would do a show and somebody would say "nice show". Where is your bass player? I played organ bass, it was never loud. We would always have to borrow somebody's organ in the town we was in. If he would have put some money into the sound, we could have lasted and we could have made some money. Steve was drunk, I was high on smoke. We were all unprofessionals.

(57)

7/8/93

We might have been drug addicts, and drunks but we
were not thieves. I don't know, Mort went mad he just
took everything. I was too stupid then to know I was
getting ripped off. For that matter, we all were like that
even through like I said before we played with some great
bands like Paul Butterfield, I met Trevor Lawrence he
wrote "I'm So Excited", Buzzy Fietien, he plays the guitar
for everybody, like Al Jarreau, Olivia Newton John, Stevie
Wonder and so on. Steve Madio he played trumpet. He's
now a session musician and a producer. He played with
everybody. Like I said, I met so many great people. In
our group, Steve would get so frustrated that he would get
so drunk that he would fall out.

(58)

7/8/93

It was so embarrassing, we would get to a city, I would be
high Steve would be drunk , Stoney would throw up all
over the place, Kenny would have an assortment of pills.
We were so unprofessional. We had a hit record, but we
were not cool. Now that I know a little about the business
of music, Mort was pocketing all the money, so with
Motherlode, Kenny was Italian, Stoney & Steve are white,
I felt sort of funny, I was the only black in the group. I felt
sort of funny. The only time I'd played with an all white
group was Grant Smith. So I left the group. I didn't get
along with Steve anyway. At one time, we actually
grappled. That's when it was time to leave.

(59)

7/8/93

That was about Dec. of 1969. Now remember when I had
mentioned Eric Mercury singer with the Soul Searchers?
He went to New York and perused a record contract. He
put out a record album called Electric Black Man.
Produced by Gary Katz. He did a show at a club in
Toronto called The Hawks Nest. He took his date with
him. At that time her name was Pam Grizzle she brought
her sister with her I won't mention her name for fear I'll
get sued. She was a nice looking girl. She said she could
write lyrics. Boy I needed lyrics in my life since I was
going to leave Motherlode and Steve and I were so
successful as writers. I guess I was looking for that Steve
Kennedy.

(60)

7/8/93

We hit it off nice she was nice looking and I thought she
could write. Mort was pressuring me, the record co. was
pressuring him. He had already gotten paid. I was
thinking about writing some songs. I wasn't in with the
white Motherlode anymore. So I called this saxophone
player named Trevor Lawrence with Paul Butterfield and
ask him to join the group. He didn't want to leave New
York. He was doing alot of sessions there. So he
recommended the drummer with Paul Butterfield named
Philip Wilson. So many things were happening at that
time. I don't know were to begin. Lets see....... I left the
white Motherlode to form a band with the black
Motherlode. They consisted of Philip Wilson drums,
Anthony Shinult guitar, Doug Richardson sax, and me.

(61)

7/9/93

I wrote a song with Phylis Gorman. At that time my girlfriend was Stephanie Smith, her roommate. Boy I had so many girlfriends then what's the saying? Young, dumb, full of cum. I even wrote with Pam's sister to try to recapture that feeling I had with Steve Kennedy. But I couldn't get it. The black Motherlode stayed together for about 7 months. In the meantime, the girl that Eric Mercury was dating, had come to Toronto to visit. She got sick. I think it was from exhaustion or something. She went to the hospital everyday to see her. Once again, I think she's a great lady. John T. is a friend of mine. I call him my friend because he's a person I've known for years. When we were little kids. He played keyboards the same as I did. We made a pact that the first one to make it in music would help the other.

(62)

7/9/93

I made it first. So, I went to John T. to come to Toronto his full name is John Thomas Davis. When I was a teenager, I got into trouble alot. When I was little, his mother took me in. I'll never forget it. Thanks Miss Davis. So, John T. came to Toronto with his group which consisted of Jorge Brown Sax, Doug Walker Drums, John T. Davis organ and Jimmy Roberts tenor sax. They came to Toronto around the fall of 1969. I got them a job at the Sapphire Club. I knew the boss there, Moe Stone. Anyway, eventually Jimmy ended up playing with people like Rod Stewart etc.

(63)

7/9/93

Like I said so many things were happening at the time. I don't know where to begin. I remember we had the black

Motherlode. Philip Wilson didn't understand the way
Mort the manager was taking care of business. Phillip
would fulminate at Mort and would berate him until he
finally left. Now in the meantime, I had a great two
bedroom apartment well furnished. The girl or should I
say one of the girls I was seeing was Stephanie Smith's
friend. She was in college studying to become an interior
decorator. So she used my place to start buying what
looked nice (my place) I lived on Woodlawn that was a far
cry from sleeping on Kenny and Stoney's couch on
Madison Ave in a rooming house in Toronto. I still saw
Delores somehow I held on to her. She had great sex, I
didn't understand her though.

(64)

7/9/93

Back to Motherlode. Pam's sister was trying to write some
songs for the group. But, it didn't work. Like I said before
I don't want to say her name for fear of a lawsuit. You see,
she is a vaxatious litigate. Pam is not like that kind of a
human being. At that time around the spring of 1970, I
got a call to pick up my reward. You've sold so many
records, we have to give you a certificate. Huh, funny no
money for the record but plenty of recognition. Anyway, I
was seeing a girl by the name of Carol Shannon. I had
known her for sometime. Boy, there was so many girls.
Now the dinner awards was at the Royal York Hotel in
Toronto.

(65)

7/9/93

Now Carol used to frequent that place alot. The Royal
York. Some with my stupid self. I didn't want to take

Carol I was afraid somebody would recognize her and make me feel cheap. So I asked Pam's sister to go with me. She was a pretty black girl. This made Carol mad. Carol got mad she fulminated with Pam's sister. She got berate. Pam's sister just sat there saying nothing to defend herself. I always thought about that. I was young and up and coming trying to find myself. Back to John T. When he came to Toronto, I gave a party for him. So I invited my two bros. Sammy and Reggie to Toronto.

(66)

7/9/93

I was on my way to the airport to pick them up. I went past Eric Johnson's house to pick him up. I picked up my bros. dropped off Eric, he played me an album by Dick Gregory. It was about food. How it was in the states. The album affected me so much, that I became a vegetarian. I was looking, searching. I knew it was wrong the way I was living. But I didn't know any other way. I was talented, but I didn't have common sense. I got alot of work but I didn't know what to do with the money.

(67)

7/9/93

Me and Pam's sister got real close as buddies. Then after about 3 months, after I knew her, she asked me are we going to have sex? I said I don't want to have this kind of relationship with her. To myself, she was a black girl. She was pretty. I don't know what that had to do with anything, so I did it anyway. I don't know why. I guess I wanted companionship. Carol was really mad. Eventually I thought that was the right thing to do. A friend of hers that did T.V. shows with her told me don't do it. Don't have that kind of relationship with her. She was one of the token blacks in Canada.

(68)

7/9/93

Anytime the Canadians needed somebody black, they would call her. Or when they would need to fill their black agenda, they would call her. I was trying to subcontiously trying to change then. So me and this girl lived together. Even though I had other girls, I couldn't give up that. Boy, was it cold there. I was into so many things in Toronto. This book would look like a dictionary if I were to mention them. I remember David Clayton Thomas. A guy I met in Toronto who had got with a group called Blood, Sweat, and Tears. He wrote a song called "Spinning Wheel". He used to play that song for years as a folk song.

(69)

7/9/93

That song sold millions. He became a star. He moved to San Francisco. I stayed in Toronto and traveled in Canada with the black Motherlode. I would run into the white Motherlode I became good buddies with Stoney's girlfriend. We would talk all of the time. I had a influx of accessories. I like to have people around me. My mother was like that. That's all I know. The things I did wasn't normal. I was always trying to be normal. But I guess it wasn't meant to be. Anyway it was cold one day. I was walking down the street and I saw a sign with a girl in a bikini lying on a beach. The sign said "would you like to be in the sun now?" I said to myself yes.

(70)

7/9/93

So I walked home. All hunched over because it was so
cold. Eric Mercury called me from Memphis. He wanted
me to come to Memphis to play on his record. It was
produced by Steve Cropper. I remember going to the
airport, it was so cold, then when I arrived in Memphis, it
was nice and warm. I said "man, this is for me". Me and
Eric lived in the same motel that Martin Luther King got
shot in. I don't know the name of the place. I ended up
writing with Steve Cropper. I met Mack Rice, the guy
who wrote Mustang Sally. It was nice down there, thanks
Merc. That place convinced me to get out of Toronto. It's
too cold up there. And the music business down here is so
much better.

(71)

7/9/93

So I went back to Toronto. I had brand new furniture.
Like I said before, I had a nice apartment. I told Pam's
sister that I've got to get out of here. It's too cold. I said
were should we go? New Orleans, Florida, or Los
Angeles? We picked straws. Los Angeles came up. So I
put an ad in the Toronto Star selling my furniture. It was
some good stuff. That was about 1971. Doug Riley
answered the ad and bought most of the furniture. He
still has some of it today. I sold the furniture. I did a T.V.
show called Black Hallehluhah. That was a black play, so
naturally, I got the call. I took the furniture money and
the T.V. money and bought a truck. A carpenter by the
name of Dave Nichols decorated my truck for me. He
made the front part livable and the back half for storage
space.

(72)   Moving to L.A.

7/9/93

By this time, I was seeing alot of girls. I was getting phone calls from them from Stoney's girlfriend. They were having confrontations. Anyway, we packed the truck, went to my girl's other house. Pam had a premonition. She said don't you know something's going to happen? I said nothing is going to happen. She said It already did. My sister's pregnant. I said "Oh boy not again" She was married before she met me for 5 years. She or he never used no protection. I was like a rabbit. I looked at a woman, she got pregnant. So I said pay no attention to your sister. You drive first. I'll go to sleep and drive later. So she drove about 85 miles from Toronto with ice on the road. She hit an ice slick.

(73)

7/9/93

When she hit the ice slick, the truck went into the ditch. So we called a tow truck. So the truck people tried to pull my truck out of the ditch. Every time they tried to pull, the truck out of the ditch, it would fall back in the ditch. After about an hour of doing that, the right hand side of the truck was caved in. But you could still drive it. We checked into a motel. She started to cry saying she was sorry. I started to laugh at her and said instead of going to L.A. we'll go to Virginia. Where I was born to see my mother and get the truck fixed okay? Okay she said. So off we went. It was my turn to drive. Boy was it icy. I remember I slipped on a bridge in St. Catherine Ontario. Boy was I lucky.

(74)   Living in Portmouth VA
7/9/93

We arrived in Portsmouth around Jan of 1971. I
introduced my mother to my girlfriend. She was glad
that I didn't get hurt in the wreck. It was just like being a
kid living again at home. I had to sleep in my old room.
They had bunk beds. I slept on top. My girlfriend slept
on the bottom. This wouldn't work. I was 27 years old. I
was set in my ways at least. I was use to having my own
place so, any ways, at least I was use to having my own
place. So we went to the local Chevy dealer in
Portsmouth. The guy took one look at my truck and said
it was nothing he could do about it. He new I would have
to go to the head office in Norfolk. Figured it would take
about two weeks at the most to fix the truck. I said to
myself "oh, oh, I don't have enough money to stay here
that long."

(75)   Living in Norfolk VA
7/9/93

So I went back to my mothers and told her that we had to
get the truck fixed in Norfolk. It wasn't far. So I had to
look for a furnished apt. over there before I put the truck
in the shop. We went to look for an apt. in Norfolk. We
went to one white lady's building and saw a sign outside
her building. It said apt. for rent furnished. So we went to
her door to inquire about the apt. She flat out told us that
she didn't rent to blacks. We heard that enough, so we
finally got a hotel room in VA. Beach. My money was
really getting low. So I ran into a singer, a white guy who
told us he needed an organ player. For that week he was
nice, as long as I kept my place. The whites on one side,

the blacks on the other side. He didn't believe in mixing.
That's how most whites are like in the U.S.

(76)   Living in Virginia Beach
7/9/93

So before we put the truck in, I drove to Norfolk, to a bar
and grill place and ran into an old drummer buddy. I
knew a guy named Leonard Mason. I spoke to him. We
hugged each other. I ask him where the happening place
to go at night man. He told me a place called the African
Lounge. My hero was playing there. I told my girlfriend
he's going to knock your socks off. We got there that
night. He was playing. He was so dated. My girlfriend
looked at me as if I was crazy. I used to listen to him
when I was a teenager. He used to sound great. He was
still playing the same songs the same way. So I went up
there and played. The people really liked what I had
done. I went back to my table. Just then, this guy came to
my table.

(77)
7/9/93

He introduced himself. He said his name was Joe Riley.
He said where are you from? I've never heard anybody
play like you. I told him that I've use to live in Toronto.
And I'm here to introduce my girlfriend to my mother and
also to get my truck fixed and looking for work. While
I'm waiting, my girlfriend's pregnant so with her I have to
be careful. He said where are you living? I told him
Virginia Beach in a motel. He said don't worry I'm
holding the pink slip to Archie's Bar and Grill. You can do
the door on the weekends. I said to myself that's just Boz
talking. He's just bullshitting. No kidding, he called me

three days later and said are you ready? This guy wasn't joking, I told him yeah, I would do it. But, first I made a phone call to David Clayton Thomas.

(78)

7/9/93

Can you believe it? I was staying at a motel in Virginia Beach. I remember when you couldn't walk down that street let alone get a motel room. Pam, my girlfriend's sister wrote me a letter. In it was a funny joke. The white lady at the desk opened my mail and berated me for getting such awful mail using that kind of language. I don't have to tell you that she didn't have no business opening my mail. Oh, I'm black so that makes it all right. Now back to David. Thought I would mention that so after talking to David, he sent me a ticket and told me to fly to San Francisco for a week. He would show me around. I stayed in his guest room. He was with Blood Sweat & Tears. The original group.

(79)

7/9/93

It was a nice party. I met the guys in the band at that party. Steve Katz, Guitar. Jim Fielder, bass, Lewis Soloff, trumpet, Fred Lipseus, sax. It was about guys in the band so we had a jam session. Half of the guys wanted me to play jazz. The other half wanted me to play rock' n roll. That's the way the band was. They had nine leaders. The drummer of the band who originated the band, being that they were successful, wanted to keep the band all white. It's not that he was prejudice or nothing like that. That's the way the band started, and we wouldn't want to upset white America.

(80)

7/9/93

David is a halcyon person. When it comes down to
manners, he's garch. He is more of a fractious person.
Alot at you he'll fulminate. At you he'll berate. A great
singer other than that. When I stayed at his house, when
it was time for him to take me to the airport before we left,
he searched his living room to make sure I didn't take
anything. You see, he knew me as a talented person, but
he didn't know me personally. If he did, he should have
known that I would not have taken anything from his
house. I was so grateful for him sending for me, anyway I
went back to Virginia Beach and I called Joe. His wife
Lucille answered the phone. I told him that I was ready to
play the club.

(81)

7/9/93

So I played at Archies Bar & Grill for about two months.
Eric Johnson on drums, he was having some
confrontations with his wife, so he was there visiting his
parents trying to get his head straight. This white guy by
the name of Ezra,(I can't remember his last name) It was
so long ago. Boy, it was a crazy place. Gangsters would
come in the place and hold up the front part of the bar. By
this time, my girlfriends stomach was sticking out. This
old country guy was trying to put the make on her. He
said "baby, come on out with me". She told him "Okay,
for 250 thousand dollars". He looked at her like she was
crazy. He didn't bother her no more. Some nights, we
would make about $30.00 a piece.

(83)

7/9/93

Being that I got a job working in Norfolk, I moved closer to the job. So, I moved to a motel called The Lafayette Motel. I remember when Eric Johnson was playing drums. His parents, his bros, and his sister were there every weekend. The minute he went back to Canada, I never saw them again. I had known them ever since I was 15 years old. I was 27 then. Just goes to show you blood is thicker than water. Joe and Lucille treated me like family. As long as I live, I'll never forget them. After Eric Johnson left, Frank Wilson a drummer the first drummer that I ever played with U.S. Bonds and Jimmy Soul. So, finally the truck got fixed. But, my pocketbook wasn't. I wanted to go to L.A. real bad. Joe ask me did I have enough money to go. One day I was at his house, he said "look under my sofa".

(84)

7/9/93

I looked under the pillows of his sofa. There was a brown bag. He was down home. It was full of bills, about two thousand dollars. I said "Is this for me?" He said take it. I said you don't know if you will ever see me again. He said yes I will. I was so elated I didn't know what to say. Him and his wife saved my life. I thanked him and her very much. By this time, my girlfriends stomach was big. She couldn't drive out there with me so now we had the money to fly her out there. So she rolled me enough marijuana to drive to L.A.

(85)   Going to L.A.

7/9/93

This was about April of 1971. I headed out for L.A.
Stopped and said good bye to my grandmother in
Belleville VA. And headed on out smoking a joint. Not a
care in the world. I was pulling over on the side of the
road to sleep. I didn't have no radio. They didn't make
cassettes in those days. I remember pulling into Tulsa,
Oklahoma. I pulled into a motel. I spent the night there. I
went to a restaurant had some great food and relaxed. I
said to myself, I think I'll go and catch a movie. Boy, was I
shocked. I saw my first porno movie there. I couldn't
believe it. Some guy was there screaming. I don't know
who put on a better show, the guy or the girl in the movie.
The next day, I headed out I was groovin' along and I hit a
deer. I didn't kill him thank God.

(86)

7/9/93

Finally, at last eureka. I made it to LA. I was there once,
that was when I was with the white Motherlode. "When I
Die" was on the charts and climbing. I was drafted so
Mort sent me to L.A. to beat the draft. I saw two doctors.
One was a therapist, the other one was a GP. The
therapist put down that I was gay. The GP put down that
I had high blood pressure and flat feet. That kept me out
of the service. Anyway, I went to a buddy of mines house.
His name is Donnie Troiano. Donnie's group was in L.A.
He was from Toronto, I sang backgrounds on his group's
record The Mandela. Before that, they were called the
Rougres. Their name was changed again to Bush. Whity
Glen on drums, Precash (Elephant Boy) John on bass, the
late Huey Sullivan on keyboard, Donnie Troiano on
Guitar.

(87)   Living in L.A.
7/9/93

So, Donnie took me in. We hit it off good. Him and his girlfriend Donna Talbert was nice to me. I met alot of people through Donnie. I stayed at his house for about three days. We wrote some songs while I was there. We wrote three songs. All I can remember is one of them "What you can't see won't hurt you". Donnie really opened up his house to me. Philip Wilson was in town. He's the drummer that used to be in the black Motherlode. But, he lived in San Francisco, so I went up there, me and my girlfriend. I stayed there for about a month. I tried to contact David Clayton Thomas. He was never home. By then, my money was running low. We were in a motel called The Village Motel in Marin County. Donnie Troiano was living in an apartment on Sycamore Avenue in Hollywood.

(88)

7/9/93

So I went back to San Francisco. The only thing I had going for me was rehearsing with a guy by the name of Bobby Trotter. He was a pimp. Had alot of money. He wanted to sing. But, never worked hard at it. How can you be a singer and pimp two women at the same time? So, I went back to L.A. I had just enough money to get us an apartment. So, we got an apartment where Donnie lived. In his building where he was renting then. Donnie started to show me around. Donnie was a workaholic. When we got an apartment, we had very little money left. So, we got on welfare. It was then I was standing in the welfare line when I saw Mongo Santa Maria's drummer applying for welfare. Only in America do we not take

care of our artists. Anyway, I was on Hollywood
Boulevard. Ronald Regan was governor then. An elderly
lady made a wrong turn.

(89)

7/9/93

The cops pulled her over. He cuffed her and searched her
all because she made an illegal turn. The land of the free?
Anyway, Donnie introduced me to the girl Tessie Cohen.
She could play congas, sing, make shoes, sew a rug, do
everything. She introduced me to her then boyfriend
Jorge Calderone. She had a little girl about eight months
old named Qually. I think that's how you spell it.
Anyway, we hit it off great. They lived in Laurel Canyon,
next door to Danny Kortchmar and Joel Obrian. Oh, Jorge
played bass guitar, sang and wrote songs. Me and him
started to jam. It was nice of him and Tessie. We were
playing locally, not only was I introduced to Kotch and
Joel, but I ended up playing with Jorge and Tessie.

(90)

7/9/93

Like I said before, thanks to Donnie, I met Jorge. We
became very close. Through Jorge, I met Danny
Kortchmar. He played guitar for James Taylor. That's
when Russ Kunkel played with James. Lee Sklar played
bass. Now I played with Kotch in those days alot. He got
me on a lot of sessions. Through Kotch, I met a producer
named Robert Appere. He worked out of a studio named
Clover. That's in Hollywood. Kotch and Joel also played
Carol King's "Tapestry". Lets see, I don't know where to
start. Through Kotch, I did a session. Through Joel
Obrian I met Jackie Deshannon. Then I got an apartment

in Laurel Canyon down the road from Kotch and Joel and his ex-wife Connie. I took the money I made with the Rob Foster Agency. I had made 16 hundred dollars a day with him, thanks Donnie. He turned me on to that job. Joel and I got to be good buddies.

(91)

7/9/93

Through Joel I got to play with Jackie Deshannon. I played organ, Randy Ellerman played piano, then her boyfriend. Boy, I was moving on up. I've left out a lot of stuff. It is so much stuff that this book would be as big as a dictionary. So, I put my bio. in another book called Friends of a Stroke Victim. I got to know Randy professionally. Well one day, I think it was Valentines Day 1972, me, Kotch, Joel Eviesands, the Brecker Bros. was at my house or my apartment jamming. David Clayton Thomas came up and convinced us that we should have the jam session at his house, then he asked me if I would put a band together for him. He was leaving Blood, Sweat & Tears.

(92)

7/9/93

I told him I wanted to do my thing. He said you could man. Write with me, I'm a star. Give me your publishing you'll be big too. Here's $1500 dollars that's alot of money, at least it was in those days. I said to myself, I'll do this one record with David, after that I'll pursue my own career. The song I wrote with David, "Yesterday's Music" had a duet on the chorus. I sang it with him when we did the Carson Show, on the Henry Mancini Show, Mike Douglas, Dick Cavette's Show, etc. They split the

T.V. screen. You could see the both of us. That not only made me popular on T.V. but also popular in the music world. You wouldn't believe the calls I got from producers, singers, etc.

(93)
7/9/93
White guys especially white producers were calling me. They figured I was a cool black guy to play with. A big guy like that he must be a black Canadian. He can't be from the states. Boy, what a prejudice place to live. I tried to tell people that I was from Virginia. Anyway, through Jorge, I met the great Kenny Rankin. I said to myself, this must be luck. I'm not this good. The money was coming in so fast, that I just kept putting off my thing. That's when I started to do cocaine. I was a vegetarian but I did alot of coke. When I met Kenny, he had a nice version of Penny Lane by the Beatles. We hit it off good thanks to Jorge. I did some coke and wrote with Kenny. Not that his music was awful or nothing like that. I was trying to forget what I was supposed to do.

(94)   In Route to L.A.
7/11/93
Hold it, wait a minute. This is getting complex, this period. I didn't do no research. This is all from memory. Let's start again. I left Toronto and arrived in L.A. Stayed with Donnie Troiano for 3 days. Went and moved to Marin County for one month. Money was getting low so me and my girlfriend moved to L.A. in April of 1971. We got an apartment in the same building as Donnie. I drove him around alot in those days. He didn't drive. By doing this he introduced me to alot of people. Jorge Calderone,

bass player, Keith Olsen, producer and engineer David Foster, writer, keyboard player, producer and now very successful. And alot more people. Me and my girlfriend at the time had no money so we got on welfare. Then Donnie, Whity, Precash and me did a recording session with David Clayton Thomas. Because of Donnie, I got alot of work. It enabled me and my girlfriend to move out of that place in Hollywood.

(95)   Living in L.A.
7/11/93
So we moved to Laurel Canyon, down the street from Jorge and Tessie his girl. That was September of 1971. Jorge liked the way I played so not only did I play in Jorge and Tessies band, but he introduced me to Danny Kortchman. Then, he was with James Taylor. We hit it off good because of Danny. I met his roommate Joel O'Brien who played drums for Jackie DeShannon and Carol King. I said to myself, oh boy I'll play my songs and play for them. They really like me. They liked me so much that Jackie offered me a job. Well I said to myself, I can't do that. I can't sight read. No problem. She said there's no sight reading on the job. So I talked to my girlfriend. She said you know you got a baby coming. We need all the money. I said to her trust me, we'll get the money. We already have, Jackie made you an offer. So I smoked some marijuana and said just this one time.

(96)

7/11/93
So off to the road I went working with Jackie. Writing on the side, putting my career off till tomorrow. Even though I was fractious when I smoked marijuana, towards people

it made made me gregarious. You see, in those days, I
smoked alot to forget about my feelings. Then, there was
Danny Kortchmar. He liked my talent so much, he
introduced me to an engineer/producer named Robert
Appere. Robert hired me alot. I was on a roll making
money, spending it as fast as I made it. Me buy a house?
Have a savings account? That might interfere with my
drug money. I could never do that. Drugs came first.
That made me forget why I really came to L.A. To pursue
my own career. Lets see, back to Jorge. Boy, could he
play guitar and write. Through him I met Kenny Rankin
about February of 1972.

(97)

7/11/93

Like I said before, I loved his version of Penny Lane and
Black Bird. He was pretty big then. Once again he liked
my talent. I played for him my songs. I sang them for
him. He liked them so much that he offered me a job
playing and writing with him. I told my girlfriend about
it. She said take it. But I said once again I wanted to do
my own thing. When I came here I had made a hit record.
She said that was then. We spent that money. If you can
work with Kenny why don't you do it now. Some people
would die to get that job. And besides, we need the
money, the baby is coming and the money you made from
Jackie was spent on drugs. I said, okay one more, so I lit
up some marijuana and smoked it and said okay.

(98)

7/11/93

So I went on the road with Kenny and wrote a song with
him called "Lost up in Love with You" which Carmen

McRae recorded. She did a nice job. Wish I could have recorded it. Who you? Who do you think you are? Don't even dream about it? You're not in that class as her boy. I know but, I wrote a hit record before. I couldn't even try in those days. I had great talent. But, I was beginning to feel comfortable behind people as long as I could have my drugs that was all the time. Unlike Eric Mercury and David C. Thomas and Donnie Troiano, I didn't even try. You see, I could play piano well enough to back up people. And why not? The money was good, the drugs were good. I had enough money to buy drugs and to support a pregnant girlfriend. I'm not hurtin nobody. I'll work on my career tomorrow.

(99)

7/11/93

Around February after I had just met Kenny Rankin, we met Kotch, Joel O'Brian, Charlie Larky bass player, Carol Kings husband Eviesands, the Brecker Bros. We were jamming at my little small place up in Laurel Canyon when David C. Thomas came to my house and moved the session to his place. You see, he lived in Brentwood. What can I say his place was bigger, better, so we went there. We jammed. He liked that. He made me an offer. He said could I get a band together for him? I could write with him. He said he would keep all the publishing because his name was bigger than mine. I thought about that. Once again, I talked to my girlfriend about it. She said why don't you take it? We've spent the Kenny Rankin money on drugs. We have no more money. But I want to do my own thing. She said you can do that when you finish working with David.

(100)

7/11/93

Once again, off to the road. I went playing making a
record with David writing the songs. The great Mike Post
was producing us. I said to my girlfriend, this is it. The
album will hit. It didn't so I said to her now I can do my
thing. David was talented but with people and his
personality, he was an invidious person. Then about the
spring of 72, Eric Mercury moved to L.A. Boy, alot of
Canadians heh? His wife stayed at my house while he
was moving down to L.A. Then he said why don't we get
together and write? I said to myself at last I found
somebody like Steve Kennedy. We'll write and I'll record
the songs. The name of our first song was "What's Usual
Ain't Natural". I said Wow, good song. I'm going to see if
I can get a record deal Why should you do that. He said
Sam Russell wants to record it. He produced Jackie
DeShannon's "Put a little love in your heart". Okay I said.

(101)

7/13/93

He's got the record deal. The next song we write I said,
I'll use that so I can get a record deal. So I smoked a joint
and justified it. In the meantime I had my first argument
with Eric Mercury. I couldn't believe it, me arguing with
Eric Mercury. I think the problem was I wasn't a calm
person like he was, talented as he is. He is just that talent.
He has a halcyon attitude which I didn't have. So I didn't
speak to him for a while. Back to David C. Thomas. I got
a band together for him around the spring of 1972. It
consisted of Chuck Rainy bass, Kenneth "spider" Rice
drums, Danny Kortchmar guitar, Tessie Cohen
percussion, Chuck Rainy got real busy, so he left the band.

Willie Weeks replaced him. Danny had to go back with
James Taylor. After the record session Kenny Marco of
Motherlode replaced him. I was in 7th heaven when I was
playing with those guys. I didn't have a worry in the
world. I smoked about 15 joints a day no problem.

(102)

7/13/93

With all that work, I was doing , I needed a vacation. So I
took a vacation for one week. I left my girlfriend at home.
Why should I take her after all I couldn't run around and
besides she would just be in the way. So when David's
record was finished, it was about July of 1972. Remember
now, I was working with Eric Mercury, Jackie DeShannon,
David C. Thomas. Doing alot of sessions. I went to
Toronto for my vacation. There I saw my old girlfriend
Delores Murry. I found her we met at my hotel room.
Boy, I was glad to see her. We were getting ready to have
sex just after foreplay. She said no. You have a girlfriend
and she's pregnant with your child. She'd changed her
mind, she kissed me good bye. Boy, for years that bugged
me. I liked that one. Oh well, so back to L.A. and went
on the road with David C. Thomas. We went to Brazil in
September of 1972. Me and Kenny had a guide. He had
some marijuana we asked him for some. He kept putting
us off. So when we went to his house for dinner, we asked
again. Finally he said okay but the Marijuana I have

(103)

7/13/93

is no good, he said. He apologized for the smoke. But he
gave it to us. The stuff was so potent it almost knocked
me out. I've never had anything that strong. Boy was it

good. We were there for a songwriters recital where
David and I won first place. They hated Americans there.
First prize was $17,000. David finally paid me in February
of next year. I remember I had to carry him on my back.
To this day, he has the trophy and has never mentioned it
since. Oh yea, in the fall of 1972, after my return from
Brazil I had met someone (I don't want to mention his
name). He wanted me to produce him and said he would
pay me half of the money and the other half in marijuana.
I said yeah oh yeah. I remember I had so much smoke in
those days that's when the stereo guy was installing my
speakers in my house. I had speakers in every room in my
house. He had to crawl through the crawl space in the
attic. While he was up there, he found a 1 lb. bag of
smoke. I didn't even know I had it.

(104)

7/13/93

I forgot I even had it. I had a glaze on my face all the time.
Boy was I on a roll in those days playing keyboards on the
road, doing recording sessions, singing on records. As
fast as the money was coming, it was going out. You see, I
didn't know any better. It was like the late Jackie Gleason.
He had a triple bypass. He said the doctor said he would
be great so why shouldn't I smoke. That's the way I felt. I
was in good health. Nothings going to happen to me.
Why should I save, I'm talented. If I run out of money I'd
just go out and get some more. No problem. Let's see,
around that time, Danny Kortchmar and I were jamming
at this place called Clover Recording Studio around
October of 1972. With people like John Lennon, Ringo
Starr, and etc. Robert Appere was the engineer. Then this

"has been" approached him to produce him named Neil
Sedaka. He was on Elton John's label.

(104)

7/13/93

I remember Robert calling me, Russ Kunkel, Lee Sklar, Jim
Horn, Danny Kortchmar to do the session. I said Robert,
this needs some backgrounds. Robert said he does his
own backgrounds. I said, he needs a change and besides I
got this friend of mine from Canada, she's great. He said,
I don't want to meet new chicks. He was kind of fractious.
So I did some coke, and I convinced him to call her. Her
ex-husband married one of Charlie's Angels. So finally, I
convinced him to call her. Neil started to play the song. I
said, Neil you need backgrounds on the chorus, so he said
go ahead. The name of the song was "Laughter in the
Rain". Being that I was the leader, I made more money
than anybody else. I made $400 for the record. Neil made
about $2 million. I didn't even receive a gold record. That
record sold about 5 million copies. Oh well, I could smoke
a joint and everything would be all right. No, 3 joints.

(105)

7/13/93

Let's see what else happened around that time. My
girlfriend had a little girl named Sala Smith on November
27, 1972. My girlfriend was going to have an abortion, but
Carol King convinced her that she should have it. We
already had one baby. We couldn't have any more. That
might interfere with our drug habit. Boy, am I glad we
had the baby. Now she's having a baby. Oh yeah, around
December of 1972, Eric Mercury was on Stax Records. He
wanted to go to the Astrodome in Texas to record on the

Marharishi Program. He got Stax a black record co. to get
him a 45 piece group band with strings, horn section,
singers and chartered a plane to take us there to record.
Once again, we argued. I talked to him about it. He said it
was his show. I know I said, half of it was my music.

(106)

7/13/93

But, like he said, it was his show. The guy he hired to
arrange couldn't arrange all that well. He was a good
saxophone player. I said, why don't you let me get David
Foster. That was before he was a millionaire, or David
Paich, I knew those guys then. He said no. I grew up with
this guy. I said you're going to do him more harm than
good. All those great people you have in your band such
as David Palmer, used to sing with Steely Dan on "I don't
want to do your dirty work". Charles Veal, violin player,
Janice Gower, violin player, just to name a few. Anyway,
this guy is now playing in the street once again. We had
an argument, you see I take the music seriously, especially
when half of the music is mine. Let's see what else
sometime that fall or early that winter, I went on the road
with Jackie DeShannon. I played organ with her. Randy
Elderman played piano with her. He got a call from
Michael Stewart to do a record session. He had to go to
Las Vegas to do some arrangements for Jim Neighbors.

(107)

7/13/93

So, he , Randy, sent me in his place. Among other things
Randy does the music for McGiver. So, I did a session for
Mike Stewart the group was from San Francisco. Joy of
Cooking. I remember the name of the song "You're gonna

reap what you sow". Mike and I hit it off fine. He was a staff producer for Columbia Records. I remember with him working for Billy Joel. Billy use to rehearse at my house. Boy that was a long time ago. When I worked with Mike, I worked with people like Kenny Rankin, Bill Chaplin, Jackie DeShannon, Alan Rich's son, I can't think of his name, Tom Jones, and etc. Like I said this is all from memory. I didn't write nothing down, this is what I could remember. In those days, I worked with alot of white people. Then, even though whites wanted to work with some blacks, (well some whites) blacks were too bitter then. Hostile. The Watts riots was still simmering. I had just arrived from Canada and they saw me with David C. Thomas on T.V. alot. So, I must have been cool.

(108)

7/13/93

So I had this influx of work coming in. You had alot of whites who wanted that black sound. So, instead of getting blacks to get that sound, they would get a white guy that sounded black, cause blacks in those days were too bitter. Rightly so, there was so much prejudice going on that blacks weren't going to take it no more. So much as the good whites understood the blacks position, business must go on. That's where I come in. I had missed all of the race riots and being that, they saw me with a white boy I must have been all right. As a result I worked alot. The more I worked the more drugs I did. And being that I did alot of drugs, to hide my feelings I had to work alot cause like I said, I didn't save nothing. I remember when I was working with Mike Stewart. He would save his money. I would buy drugs. Why did he want to do that? There's plenty of work. He use to to tell

59

me that he was saving for a rainy day. I use to tell him
what rainy day? It never rains in California. Nothing can
happen to me. Why do I have to save?

(109)

7/14/93

Oops, I forgot before I came to L.A. December of 1970, Eric
Mercury flew me to Memphis to play on his album. I was
in Toronto then. There I played on his album. Met Mack
Rice, the writer of Mustang Sally who wrote a song for
Eric Mercury's album with the great Steve Cropper. I met
Al Jackson the drummer on Green Onions. In about April
of 1971, Cropper came to Los Angeles to put backgrounds
on Eric's Album. Steve was the producer, so Steve called
me in to sing on the album. It was then I met the
legendary Claudia Lenear. She at one time was one of the
Ike Ette's. The Rolling Stones, they wrote a song about her
called Brown Sugar. Man, what a knockout, what a sight
to see. She never knew it, but I wanted her so bad. She
knew people like Mick Jagger, she used to sing with Joe
Cocker. She knew the Beatles. I said to myself what
chance do I have so

(110)

7/14/93

I never said anything to her about my feelings that is. My
girlfriend would get crazy when she would come around.
She would never say anything when I was with Jackie De
Shannon or Linda Ronstadt, but when Claudia would
come around, she would go nuts. I used to follow her
around (Claudia that is) like a little puppy. To this day,
Claudia never knew how I felt. If she reads this book,
wherever she is now, she'll know how I use to feel.

Anyway, we got to be good buddies about 1 year later.
About April of 1972, after I came back with Jackie off of
the road, I played on Claudia Lennear's album. It was
there I met the famous Jim Keltner. He was drummer on
the session. That boy has played with everybody. I
remember being so nervous on that session that I had to
do some coke. It didn't take much for me to do that. I
can't remember when I started doing cocaine. All I know
it was a way for me to escape.

(111)

7/14/93

You see, my mother was bilulous. So that was the only
way I knew I could escape. God bless her soul. She's
dead now. That is why I never extended myself alot to
make up for things I didn't have as a child. Sure, I wanted
to do my thing, but I was having such a good time
escaping that I didn't have time to think about my thing.
All the people I was meeting such as Jim Keltner, Jackie
DeShannon, Dionne Warwick, she sat in with us one time.
Jackie's show. Dionne sang "What the World needs now".
I played with the great Jim Horn with Neil Sadaka on
"Laughter in the rain". Like I said before, anytime I felt
down I would do drugs. They would make me halcyon.
Boy in those days I was on a roll. In September of 1972 I
met David Foster. He just arrived from Vancouver with
his group called Sky Lark. They were in the studio doing
their album. His ex-wife would call and ask me for advice
all the time. I gladly gave my service. They put out a
single it was called "Wild Flower".

(112)

7/14/93

I remember doing the second album with them, I think the song was called "One more mountain to climb" written by Neil Sadaka. I wonder what happened to that album. Anyway, since then, David has gone on to become a millionaire. He's done everything. I see his name all over the place. Good Luck David. Oh yeah, that was about the time I met John Lennon. It was at Clover Recording in September of 1972. I used to jam alot with him. The studio is in Hollywood. That was a whole different level. He used to hang out alot with Harry Nilsson. Boy could they party. Let's see. Me and my girl were living in little apartment in Laurel Canyon in Hollywood. We needed a bigger place, so we moved in September of 1972 to North Hollywood, to a one bedroom house. I had money that week. Some money left over from my drugs so there we moved. My girlfriend had our second baby Sala. Like I said, before, thanks to Carol King, my girlfriend didn't have an abortion. Thanks, Carol I don't know how I came to my senses then.

(113)

7/14/93

We moved to North Hollywood. We rented a house. I wouldn't dare to buy a house that might interfere with my drug money. We decorated that house really well. The sessions were going well then. I was singing with Della Resse, Connie Stevens, backgrounds, jamming at Clover Studios with people like John Lennon, Ringo Starr, Bobby Keys, the jam sessions got too big for Clover. That was a little studio. So, we moved the jam session to The Record Plant on 3rd Street in Hollywood. Boy, that place was big. People like Mick Jagger, Billy Preston, Danny Kortchmar who is now producing Bon Jovi. All the English groups.

We called it the Jim Keltner Fan Club. We used to get
together every Sunday night. I remember one Sunday
night I couldn't make it so I asked David Foster if he
would take my place. There was so many drugs there.
David didn't do that. He was straight. All he did was
cigarettes then. Anyway, he went there and played. They
liked him so much, that him Paul Stallworth bass, Danny
Korchtmar guitar,

(114)

7/14/93

Jim Keltner drums. They formed a group. It was called
Attitudes. You see, in those days, there was so much
going in don't want to mention about nobody's personal
life. Just want to tell you what happened musically. I
don't want to get like those god awful tabloids. If I have
something negative to say about somebody, I won't
mention their names. The reason why I talk about drugs
so much is because in those days, there was so much of
that stuff going around. Everytime I played, I was high.
We were settled in our house and my girlfriend said to
me" Why don't you save some of that money? What
you're doing is not right. If I was making that kind of
money I would do that. I said "You go out and do that".
So, she did that. She and two other girls went out and did
sessions. She worked for people like Mack Davis, Al
Wilson, Jose Felisiano, Bobby Womack. She didn't have
no ear for music. But, she was smart and pretty. She got
the other girls to show her her part.

(115)

7/14/93

Finally, one of the girls said she didn't want to work with her anymore. You see, she was pretty and all that. She was smart, but she didn't have a feel for music. Alot of people like lawyers, accountants, record execs, try to do it (music that is). But, it never works. They know the business but they don't have the feel. That's what happened to her in Toronto. She got alot of work there. Here, the business was bigger. There were bigger thieves up there. There was alot of small token blacks here. There were alot of token blacks, she was just one of many. I guess she wanted to do that cause I worked so much and most of the time I was impecunious even though I had a feel for what I was doing. You could never take that away from me. Boy, if I had her smarts, I would be well off. Back to David C. Thomas. I did alot of records with him. It was the fall of 1972 I believe. It was about how David, being that I was the leader of the band in those days,

(116)
7/14/93
David wanted the horns transcribed from the original Blood, Sweat & Tears album, such as Spinning Wheel etc. I didn't know how to do that, so I had this great idea. By this time Trevor and his then wife Linda, daughter of the famed Ira Tucker of the world famous American Institution Dixie Hummingbirds. I said, we could get him to do it. So David consented. Even though David was a inimical person David was nice to him. For that matter, in those days, he was nice to me. He was impious a very impetuous person. Imperious. He would inculpate his problems on other people, but deep down, within, he was innocuous. But he came off as a insinsate person. We needed horns for Lake Tahoe. We played Ceasars Place

the Rowan and Martin Show that was about December of
1972. I remember it well. It was the first time I had been
to a gambling establishment. I walked in the lobby to
check in. They had all those slot machines. All those
people playing, people winning. I said I'm gonna try this.

(117)

7/14/93

So, I put my quarter in the slot machine. I immediately
won about 25 dollars. I said I got it, I'm gonna play this
thing. The change lady said I could put 4 quarters in at a
time. So I said, wow. So to make a long story short, I was
broke in ten minutes. So I rejoined the band. I had to if I
wanted to break even. Then, I said to myself, I got enough
habits already, so I quit. But, anyway, Trevor worked out
fine. He's a good person when he's not being imperious.
One of David's producers was the late great Gabrial
Mecker. I think Gab did the second album or a single. I
can't remember. It was around January or February of
1973. He liked what I was doing so when It was time to
produce his other act, Etta James, he called me to do it.
And Trevor, the associate producer. It was then I met the
great Etta James. I remember she had her little five year
old boy with her. Now, he's her drummer. Boy, times
change. I learned alot from her. I went on the road with
her. I played with her in San Francisco.

(118)

7/15/93

Let's see what else I remember. I have to reiterate to you
one more time. I'm doing all of this from memory.
There's no research done like Kitty Kelly did in her
unauthorized biography of Frank Sinatra. I remember

living in No. Hollywood. Our son was about a year old then. His name? Amani. I would smoke a joint, sit back on the couch and watch T.V. I would leave the back door open, cause the back yard was closed in. I would leave the front door open and the screen door locked. The hook on the lock was way up high. He would shake the door until the screen door would open. I would be on the couch sleeping. He would go outside butt naked with the dog. I would wake up and he would be gone. I would get in the car and look for him. When I would find him, he would be about 2 or 3 blocks sitting on the curb singing to the dog. When David C. Thomas would work in town, he would do some of his old songs from the Blood Sweat and Tears album.

(119)

7/15/93

If any of you know the song "And when I die", he would start the song by himself by singing, and when I die, Amani would sing it with him, then my daughter was born November 27, 1972. Thanks to you again Carol King. I remember one time my girlfriend took them to McDonalds one time to get a hamburger. They got their food. She got hers. She went to sit down while she was sitting, the two of them, my two kids, they were standing there crying. My girlfriend asked them what was wrong. They told her that the girl behind the counter didn't sing "You deserve a break today". Sala was funny. When she was a little baby, when she cried not only did you have to hold her, but you had to walk around with her while you were holding her. You know what I miss about then? Hugging them, they were so cuddly. Boy do I miss them. What nice kids. I remember Amani was always singing and the two of them were always fighting. Now my little girl's going to have a baby.

(120)

7/15/93

Lets see, around February of 1973, I got a call from a lady by the name of Venetta Fields. She told me she had a group called The Blackberry's, and she was looking for songs. Her and her partner would like to come to my house and listen to some songs being that I could write. She told me that Billy Preston was producing them. I said all right. I couldn't believe it Venetta Fields was coming to my house for songs. She's worked with almost everybody in the business singing backgrounds. You can hear here with Humble Pie, Pink Floyd. So, her and her partner came to my house looking for songs. She introduced me to her partner. I said "hello". I said "where are you from?" She was Carlena Williams. She told me Buffalo. She said I used to work the Ikettes. I said I used to know a lady I worked with that was from Buffalo that use to work the Ikettes. I worked with her at the Flamingo Club in Toronto. She said I use to work

(121)

7/15/93

at the Flamingo Club. I said Oh my God its you Carlena. I haven't seen you in about 10 years. I remember you used to tell me and the drummer horror stories about how Ike Turner would beat his wife. We used to laugh at you behind your back. We thought you were crazy cause nobody could do that to another human being. Just goes to show you, I can be wrong. Like Shakespeare said" To error is human," anyway, they took a bunch of songs.

They liked two of them. Boy, was I lucky, I had their only
single" Life is full of Joy" written by me and Eric Mercury
and "Yesterday's Music" written by me and David C.
Thomas. Since that time, the three of us got to know one
another real well. I would not do a session in those days
unless I would call Venetta. Boy she knew her music.

(122)
Back to Etta James. Around January 1973, we had finished
recording Etta James' record. Among the great musicians
on the recording session was Chuck Rainy, bass, and the
great Larry Carlton, guitar. That's when I met him. Did
you know he's a descendant of The James Gang? I played
keyboards, sang backgrounds on that recording session. I
can't think of that girls name, but she sang on Oh Happy
Day by Edwin Hawkins and Jennifer Warrens. Boy, you
know that must have been a long time ago. So, now that
the album was finished, she needed to go on the road. It
wasn't far and long. We had to get some musicians. So,
she got Trevor Lawrence, sax, Bobby Reys, sax, Steve
Madio, trumpet, Reggie McBride, bass, Buzzy Fieten,
guitar, me, piano and Greg Thomas, on drums. We
needed a place to rehearse. So, the manager at the time
was Ed Ticker, who managed Emmy Lou Harris,
suggested that we use a place called The Alley.

(123)
7/15/93

It was then and there I met the owner Bill Elkin. The place
was decorated in old jeans, old trees, cars, nuts, bolts. It
was like something from a Greatful Dead concert. I can
say truthfully I've met alot of people on this planet. Bill
Elkin is the sickest person I know. He has a bunch of

Harley Davidsons. His telephone number to his business is unlisted. He doesn't let you rehearse there if he doesn't like the music. He looks real funny riding in a car. Anyway, we rehearsed there and played San Francisco. I remember cause Reggie McBride was recording with Stevie Wonder in L.A. during the daytime and playing a club in San Francisco at night. We played at the Great American Music Hall. Reggie would fly everyday. I think the album was called Talking Book. Boy, he's a wired bass player. He would lick his fingers everytime he would play. I remember he was busier than I was.

(124)

Things were getting crazy then. My girlfriend the one that I was living with then, needed a break. So, she went back to Toronto for about one month. That was about August of 1973. Good, I said, Boy did I mess around. Once again, I got together with Eric Mercury and we wrote some songs. A funny thing, we never argued over music. I knew my place. It was over other things. Now, I understand I had no self-esteem, but plenty of talent. It was all right when we were teenagers, but this is L.A., you should treat your talent with respect. He did with his, I didn't with mine. With my talent, I was misleading. I think that bothered him, even though we were alike in alot of ways as far as talent was concerned. We were so different when it came down to business. The difference was he took care of it, I didn't. I relied strictly on my talent. Like the great Donnie Troiano once told me, you can find talented musicians a dime a dozen.

(125)

7/15/93

Anyway, we managed to write some songs. That's when I
met a lady by the name of Leah Kunkel, sister of Mamma
Cass. She came to my house looking for songs with a
Abigale Hanness, Danny Kortchmars's girlfriend. I
wonder what happened to Leah's album. Anyway, we
three got to know each other well. Abigale sang with me
on Neil Sadaka's single, "Laughter in The Rain". I went to
Leah's house for a party. Cass was there. I met her then
husband Russ Kunkel, drummer supreme. Lets see,
Kenny Rankin, Michael Stewart the producer I told you
about earlier in the book did a record on Kenny Rankin. I
met his then wife Yvonne, his little girl Chanda, his other
little girl Gena, and his boy Chris. I used to take him with
me to the record co. baseball games alot. He used to say to
me when he was about 10 years old "I want to get a job. I
need alot of money" I said "what do you need money
for?" Your daddy's rich. Pardon the saying,

(126)

7/15/93

but your mommy's good lookin. He said I want my own
money. I said to him when you get 15, I'll get you a job.
Just stay in school now. So, he did. When he turned 15 I
got him a job assisting Larry Carlton in his studio. Now,
he's a road manager. He's been to Europe a number of
times with everybody. All kind of groups. My don't we
grow up fast. He goes by the nickname of Hoover. Funny
name. His sister Gena use to work for Bonnie Raitt's
management co. Goldmountain. Hi guys. Hope you're
doing all right. I miss you. I played on the road with
Kenny Rankin in those days. I played New York, the
Bottom Line, PA, L.A., Boston, alot of places with him. I
learned alot of things from him. The one thing that sticks

out in my mind that I learned from him is how to play soft. His music was and is of a halcyon attitude. Thank you Kenny for your music.

(126)

7/15/93

Once again, back to David C. Thomas. This was the winter of 1973, maybe January. We were in the studio doing sessions with him, David that is. Boy was I busy then. Paul Rothchild was the producer. He really liked what I was doing. I was an all purpose person. Played keyboards, wrote songs, sang backgrounds, arranged, I could do it all. He was the producer that did the Janis Joplin records. He said I would like to work with you outside of David's project, that is. I said wow! I went home and told my girlfriend, at last I'm gonna make my own record. She said that's great. I got all excited, then Paul called and said you're so great Smitty, that I want you to play on Bonnie Raitt's album. I said to myself, here we go again. I was so hurt, not cause Bonnie was no good or nothing like that. I thought that he wanted to do a record on me.

(127)

7/15/93

Again, I did what anybody in the right mind would do. I said yes to Paul Rothchild. Even though, I was hurt. I soon remedied that by getting some marijuana, and cocaine numbed myself and I did the session. I remember the session. The great Jai Winding was her piano player. He had told her if he couldn't do the album, he wasn't going to go on the road with her. I don't care who was in the piano chair, she wasn't going to like them. Guess

71

what, I got fired. You see, I was Paul's the producers choice. Jai was her choice. She won. I felt funny . That was the first time I was fired from a job. Since then, I've been fired plenty of times. The bottom line is that my heart wasn't in doing the session. Even though I was multi-talented,

(128)

7/15/93

that's not what I came to L.A. to do. I'll bet you if Eric Mercury could do what I could do he would have said something, cause he has an abundance of self-esteem, as well as a talent. Like I said, before, I could easily escape by doing drugs. For an example, when I was working with the fellow that had all of the marijuana, I had so much of it, that I was doing about 25 joints a day. A nice way to escape. That's how I managed to escape in those days. Once again if that was Eric Mercury he would have all of that marijuana he would smoke about 2 joints a day if that much. I figured why not? I'm young I can handle it. And besides, It helps me to forget.

(127)

7/15/93

Also in about Nov. of '72 I had just arrived from Brazil with David C. Thomas and I got a call to do a session with these three girls. They were young black girls by the names of Carman Twillie (at that time her name was Carman Bryant), Netty Gloud, and Cathy Collier. Boy could they sing. The producer was a Motown producer. He asked me to play for them. I said yes. I started to play for them, we took a break. They started to sing in baroque. Carman started to recite Shakespeare plays. I

couldn't beleive it, they were incredible singers. I told the
producer they're great. Where are they from? He said
Pasadena. I said they should be working more. He said to
me they're just getting started, I have to keep or get them
work while I'm doing this record on them he said. I told
him not to worry I know a colleague of mine that's doing
an album. So I called him. His name was Donnie Troiano.
Donnie loved them. His engineer at the time was Keith
Olsen the famous producer whose done people like
Fleetwood Mac,

(128)

7/15/93

Pat Benetar, Foreigner, Tom Waites, and etc. He also liked
them, and the both of them put them to work. Keith Olsen
then was a staff engineer at the time at Sound City in
Panorama City. That's a suburb in L.A. So about a week
into the session one morning I got a call from the producer
screaming telling me what did you turn those girls onto
those white boys for. If you keep on doing that I'll have
you killed. I said that to say one thing, hatred comes in all
colors. Sometime around Feb. of '73 I got a phone call
from David Palmer, he use to sing lead vocals with Steely
Dan, he wrote a song called Jazzman with Carol King. He
said hello I'm one of the guys that went to Houston with
you with the Eric Mercury project. Let's get together and
write he said. I said okay, we got together. Boy could he
write. We wrote two songs. They were called, "Dreaming
as One", which was recorded by people like Jackie
DeShannon, Ritchie Havens, The Pointer Sisters, Etc.

(129)

7/15/93

The other song was called "Saved by the Grace of your
Love". Gladys Night and the Pips did it. Anne Murry did
it. Sheryll Ladd did it on her special and etc. David
writing with you is a wonderful peaceful experience.
Let's see what else happened around that time. I met
Charles Veal around that time, a great violin player. I had
a barbecue at that time. Around March of 1972. Neil
Sadaka and Carol King came. They were childhood
sweethearts. He wrote a song about her. I think it was
about her. It was called "Oh, Carol". Alot of people
showed up for that barbecue. The late Rev. Joe May's son
Charles, Eric Mercury, Jim Horn and etc. I had a
wonderful time. I can remember my daughter was only
about two years old then. She was so cute I told her if she
wanted to, she could be a brat the rest of her life. She said
okay daddy. And she was. Boy, was she ever. Danny
Kortchmar showed up too.

(130)

7/16/93

By this time it was about the spring of 1972. Maybe April
of that year. My girlfriend's career was taking off. She
was working with Mack Davis on the road. With them
were Al Wilson, Jose Felisiano, and so on. She was
making enough money to support herself and the kids,
but not me and my habits. You see, I was at an all time
low. We had a Volvo 164E and a station wagon 145. The
station wagon we were leasing. They took that back.
They repossessed the other car. I stood there watching
from the window as they took the Volvo. My girlfriend
said to me you better get some work quick or else we
won't have a place to live. I remember I was doing so bad.
I was down to about 50 women. I was down to smoking

about 10 joints a day. Things were rough. Then, I was talking to Eddie Kendricks. I met him on the Eric Mercury project. He was one of the background singers. Not Eddie Kendricks the singer with the Temptations, the background singer. I told him I needed some work. I was multi-talented. I could do most anything

(131)

7/16/93

Eddie said he would help me. He got me a job singing backgrounds for Della Reese on the Scoey Mitchell Show. That was great. That was in town. Then he got me a job singing on a Carol King Album. Oh, by the way Patrice Holloway was on the Della Reese job. Her sister Brenda Holloway wrote "You made me so very happy". For the group Blood, Sweat & Tears. Then, Eddie got me a job with Connie Stevens singing backgrounds. The stipulations were, you had to go to Las Vegas and dress up in a bunny outfit. My live-in girlfriend said no, we don't need the money that bad. Little did she know I had a woman fixation. I had to have money for that. So, following her advice, I quit Connie Stevens and stayed in town. Then, I got a call from Bill Withers office around (??) of 1973. They asked me to play a weekend in Fresno and Bakersfield with him. I said yes. I played keyboards with him. It was nice. The one thing I remember about that job was the bass player Melvin Dunlap.

(132)

7/16/93

The one thing that sticks out in my mind about Melvin is that he took the insides of the piano strings and he played them. Boy, what a groove he could get. Oh yeah, when I

was rehearsing, with Connie Stevens, she needed a
rehearsal keyboardist. She asked me did I know anybody.
I was singing, so I recommended David Foster. The group
Skylark wasn't working. Boy, things were picking up.
Michael Stewart was back in the studio, he was in the
studio producing Kenny Rankin. Then being that I was
the leader, I had to take the contracts to Columbia
Records. I then met a young executive in the other
department called Epic Records. His name was Eddie
Wynrick. We got to become good pals. He liked my
talent. I'll never forget him. He believed in me. He asked
me to produce a Canadian artist for him by the name of
Paul Sanders. I was so excited. I wanted it to be right. I
got Mike Stewart to help me. Charlie Larky played bass,
Danny Kortchmar played guitar, Joel O'Brien played
drums, and Donnie Troiano played guitar. I remember
Donnie started

(133)

7/16/93

to play some jazz riffs that I showed him in Toronto at an
earlier time. He kept saying Smith, you remember this riff
you showed me? I was trying to get him to keep quiet,
cause if the L.A. guys knew I could play jazz, I wouldn't
work no more. I wonder what happened to that record?
You see, in those days, I didn't believe in a therapist or
God mumbo jumbo. I said that's what they talk about in
therapy. Then I got a call from Steve Cropper. He wanted
me to play keyboards on The Sam and Dave record. I said
to him, "where's Booker T?" of Booker T & the M.G's. He
said he's doing his own thing with his wife Priscilla
Coolidge, Rita's sister. I remember playing the Midnight
Special with them. That's the only time that I sweated at a

rehearsal. Boy, they were good. I remember about that it was the spring of 1973. David Foster auditioned for the Etta James job, so did Brian Wray. He was a young guitar player I met when I was in Denver with David C. Thomas. I don't know if David got the job or not,

(134)

7/16/93

but I know that Brian got the job. He still plays with her sometimes to this day. Brian wrote a song for Smokey Robinson, "Just to Know Her". Back to writing, I wrote this one melody that was completed at least to other people, not to me. I wrote it. I remember writing it and giving it to a colleague and her husband. They looked at me like I was stupid or something. They couldn't do anything with it, they said. It was too complicated. They were both writers. That was about the time I was working with Bill Writhers. I said, Oh well, I guess I'll throw it away. They said it was too complicated. I played that same melody for Eric Mercury. He said I like it. He finished the song in about an hour. It was called "Down the Back Stairs, of my Life". Then Thelma Houston recorded it. Yvonne Eldleman recorded, Kenny Rankin recorded it. Joey Skarbury recorded it and etc. I said that to say this, never throw away nothing, you never know what you got.

(135)

7/16/93

By then, I was really thinking about doing my own record then. So, I asked Chuck Rainey would he produce my album for me? You might know him as the bass player on the T.V. sitcom Sanford and Son. By this time, I was making money and spending it left and right. My accountant then, Bernie Francis, told me to put something aside for a rainy day. I told him that it never rains in L.A., and besides, nothing will happen to me. I'm indestructible. I'm young. I play on hit records. He told me that you always save something. Ken Norton was his client. He used to box Mohammed Ali. I remember he wanted a brand new Lincoln. The one he had was two years old. So Bernie told him instead of spending 25 thousand dollars on a new one, spend 5 thousand dollars on a a great paint job on your old car. Paint it a different color.

(136)

7/16/93

Not only can you get a great paint job, but for that kind of money you can get it completely detailed. I never forgot what he said. Boy, did it take along time for it to sink in. By this time, late fall around Nov. of 1972, my girlfriend was really working. I was working too. But not enough to make ends meet. You see, I always lived beyond my means. That was to makeup for all the things that I didn't have when I was younger. Like I said before, I had lots of talent but I thought with my sex organs. I guess that's why I had to have alot of girls to feel validated in those days. That meant alot to me. Just as much as music anyway. My live in girlfriend said I can't take this no more. So she moved to an apartment on Coldwater Drive with the two kids. She bought a brand new Mazda. That was so much better than the piece of junk that we had. I moved to a one bedroom apartment on Arch Drive in Studio City. She was still in Sherman Oaks.

(137)

7/16/93

Oh yeah, I've got to go back a minute. I just remembered
something. I guess I remember alot of things. Some of
them are negative and I don't want to write about it.
Some of it is positive. If I were to write everything, this
book would look like a dictionary. As I was saying, by
this time, Trevor Lawrence was the associate producer
with Richard Perry on the Martha Reed album. Trevor
asked me to play on the album. I'll never forget that time.
It was about September of 1972. Richard Perry was an
eccentric kind of person. He had gone through about 6
keyboard players to do one song. It was called Many
Rivers to Cross. He liked me. It only took me two weeks
to play that song. To this day, everytime I hear that song,
I cringe. Anyway, before I moved to Arch Drive, I moved
to Oakwood Apartments with Eric Mercury. For about
one month. Boy, how could a guy work so much and be
so broke? I said now I understand. Eric and I got along
well. I was running women, doing drugs. Having a good
old time.

(138)

7/16/93

By this time, Jim Keltner was doing the Bobby Womack
album. Bobby needed a keyboard player. He
recommended me. I did the gig. He liked me so Bobby
suggested I get another keyboard player to help me. I got
David Foster. Bobby heard him and never called me back.
The short time I was there, I met his writing partner, Jim
Ford. He co-wrote with Bobbie, "Harry Hippie". Boy he
was crazy. I remember inviting him over to my house for
breakfast. That must have been before me and my

girlfriend split up. We were vegetarians then. I told him,
that I didn't eat meat. So, that morning, he came to my
house with a lb. of bacon. He said, I know you're
vegetarians, but I eat meat. I think back to those days, I
was a stupid vegetarian. Didn't eat no meat, or fish or
nothing like that. But, did plenty of drugs.

(139)
Then about the latter part of 1973, I'd say around
November of that year, my live in girlfriend and I split up.
She moved to Coldwayer Canyon in Sherman Oaks. I
moved to Eric Mercury's apartment. Then Jimmy Roberts
came to town or at least that's when I saw him. I told
Jimmy I wanted to interview him for my book. He said
yes. Here goes.
Smith: full name-- Jimmy Roberts.
Smith: When you were born-- 8/31/48.
Smith: what made you decide to come to L.A.—
Jimmy: I was in pursuit of something I had been in
Toronto following Smith for about a year. You gave me an
introduction into the music business and a learning
experience. I guess I needed to be where something was
happening. You were In L.A. I guess I figured it was the
right place to be. I needed to be around the guy who I
worshipped as a musician.

(140)
                    7/21/93
Jimmy: I guess well, worshipped is not the right word. I
have the utmost respect for you as a musician, and as a
roll model for the things I needed to do as a musician.
Smith: When did you come to Toronto?
Jimmy: The fall of 69.

Jimmy: With The John T. Davis Quartet.

Smith: When did you leave Toronto?

Jimmy: I left Hamilton Ont. Canada in 1974. I spent 6 months working Virginia with Franklin Wilson. Frank Wilson said he was going to L.A. He arrived in L.A. about October of 1974 and I (Jimmy) arrived around in the end of 1974. Cause, I remember doing my first job in Los Angeles. I had been here for a while before I called you.

Smith: Who are some of the people that you have worked with?

Jimmy: A guy by the name of Larry Ammons. He was a piano player. Roy Dent, David Benoit, Carlena Williams, some of those people I met at a club called The Parisian Room. Most of them were not big names, but they had nice club connections, and could play.

(141)

7/21/93

Jimmy: So, I started to hang out in the Crenshaw District, like places like, The Name of The Game, The Tiki Room, Renado Rey were doing some of those jams. Cadelo Demilo was an M.C. She used to M.C. the Red Holloway Show. She was like a floating M.C. who hosted alot of those shows. She was one of the first people who tried to get me work. Cardelo was hanging out with people like Redd Foxx, Della Reese, etc. She had alot of nice parties at her house.

Smith: What about Greg Allman? When did you start working for him?

Jimmy: I started working with him down the road a piece I met him indirectly from you. I met Gene Dinwiddy who played saxophone who used to work with you. I met Gene when you and him was working with Etta James.

Then, I ran into him on the Jackie Lomax record session.
You did that record didn't you?
Smith: Yes
Jimmy: Gene did the record session with me. He was a
member of the Gregg Allman Band.

(142)

7/21/93

Jimmy: Their management was putting a horn section
together 'cause Gregg Allman and Cher had performed on
an album together. So being that, Gene was the leader.
He hired me for that. I think that tour was around '77. So
again, that was related directly to you, you see alot of
things I did in this town were related directly to you.
Smith: Well, I guess it's got nothing to do with your
playing right?
Jimmy: Sure it's got something to do with my playing.
I'm not saying that to give you alot of an image or nothing
like that, but I'm just saying that to show you how you
were important in the space of my life. I'm not saying that
I owe you except to say thank you. You see, everytime I
say that to you you kind of respond to me in a defensive
sort of matter.
Smith: Am I being defensive by merely saying I can take
you to the water but I can't make you drink it?
Jimmy: Once again, I kept the job because I could perform

(143)

7/21/93

Jimmy: Once again, thank you. You see, everything has a
purpose in life for an example, did you see the movie It's
A Wonderful Life?

Smith: Yeah. With Jimmy Stewart and Donna Reed

Jimmy: He, Jimmy Stewart didn't realize that what he was doing was helping people until an angel came down and made him aware. You see, the same thing, the things that I've done have been directly from off shoots that you've made to me.

Smith: Yeah, I guess I was looking at you as though you were a good player, or maybe they just hired you cause you were black in America or something. That becomes a secondary part of it. I can be a good player sitting back in Suffolk, VA. If I hadn't been working with John T's band, at the time, when you invited him to come to Canada. He didn't want to go by himself so he invited us to go with him. Instead of one guy showing up, four guys showed up at your door step. You didn't turn us down. Instead, you tried to help us.

(144)

7/21/93

Once again, if John T. hadn't made that connection, with you I would have still been sitting in Suffolk till this day.

Smith: Well, I guess I could have come to Suffolk and put a gun to your brain and made you leave.

Jimmy: You could have, but you probably wouldn't

Smith: Yeah, but you did it yourself

Jimmy: I made the decision to leave

Smith: What about Rod Stewart?

Jimmy: What about Rod Stewart?

Smith: When did you start working with him?

Jimmy: My first tour with Rod was in 1986. I was working with Chuck E. Weiss at the Central in Hollywood. And I ran into Lee Thornberg. We were working together in Ventura one night with a guy by the name of Johnny Flynn. Just as we were leaving, Lee, who played trumpet for Rod, said man, Rod's looking for a a saxaphone player. He said, I think you'll be good for that job. I'll set up an audition for you. So Lee got me a spot to play.

(145)

7/21/93

Jimmy: So I went on the audition and they hired me. I've done every tour since then with Rod.
Smith: So you've done alot of studio work too.
Jimmy: A fair amount. Not as much as I could have done. Alot of it I didn't do by choice. Like you said earlier, the dollar value do I want to do this? The other thing I know, that you have the confidence to be able to do it. One of the reasons for not doing alot of studio work is not being able to read anything they put in front of you. Not being prepared as a reed player. I was a little insecure about doing sessions.
Smith: Does that make you an awful player?
Jimmy: No. That doesn't make me an awful player but it would make me feel insecure every time I went to a recording session. And I made it, and I would say Thank God I made it. So what I'm trying to say is never bite off more than you can chew. For the money that is.

(146)

7/21/93

Jimmy: I remember one time I got a call to do a T.V. show. The guy asked me do you play alto flute? I said yeah. I didn't even own one. I rented one from a buddy of mine. I went to the T.V. show. The parts were all written out the first song was the alto flute song. I pulled it out. I could even get a sound of it. The guy politely canceled the session. When he called back everybody, he didn't call me back. I'll never do that again. I play tenor alto and soprano saxophone. If that's what you want me to play, I'll play that. If somebody calls me for a job and I think I can't do it, I don't except it. The humility taught me to do what I only can do. It was an ugly learning experience for me but it didn't kill me.

Smith: How do you feel about playing behind people?

Jimmy: I don't mind playing behind people if I enjoy their music.

Smith: Do you want to make that a career?

Jimmy: I don't know if I want to make backing people up a career.

(147)

7/21/93

Jimmy: I guess I'm living my life that's a career. Being a solo artist, I've never done that before. It's not going to make me feel like I've had a disappointing life if I don't do that. The things that I've already done I feel that it has helped me to utilize my talent and I have brought joy to alot of people's hearts by playing along with them.

Smith: What about that feeling of needing to express yourself?

Jimmy: I could have not expressed myself more than when I've played with you, or anybody else.

Smith: Maybe I should look at things like that

Jimmy: You don't have too. You have your mind and I have my mind regardless of whose name's on the marquee, even though people come to see Rod Stewart, they tell me man you played very good. Just because they came to see Rod they appreciated the way I sounded.

That doesn't mean that because my name wasn't on the
marquee I'm gonna not express myself

Smith: I know I wanted to write a book. The guy wanted
to charge me 7 thousand dollars to express myself.

(148)

7/21/93

Jimmy: Does that mean you're going to express yourself
any less cause somebody was going to help you or what?

Smith: I'm just saying that I'm able to express myself and
I thought I couldn't by writing a book I've never done that
before. But what my girlfriend says, you can do that
yourself.

Jimmy: I know that you can do any of that.

Smith: Now, I know first of all I don't have 7 thousand
dollars

Jimmy: You'll always find a need to do all of those things
you need to do. I've got to go now. I've got to go and
help some people.

Wait a minuite, by there you have it. Jimmy's own words
that's what I'm trying to say in this book. You see, that
was a homeboy from home that could play that was
heuristic. I thought I was doing myself a favor by hiring
him. Instead, I'm his hero and all the time I was a nervous
wreck. Oh well, what you gonna do? Anyway, Venetta
and Carlena wanted to peruse their own record deal. She
ask me to produce some demos for her. So, we got
together around the spring of 1975. I used Frank Wilson

(149)

7/21/93

on drums, Larry Nash on piano, Jimmy Roberts on sax.
Boy that was fun. Boy can she sing. As usual, the tapes
got lost. Joe Gottfried the late Joe Gottfried who owned
Sound City, that's a recording complex in the valley of
L.A. He told me that I could use his place anytime I
wanted to. So I asked Roy Gaines if he wanted to make a
record. He said yes. We did it. It was fun. Then I
produced Jimmy Roberts out there. I used David Foster.
You see, I remember Foster when he had only one car. I
used Keith Olsen as an engineer. That was all right too! I
don't know how I did that back then. Boy, was I high.
Then about the fall of 1975, we went in. Keith was just
starting to produce then. So he started with Jorge
Calderone. In the meantime, David Mancini's, studio
Devonshire, Mike Stewart was doing a record on Kenny
Rankin. Boy, was I busy then. Not only you're good as
your last hit, but what have you done this morning?
That's the way it is in L.A. Anyway, back at Sound City, I
get a call from a guy named Glenn Spreen. That was
about the time I was working with Kenny. He asked me if
I could work with him on an album that he was

(150)

7/21/93

producing. A guy by the name of Dave Loggins. The
album was called Back To Boston. I said yeah. I got a
chance to work with great Max Bennett, bass and John
Geurin, drums. It worked out great. Since then I've
worked with Glenn on alot of projects. On one hand, I
wanted to do my own thing. But, on the other hand I like
the money. I needed that to buy drugs. Then around that
same time, I got a phone call from Robert Appere at
Clover. He said that Tom Dowd was producing Rod

Stewart and he was using Steve Cropper, Al Jackson,
Duck Dunn, and did I want to do the album? I told him
that I would think about it. I was pondering over it. I said
to myself Steve Cropper and the cats Wow! I've got to do
my own thing, but wait a minute. I said to myself I could
do just a little drugs and make it all right. So, I'll do it. So
I did the album with Rod Stewart. It was Atlantic
Crossing. I remember playing with the late Al Jackson on
drums. When it would get good to him, he would stand
up and play.

(151)

7/21/93

The one thing I remember about Rod not only is he
heuristic, but he's a good business man too. I guess that is
why he's been around so long. Then around that time,
Eddie Wynrick and Willie Leopold who I was signed to in
a production deal, they said I needed a manager. So, I
talked to Ken Fritz then I played one song for him. He
liked it. So, I went with him. Before, I went with Ken I
was fed up. I remember cutting back on my intake of
smoke. Maybe 10 joints and I said I've got to get a record
deal. So, I got a bunch of musicians together at a place
called The Troubadour. That is a club in West Hollywood
near Beverly Hills. So I auditioned. A representative
from Warner Bros. by the name of John Salstone heard me
and liked what he heard, so he wanted to sign me to
Warner Bros. The president then was Joe Smith. They
offered me a little money to sign. But, as soon as Ken Fritz
came in the picture, I got more money. I bought with the
money eleven keyboards. Boy, we got along great then,
until Joe Smith called him and told him that this new artist
that had just signed with

(152)

7/21/93

them, he had a hit record. It was called Breezin. His name
was George Benson. George had a meeting with Ken. He
told Ken sure you can manage me if you can make me a
million dollars cash in a year. Ken did it. The rest of his
clients caught hell. Finally, after his other clients were
bugging him, he got some help. A guy by the name of
Dennis Turner. I don't think they're together. Now,
Dennis is on his own now. Among Dennis' clients are
Kenny G. Good work Dennis. Just before I was to go to
New Orleans, to do my album. I was talking to James
Gadson. He advised me not to go. You're a fixture here.
Anyway, Brian Ahern called me to do Dianne Brookes
album. It didn't take much to convince me to do that
album. I was a Dianne Brookes fanatic. I loved her music.
Anyway, and besides I was going to do my own album.
Brian asked me to be the leader, so I got Jimmy Roberts on
sax Wah Wah Watson on guitar, Carlena Williams on
backgrounds, James Gadson on drums. All of my favorite
people.

(153)

7/21/93

Oh I've got to back up a minute. Just before all of that, I
was working with Etta James at the Troubadour with
Gene Dinwiddie on Sax. That's right, it was the Spring of
1974. Boy it's hard to keep all this stuff up in your head
for 20 years, especially when you have all those drugs in
your head. It was Etta's Birthday. We were throwing
cake all over the place. Joe Riley, you remember me
telling you about him? He was managing a group called

Jade. He asked me to produce them for him. He said we
could make the album cheap. He said he knew a college
student who could do the album cover for next to nothing.
I wasn't used to working like that, but since it was Joe
'cause he helped me when I was down. I said one day I
would repay him. So, I agreed with him. So, I got the best
engineer around, Keith Olsen. Him and I flew to New
York and recorded the band. We did everything in one
day. Hell, Joe only paid the man for one day. We
recorded about 10 songs. Jade sang the backgrounds.

(154)

                            7/21/93
So, Joe said after we didn't have time to finish 3
background vocals on 3 songs I told him that I would do it
myself in L.A. at Sound City. I told Joe that I would get
Joe Gottfriend to give me some studio time and I would
do it myself. I could sing. So, he said great. So, that I
didn't do in New York at the studio, I could do in L.A.
Like percussion, horn sections and etc. So, I got back to
L.A. and was talking to Carmen Twillie. She was the girl
working with Cathy and Netty. I said I've got a great
idea. Instead of me doing the backgrounds myself, why
don't I get you girls to do the backgrounds. I said Cathy is
suffering from malnutrition. That would be some money
for her. I could call Joe. Get some money she said she
wouldn't mind, but the other girls would. I said to her but
they don't have any money they'll do it for me I told her.
They won't mind. I'll call Joe and get a little money. I
know Joe didn't want to spend any extra money. That's
why he wanted me to do it.

(155)

7/21/93

I asked Joe for the extra money. Against his better
judgment, he mailed me the money. That night, we did a
session at Sound City. Cathy was really hurtin. You could
hear her stomach growling. That's how bad it was, so I
told her not to worry. She would get her money. Besides,
I never did anything unless three of them were on it. So,
Netty and Cathy were really bugging me, rushing me.
They kept telling me they had to leave. They wasn't
making enough money to keep them there for a long time.
The more Cathy's stomach growled, the more frustrated
she got. I told Netty and Cathy don't worry, the minute
that Joe's money got here I would pay them. The next
morning about 8 o'clock I heard a knock on the door. It
was Netty & Cathy demanding their money. Netty said I
want it now or I'll report you to the union. So, I borrowed
the money to pay them. That was 20 years ago. I have a
long since forgiven them. But, them I'll never forget since
then Cathy did the movie Uptown Saturday Night with
Bill Cosby.

(156)

7/21/93

Cathy was with Ray Carles' Rayettes. Netty had done
countless sessions. Carmen movies, Smoky Robinson
commercials, etc. You see, no hard feelings. Oh yeah, just
before my record, I got a call from Paul Rothchild to play
on Bonnie Raitt's album. Wow, Bonnie Raitt! I said. I
remember going to the record session. Lets see, that was
before Diane's session. So, that must have been the
summer of 1975. I got there. She was disturbed because
her piano player wasn't on the session. He was the great
Jai Winding. Madonna's piano player. He told her that if

91

he couldn't play on the album, he wasn't' going on the
road with her. Boy, was she mad. She wanted him. The
producer wanted me. I was vibed out so bad that Paul
asked me to leave. Boy, I remember getting fired so much
in those days. Oh yeah, after we got finished celebrating
Etta's birthday party at The Troubadour, about 6 of us 4
white guys and me and the drummer he was black. His
car was parked in back of the Troubadour the club was
about 1/2 block from Beverly Hills.

(157)

7/21/93

So being that everybody parked in the back of the club,
the 4 white guys was in one car. Me and the drummer
was in the other car. The white guys pulled out first. We
pulled out behind them. Being that we were 1/2 block
from Beverly Hills, the cops pulled me and the black
drummer over. He wanted to know what we were doing
in that alley. Just then I lost it. This was about 1975. The
cops were harassing me. For 3 years you see, I lived in
Hollywood. I used to write with David C. Thomas
everyday. He lived in Brentwood. I would leave his
house late at night from writing. And every night the
cops would stop me to ask me what was I doing out here.
Your lights need fixing. I had a brand new truck with my
name on the door. You know why they were stopping
me? Anyway back to the Troubadour. When the cops
stopped me, like I said I lost it. I cursed the cops out. I
was fractious I fulminated. I was so loud that they put me
in jail for three days. I wouldn't tell them my name.
There is no justice for a minority in this town.

(158)

7/21/93

Lets see, around that time, about 1973, as I told you I was
moving to Arch Drive in North Hollywood 'cause me and
my girlfriend were breaking up. She moved to an
apartment on Coldwater Dr. First, I moved in for about a
month with Eric Mercury. Damn, I missed those kids.
She had gone to South Africa with Al Wilson. Even
though I pursued her to get back together in between
girls, I wanted to have a family, or at least try at it. After
living with Eric Mercury for a month, I moved to Arch
Drive. My girlfriend was still in South Africa with Al
Wilson. When she came back, I don't know why she
changed her mind. I don't know maybe the other girls got
fed up with showing her her parts. Or maybe she could
put up with my idiosyncrasy. I don't know what it was,
anyway we moved in together on Coldwater. By that
time, I had started to work. I remember one time she told
me if it wasn't for her, there wouldn't be no money
coming in. I know why there was money coming in.

(159)

7/21/93

See, she was a pretty Canadian girl with plenty of smarts.
No talent, but plenty of brains. You see, the white
producers like that as long as she had the two girls
showing her her parts. Whenever I had projects, I would
never call her. Not because she was my girlfriend or
nothing like that. She was already working with other
people. I was never jealous just embarrassed. Till this
day, other than the fact that we had two lovely children, I
don't know why I got married to her. I guess I wanted a
family unit. I never had that and the fact that she was
pretty, but that didn't stop me from seeing other women.

So, we got married just before I went to New Orleans to do my record. Boy, I remember playing table tennis with Mike Stewart jogging in the park in the mornings, going for walks with him in the afternoons, going to Toronto to get together with Motherlode. Things were looking good. I had plenty of girls, plenty of drugs, I had a record contract. I remember around the fall of 1975, my record deal was finalized.

(160)

7/21/93

At last!! My own record deal. What could go wrong I said. I arrived in New Orleans October of 1975. Finally, I met the great Allen Toussant. He came to my hotel room on a Friday night. He said we would go to the studio that Monday. Monday morning came. He had his secretary call me to tell me that something came up till Tuesday. Tuesday came, he got his secretary to call and tell me that he couldn't make it. Could we move it to Wed? That went on for about 2 weeks. I was going nuts. Thank God for that girl I met in New Orleans and that pound of smoke I had with me. So I got frustrated that when we did go in the studio, I asked Allen if I could send for somebody I knew from L.A.? I sent for Jimmy Roberts. He played on my album 5 of the songs I wrote. Some of the songs Allen wrote. He would take my songs that I wrote do his own arrangement on the songs. He didn't ask me what I thought. Or would you like to try it or nothing. I was getting so frustrated. I called my representative out at Warner Bros. Pete Johnson was his name.

(161)

7/21/93

Pete told me that Allen Toussant was the star. What he
says goes. If it's not like that we will have to let you go.
Boy did I get frustrated. I smoked about a pound of pot.
In a month, my phone bill was about 3,500 dollars. The
only time I felt good is when I sent for Joe Riley and
Jimmy Roberts. The album finally got finished 2 months
and 1 lb.of pot later. When Warner Bros. heard the album
they didn't like it. Guess what? They fired me. What was
Allen doing? Driving around in his Rolls Royce. I'm not
saying that all of it was his fault, but in spite of everything,
I had talent. Just because they didn't like the album they
could have given me another chance. You see, the talent
never went no where. I still was talented. Like I said,
before you're as good as what you did this morning in this
town L.A. The kids then I remember taking them to
harmony playhouse, that was a nursery school.

(162)

7/22/93

I remember those kids used to fight all the time. I
remember when me and my then wife split up at the time.
Oh yeah, we had children before we were married. She
was doing shows. I don't know who it was with? Maybe
Bobby Womack or somebody. And The Friends of
Distinction was working with them. She met the leader of
the group Floyd Butler was his name. I remember her
staying out all night with him. You know the worst part
about that was? I didn't even get mad. I was more
concerned about getting a song to him. So, the next day,
she came in from staying with him all night and the first
thing I asked her was you didn't bring him with you?
Now, if that would have been my first wife, Helen, I

would have been furious. Anyway, Floyd came over and
listened to about 60 of my songs. Out of those 60, The
Friends of Distinction recorded two. "Goodbye" written
by myself and Eric Mercury and a song called "When I
Die" I hate to say this, but that's all to me that mattered.
And of course the kids.

(163)

7/22/93

Boy they were some pretty kids. I'm not saying that cause
they're mine. They're grown ups and they still look that
way. That's something I did right. As I was literally
leaving out the door to go to New Orleans to do my
record, I was so excited. I got a call from Al Jarreau's
office. His manager wanted me to go on the road with Al.
I told him that I couldn't, I was going to New Orleans to
do my record. I don't know, he must have took me the
wrong way. I never heard from him again. That was
around October of 1975. Things were going pretty smooth
then. I had plenty of drugs, I had finally gotten married to
the girl I was living with, even though I didn't love her.
But, that's all right. I had plenty of drugs. I could justify
anything. We had moved in next to David Foster on
Coldwater. His little sister, and his ex-wife's little girl, his
step daughter would baby-sit for me and my wife. That
made it possible for the both of us to work. We used to
have great parties at that place. People like Trevor
Lawrence would come.

(164)

7/22/93

So off to New Orleans I go. We finally got finished doing
the album. Allen Toussant and I. Even though I wasn't

happy with the finished product, I was excited that I had
an album. So, I would play it for some of the people I had
worked with. People I looked up to. When the album was
finished, I would ask them "how do you like it?" They
would say "Man, it sounded good, when can I book you
for my session?" You know what that means? They
weren't listening with their hearts. Anyway, we were
living on Coldwater Canyon. I needed some book shelves
installed in the apt. So, I called this carpenter, I can't
remember his name, anyway, he did a good job. Him and
I got into a conversation. He was telling me that he was
from Chicago, that he worked in this big candy factory. I
won't mention their names. He told me that they would
make 100 gallons of candy and sometimes a rat would fall
in. They wouldn't throw away a 100 lbs. of candy. They
would just grind up the rat in it. From this I haven't eaten
that candy or no other candy bar. Ben? Are you in there.

(165)

7/22/93

I remember just before I moved back to Coldwater
Canyon, I was living with Eric Mercury, we were writing
and I adulated with him. I said "man, you write great
lyrics" I said where did you get your inspiration? He told
me Winston Churchill. I said what do you mean? He said
that Winston Churchill was a great speaker and he knew
the english language well. I said what do you mean? He
told me a story about Winston. He said Winston Churchill
had come to Congress to speak. Winston was known for
asking for money when he spoke. So, when he got up to
address Congress, he said "Members of Congress,
President, distinguished guests, I didn't come here today
to ask for money" then everybody applauded and gave

him an ovation, they cheered, they did that for about 5 minutes. Then everybody quieted down. He finished speaking. Then he said, for myself. To me that was smart and witty. Winston Churchill was a great man. That goes to show you it's not what you say, it's how you say it.

(166)

7/23/93

Anyway, I finally or should I say me and my then wife got enough money to move. Even though she was a perucrious person in those days, I found a way to make ends meet. I supported my family and my habit. You could call me a white collar drug addict. Anyway, we moved to Van Nuys, CA. It was on Ranchito Avenue. A nice house. I remember It had 15 fruit trees. We had fruit coming out of our ears. The kids were fighting as usual. In those days, talk shows were getting popular. They were talking alot about child abuse. So, we stopped spanking our kids. Besides, it didn't do no good anyway. So whenever they would fight, I would tell them "I'm gonna send you back". That would scare them. That worked for about one year. Till one day my daughter and son were fighting and I said to my daughter O.K. I'm gonna send you back. She was really mad at my son. So she said "OKAY I'M READY LETS GO". I didn't know what to do. I was caught between a rock and a hard place. One time, my son, Amani and my daughter Sala was fighting. I was so frustrated. We, my wife and I

(167)

7/23/93

finally broke both of them up. Sat both of them down. We had a sensible conversation with them. So, we asked

Amani, our son, we said "what do you think we should do about you and your sister's fighting?" He said to us calmly "If you send Sala away, she wouldn't be around for me to fight with". We said "okay". Now Sala, what do you think we should do about your brothers fighting? She stood there laughing and laughing as she fulmitated and said nothing. Just then I came to a conclusion. It's nothing you can do about it. It's a stage they go through. Back to music. Before David C. Thomas went back to Toronto, we went into the recording studio with a guy by the name of Jeff Lathom. I don't know if that record came out. This is my comprehension of David C. Thomas. David is an imperious person. Also, he is an impetuous person. He would make you feel like an imprecate person. In the end, he would implicate you. Sometimes, he was enough to make you inimable.

(168)

7/23/93

Even though you were where an innocuous person. Sometimes, he would make you feel like an inxidious person. Even if he is a vaxatious litigate at last, I got it on paper. I've been working and knowing him for a long time. With him I wish I could adulate about him. But, chances of that would be pretty slim. When he says something to you, it's so falacious. He is not gracious. With him I would not berate or abhor him. I would get to the point where I would fulminate with or without him. I would never get fractious. Instead, I will vent my frustrations into a halcyon person. That's my compendium of David Clayton Thomas. Now on to something positive. I got a call from David Kirshenbaum. After I had arrived from New Orleans from doing my

record I played it for him. He said, I like it. Hey man, I'm
recording a record with Ritchie Havens and I want to get a
personal affect. Being that you have your group from
New Orleans, here in L.A. how would you and your
group like to do Ritchie's album? I remember I was
practicing

(169)

7/23/93

so hard with my own group looking for some kind of
validation from peers. But, once again, I would always get
your record sounding good. When can you work for me?
So instead of doing what Ritchie Havens did along time
ago, going for it. I took the easy road. I backed him.
Why? Cause my contract was terminated from Warner
Bros. I would never think of going out there and trying to
get something going. Instead, I took the easy road because
I could do sessions. Me and my group from New Orleans
backed up Ritchie. Now I'm not saying that's bad. That
was good. I made alot of money. I had alot of fun even
though it wasn't my project. I tried to explain that to
people today. The first thing they say is "Wow, Ritchie
Havens" boy, I wish I could do that. You should have
been glad to get the work. They make it sound like I'm
not grateful. Man, I'm glad and I'm greatful, but what
about my project, even if you don't like it? Why can't you
say try try again? Naturally, my wife's not going to say
nothing. She likes that sideman money.

(170)

7/23/93

She could care less one way or the other. I couldn't
confide in no one. You see, everybody was trying to do

what I was doing, get work behind somebody. When I arrived In L.A. I arrived here with a hit record. I co-wrote a song called "When I Die". That what I wanted to pursue, a career. In doing my own thing, it's not a disgrace to back up no one, but I felt I was taking a step backwards by not pursuing my own thing. So, I stayed high all the time. That always made me forget about pursuing my goal. By this time I had been doing commercials for about 2 years, T.V. shows, you name it. I've done it. That's why in other peoples eyes I was doing great. That's what they wanted out of life, that was them that wasn't me. I remember when I was 13 years old I would go to a place called Sunset Lake in Portsmouth Virginia. I used to watch some great performers there. That was a place where blacks were allowed to go. I would watch those great performers.

(171)

7/23/93

I would say to myself "Man, I want to play like them". Only one thing, I will never do drugs. Believe me, I saw everybody. Now, I'm older. I can see how you can get caught up in the drug gang. It is so subtle. One joint leads to another, the next thing you know, you're doing 10-12-15 joints a day. No harm done cause you can pay for it. Somebody comes to a club and hears you. They like the way you sound. You make them feel good. So they want to make you feel good. You get three or four people like that, the next thing you know you're quietly doing 10 to12 joints a day. Boy, that stuff makes you like superman. You can do anything. That's why I didn't worry about pursuing my career. I could always put it off. Cause I could always put it off. Cause I would always afford to buy. You see, the cops very seldom bust people who can afford it. It's the ones who rob stores, steal to support their habits.

(172)

7/25/93

Around that time, Dianne Brooks was still in town. She was on Warner Bros. Records. Her album didn't do too well. So, she started to do background sessions. I had previously met Venetta Fields. She was with Boz Skaggs singing background for him, that is. I told Venetta that Dianne Brooks was looking for work. So, I recommended that Dianne, for her to sing with Boz Skaggs. She sang backgrounds for Boz Skaggs. I'm glad she got that job. That was about 1975 or 1976. Lets see, around that time, I was dropped from Warner. So, around that time I was working on the road with Kenny Rankin. Boy was I busy in those days. In the band were greats like Wendy Hass on piano, Martin Mulls' wife, Roy McCurdy, the drummer who was with Cannonball Aderly, Kenny was doing one of the songs we had written with me and his ex-wife Yvonne Rankin called "Lost up in Love With You". We were performing at a club called the Roxy. That's in Hollywood. Carman McRae was in the audience. She heard the song.

(173)

7/25/93

She said she wanted to record our song. I said Okay. I'll send it over tomorrow. So the next day, I called her to ask for her address. I said I would messenger the song over. She said no, you bring it. I remember I was so nervous. I was so nervous, I had to take a valium. The first time I ever did that. I remember going to her house. I got all choked up. It was hard for me to talk. She asked me to play the song for her. I couldn't. I was too nervous. So, she played it for me. Boy, can she play piano. I remember she called me William D. I don't understand it. I have worked with people like John Lennon, B.B.King, Bonnie Raitt, etc., and I didn't get nervous. But, Carman McRae. I almost jumped out of my skin. She did the song, thanks Carman. Boy, I was working so much in those days. Oh yeah, my group was still in town. Even at that time, I didn't have a record contract with anybody. It was about the fall of '76 when I was recording a record with Ritchie Havens, David Kirchenbaum was the producer.

(174)
                    7/25/93
We were recording his record at A&M studios in Hollywood. That's where the owner of A&M Jerry Moss's office was. He heard what I was doing with Ritchie Havens. I guess I was making so much money as a sideman, he asked me was I interested in a record contract with A&M? I said yes, on one condition. that you build me a recording studio in my garage so I can make demonstration records. He said yes. So, I made a record with A&M records. Out of 10 songs, 9 of them I wrote. People liked the one I didn't write. I recorded that album in Muscle Shoals Alabama. It was with the producers Clayton Ivey & Terry Woodford. Once again, I asked my music colleagues their opinion of the record. Once again, they said they liked it, but when can I start work for them. Oh well, I got enough money out of the deal to move to a two bedroom house in Van Nuys, CA. I got the kids a

bike, even though I was impecunious, I loved those kids. They were the family I never had.

(175)

7/25/93

When finally the studio in my backyard was erected, people like the great Chuck Rainey, Larry Carlton, Jeff Pocaro, David Paich, Steve Lukather, Mike Baird, James Gadson, Greg Puree, Roger Betholomey, Ritchie Zito, Reggie McBride, "pop" Popwell, etc. Guys, thank you ever so much. I remember we used to have a fridge in the studio. We used to keep beer and pop in there. I remember we got a case of beer for the studio and one of the cans had a dent in it. My ex-wife wanted to sue the beer company. Instead of getting the can replaced or just drinking it. I don't think it was poison or nothing like that. Like I said, before she's a vaxatious litigate. Boy, I had fun at that house. Playing table tennis with Willie Weeks. I saw on the Jay Leno Show Willie's working with Winona Judd. I wonder does she know that her bass player is a genius? Anyway, Rick Wilson, the engineer that was working in my studio did alot of records with alot of people. I remember when Toto used to come over to my studio to help me. Ali Willis used to use my studio to record.

The Man Beyond

It was the spring of "77. I was doing a tour with Mike Finnegen. He had done one of my songs (Saved by the Grace of Your Love). I was on the tour bus sitting there reading a music industry magazine when I saw this ad saying that they had home recording equipment that you could use in your home. I was excited cause now I could

make records at home. One of the roadys told me that the
sound would be bad. I told him that I didn't want to make
records, I wanted to do demos of the songs that I wrote.
To make a long story short, I got the equipment. The
other roady, Tommy Yuill, agreed to put it together for
me. He started and he had to go back on the road again.
So I asked a friend of mine Eddie Wynrick did he know
anybody else. He said that he knew a young guy named
Rick Wilson. I said great, I would love to meet him. So I
met Rick. He was a cross between Tom Cruis and Pat
Paulsen. Man, was he layed back. I asked him could he
wire my board. He thought about it for a while, then he
said yeah. He wired that board in 3 days, 3 weeks it
would normally take. Even though he was strange he did
things then that nobody had ever thought of. I don't
know how to explain it in layman's terms. Eddie ask me
how did things work out with Rick. I said to Eddie, he's a
genius but he's strange. Eddie said what do you mean. I
said that guy acts like Bob Dylan. Now he's head of sound
at The Post Group. That's a company puts effects to T.V.
shows and movies. The majority of the T.V. shows and
movies you see, The Post Group had something to do with
it. One of the things Rick did was the sound at the MGM
Studios at Epcot Center at Disneyworld in Florida. Rick,
even though you're famous now in the music world, you
started out in my garage. Upon reading this compendium
of Rick Wilson you can see why I call it The Man Beyond.
He's light years ahead of most people. Rick thanks for
everything including the late nights in my garage. Peace!

(176)

7/25/93

Boy, that was some good days then. I remember getting a
call from Gladys Night and The Pips' producer. Her name
was Rana Seneka. She was interested in recording one of
my songs that I had co-written with the great David
Palmer. He sang lead with Steely Dan on "I don't want to
do your Dirty Work". Anyway, I messengered the song
"Saved by Grace of Your Love" to her in Philly. They
recorded it. Boy I was in LaLa Land. Gladys Night and
The Pips recorded one of my songs. Boy, I've had such a
good life. I didn't realize I had it so good. I'm writing this
so young people that are pursuing a career won't make
the same mistakes. Never look a gift horse in the mouth.
Like I said, Rick Wilson and I were working in the studio
when I finished recording, I invited Jerry Moss to my
house to listen to what I had done. He liked it. Oh and by
the way, thank you Tommy for helping me to build the
studio. Chuck Rainy thank you for giving me that bass.
One of the basses that you owned.

(177)
7/25/93
It was around that time I got a call from Michael Stewart.
He said he was producing a girl by the name of Nancy
Shanks. Would I be interested in working with her? He
let me listen to some of her work. I listened. I liked it. I
worked with her. Me and her and her boyfriend hit it off
great. Not only did I play on her album, but I wrote some
songs with her. That was fun too! In those days, I
couldn't see for looking. I remember in those days
working with Jana Felesiano, Jose Felesiano's wife. She
got me an audition to star in Dustin Hoffman's movie
"Straight Time". The producer wanted a musician who
didn't act for a living. But, they finally ended up using

actors for the job. Boy, they were some good times. We lived on a piece of property that had about 15 fruit trees. My ex-wife had a garden with all kinds of vegetables. The kids had a tree house, they had just started school. Around the property was a wooden gate. I remember I was producing a Japanese film called "Mach 78". I had hired a professional mobile recording studio.

(178)

7/25/93

The name of the studio was Haji Sound. It was owned by Alex Kazanegras. I remember hiring a violin section for 12:00 a.m. in the morning. I can remember it was real dark out. You could smell the fruit trees. It had rained about 2 days prior. All you could here was violins at 12:00 a.m. Boy, that was sweet. The property was full of violin music. The kids were asleep. It was so peaceful. The dogs were at rest. Boy, that was a great time. I remember getting the job. Ken Fritz, my manager called me and said that this Japanese movie co. was doing a movie and was wondering could his client George Benson do it? He told them that he couldn't cause Benson was traveling at the time. But, he had another client that could do it. Boy, I'm glad he recommended me. I learned alot from doing that film. Oh yeah, a funny thing happened. I was working with Ritchie Havens at the time, he had just got his false teeth and he was singing a song called "Freedom".

(179)

7/25/93

Ritchie was jumping around on stage singing and his teeth fell out. There they were laying on the floor. When they fell, he didn't miss a beat. He kept right on singing he just

danced over to the side of the stage where his teeth were.
He picked them up and he kept on singing. It was so
funny. You had to see it to understand it. Teeth or no
teeth, you sing your ass off Ritchie. Anyway, I recorded a
record album for A&M records. I went to Muscle Shoals
Alabama to record my record. It didn't come out the way
I pictured it. Maybe one of the reasons was I wasn't
authoritative enough. Once again, alot of talent no self-
esteem. It was the same as my first record. They told me
what to do. The producer that is. I know that's their job,
but I was supposed to have some input. Well, how could I
do that if I stayed high all the time? I don't say nothing
the producers will. When you're high It's hard to take
charge.

(180)

7/25/93

Once again, the record co. heard the finished product.
They didn't like it. Not enough life in the record they
said. Little did they know about all the drugs that I did. It
was the same as my first record. I was in a state where I
didn't know nobody. So, I sent for the great Jim Horn.
Not only could he play, but I knew him. He was a familiar
face. I remember the producers wouldn't let me smoke
pot in the recording studio. They had alot of friend cops
down there, so I got the record co. to rent me a trailer so I
could smoke. I remember coming to record one night. I
had a bag of smoke in my pocket. I was going to my
trailer to get high and there were two cops in my trailer
and the two producers and a lady engineer white girl.
The two cops ask me did I have any smoke? I nervously
told them no. They were sitting around talking about

Alabama Law. How it was all right to shoot a man if you catch him with your wife.

(181)

7/25/93

I sat there nervously as they smoked. Finally after they smoked they left the trailer. Leaving me and the white girl in the trailer alone in Muscle Shoals Alabama. Boy, was I scared. I think that's the most frightened I've ever been. Even if things have changed in the south, I don't know maybe because I'm from the south. There's still smoke from the fire that's been put out a long time ago. Just think, a place like that, so much good music came from there. Once you get past the prejudice, you got it made every way. Thank you Terry and Clayton for helping me to make my album. Even though it wasn't a success, I thank you anyway. Just think all that money I was making, I had to borrow money to pay my rent. Talking bout money management I wasn't no H.F.C. Jim Horn, it was a pleasure working with you. I hear you're producing Delbert McClinton. Good luck with your project.

(182)

7/26/93

Before I move o there is one thing I would like to remember. One more thing. I remember my daughter by my first wife. Her name is Jeneanne. She came down to visit me when she was about 12 or 13. I don't know her exact age. But, I was glad to see her. That was one of the times I was with her. I was so irresponsible, my first wife Helen raised her. I remember taking her to my dope dealers house to purchase dope. Now, what kind of a way is that to raise a kid? Helen you did a great job. Jeneanne, I'm sorry I wasn't there for you. I hope some day I can make it up to you. Anyway, we moved from Van Nuys out to Woodland Hills. That's a suburb in L.A. It was a bigger house. It had a swimming pool, a barn. Kim Gardner helped me to move. He's the proprietor of the Cat and the Fiddle. That's a pub in Hollywood. Boy, that was a nice house. We had two dogs we used to have chickens, but the Coyotes ate them. It was great, I remember the kids and I swimming on Christmas Day. We were looking at the mountains, they were far away. They had snow on them. The kids asked me what that white stuff on the mountains was.

(183)

7/26/93

I told them that it was snow. They had never seen snow before. So we got dressed and drove to Lancaster CA. That's about 20 miles from Woodland Hills. You should have seen their faces when they saw the snow. They played in it. They threw snow balls. After, I showed them how to make them. What an experience watching them. Anyway, we went back home and got in the pool. You see, I've seen snow. I'm from back east. I used to live in Toronto remember? Anyway, back to projects. Like I said before, I was a multi-talented person. I could do alot of things. So, I did alot of things. For an example, I got a call from Eric Mercury to co-write with him for a segment in the movie "The Warriors". Great, I said when and how do we get paid? I ask. He said we don't up front but we get a chance to keep the publishing. That was around 1978. So him and I wrote a song for the movie called "You're moving too slow". It sounded good. Just before the movie came out, the producer called me and said that he needed the publishing, his mother was sick and he needed it.

(184)

7/26/93

I didn't give up my end of the publishing. To this day I still get checks. We'll, my ex-wife gets checks from that movie. Only in L.A. does that happen. I remember getting a call from Robert Appere to play keyboards for David Cassidy. So, after talking to me for a while, he convinced me to do it. I smoked enough pot, and numbed myself and did it. The session went on and on. I was so bored. Jim Keltner was playing drums. He saw my situation so he took me in his Mercedes and we listened to this tape he had. He said "Man, you've got to listen to this song I played on with Ry Cooder called "Down in Hollywood". Chaka Kahn was singing with him. We did this after the session. I remember listening to that song all night. Boy, that sounded good. About 6 in the morning, after listening to that song all night, we went to the corner bar. Opened it up we were the first customers. We proceeded to get pissy drunk. Keltner got real high. He called Ry Cooder about 7 in the morning and said to him " I know this keyboard player, he's good. You've got to use him on your next project".

(185)

7/26/93

Sure enough about a week later, I got a call from Ry Cooder. He asked me if I would like to go to New York and play Madison Square Garden with him. At the No Nukes Festival with him. There will be all kinds of artists

there. Bruce Springsteen, Jackson Browne, Graham Nash.
We only had to backup Chaka Khan when she sings
"Down in Hollywood" with me. I said yes. So, I went to
rehearse with him for the project. We rehearsed at a place
called The Alley owned by Bill Elkins. It was there that I
met the great David Lindley and the dynamic Bobby King.
I remember listening to Bobby sing. Man, he's great and
David Lindley sounds like 10 guys playing when he plays.
When Ry Cooder took his solo, I thought another person
was playing with him. Ali McGraw was at that rehearsal.
I remember cause I kept looking at her legs. Anyway, the
rehearsal was great. We went to New York, we arrived at
Madison Square Garden. I remember seeing and meeting
alot of celebrities. Bruce Springsteen, James Taylor, Carly
Simon, Jackson Browne,

(186)

7/26/93

Leah Kunkel, and my brother was there. His name is
Reggie. Boy, that was a treat backing up Ry Cooder and
Chaka Khan. Oh, by the way, Leah Kunkel is Momma
Cass'es sister. So when we got off the stage, I went over to
Leah Kunkels' dressing room. We started to talk. She was
telling me that she was doing some work around L.A.
locally. She said that she was doing it by herself. She said
I could join her. She said that she would like that. So
along with the other things, I was doing, I played locally
in L.A. with Leah Kunkel. That was real nice and
intimate. I liked playing with Leah. I learned alot form
her, she's real smart. She's a friend of Steven Bishop's.
She got me a movie session with Stephen Bishop. It didn't
pay no money. He said if I would give him a tape of my
songs, he would play it for some people for me if I would

do the session. For it's just one song and besides, people
like Donna Summer, Yvonne Edleman are going to sing
backgrounds on that one song. The movie is called
Hollywood Knights.

(187)

7/26/93

So I said to myself: What the hell, I'll do it anyway. He's
a friend of Leah's and he's a good writer. I knew Kenny
Rankin for a long time and Kenny did one of his songs.
What the hell, I'll do it. I'm not worried about the tape.
You know how people make promises. I did the session. I
sang backgrounds on the session. I gave Stephen the tapes
and forgot about it. It's about a month later I get a call my
ex-wife told me that Quincy Jones' office called me. He
wanted you to call when you get in. I told her yeah. It
was probably some people I knew pulling a prank on me.
That wasn't Quincy's office calling. About two weeks
later, Quincy himself called. I picked up the phone. It
was actually him. I choked and said hello. He told me
that he liked my music. He had a tape of my music from
Stephen Bishop. I would like to use your songs for James
Ingrams' album. It goes to show you, never judge a book
by it's cover.

(188)

7/28/93

Boy, there was so much going on in those days, I don't
know where to begin like I did before, I'll take it from
house to house 'cause I moved so much in those days.
Like I said before, even though I worked alot, I was an
impecious person. It was like clockwork. We would
move to a place, I would pay the rent for a while, then the

rent would interfere with the drug money. Then we
would move. Let's see. . . .it was around 1978, Eric
Mercury and I had just written some songs. He was
divorced by then. He started dating this big singing star.
He told me not to mention her name. She's a vaxatious
litigate. He told me so I won't mention her name.
Anyway, she came to my house to listen to some of my
songs. She recorded three of my songs. One of them was
in a movie. Thank you Eric for introducing her to me.
Back to Leah Kunkel, it was around the time that Leah and
I recorded the Stephen Bishop soundtrack. It was
February 1980. We both convinced each other that it
would be nice if we could take our act that we had
together on the road. Graham Nash had asked her if she
could open the show for him. She said yes. So she asked
me did I want to

(189)

7/28/93

open the show for Graham Nash? I said yes. So we
rehearsed at her house. I remember going to her music
room. Her then husband, Russ Kunkel had so many gold
records on the wall. It was wall to wall gold records. I
had never seen nothing like that before. So we rehearsed.
She did some of my songs. It was great. It was so nice.
Just piano and her. What a nice sound. So we went on the
road with Graham. When we got to L.A. some of his
music colleagues that played on the Crosby, Stills, and
Nash album appeared on the show with us. Such as
David Lindley, Gloria Coleman, Lenny Castro, Greg
Doerge and etc. Graham was traveling light. He had a
piano player and a guitar player. It was sort of an
acoustical atmosphere. All of a sudden, Graham didn't

like what the piano player was doing. He wanted to get another piano player in the middle of the tour. He asked me I told him no. Me and his piano player had gotten close and I knew him. He said if I don't do it, somebody else will. He said I thought you would like to do it being that you're out here anyway. Besides, you could make double money.

(190)

7/28/93

I thought about it for a while. Discussed it with my ex-wife, we both agreed that I should do it. Leah didn't think it was cool. She said it would break up the act. I told her that It wouldn't. I could do both I said. So, we had an argument. So against her wishes, I did it anyway. So, I got on Grahams tour bus, listened to the tape one time and did the show. Boy, that was some hard work. What I would do is get high before I go on stage then when I would go on stage, I would tell the roadie to put a beer on the piano. I don't know how I did it , but I did the show. It went over well. The white kids in the audience couldn't understand what was this black piano player doing knowing Graham Nash's music? I remember playing with Graham at Penn State. The girl who was the president of the entertainment committee. We were talking about the Rolling Stones. I said Stevie Wonder opened the show for them one time. She said isn't that that blind guy who sings? I said yes. Have you ever heard of Marvin Gaye?

(191)

7/28/93

She said no. Here was a college girl an American college girl raised in New York City all of her life, and she had

never heard of Marvin Gaye. He's only had tons of hits.
It's funny how the music system is so different here in
America. If you're white, you're pop. If you're black
you're R&B. Anyway, the tour was fun. I'm glad I
listened to Crosby, Stills, & Nash. That's right, I'm not
supposed to listen to that music. Oops, that's right I'm
black. The next time I won't listen to it. Let's see... around
that time around 1980, I got a call from Leslie Morris. She
was a contractor in L.A. at the time. She's a great lady.
She asked me if I wanted to do a movie soundtrack called
Breathless with Richard Gere. She said you have to be
able to read, but I can't read fast. That Monday, I
remember it well. We was supposed to be in the session.
She called me that Friday and told me the session was
canceled. You'll get paid for the session she said.

(192)

7/28/93

As long as you agree to do the session when we re-book
the session. I said all right what away to make a living.
Stay at home and still get paid. So when Leslie called me
back for the session, I said yeah. So, I got to the session, it
was in Hollywood. It was a big session: 5 guitar players,
percussionists, violins, 2 piano players. Jack Nietzsche
was the musical director. They put the music in front of
me. It looked like somebody had put pepper on the paper.
It was so many notes. Jack counted off the song. He went
1-2-123 the music looked like mumbo jumbo to me. I
couldn't play it. He counted it off again. I was so
embarrassed I didn't know what to do. There's a perfect
example of someone biting off more than they can chew. I
wished that I could have gone home, just to get a hug
from my ex-wife. Some kind of reassurance from her. I

was the only black out of 40 people in the room. I was throwing up all the way there. I had smoked about 5 joints.

(193)

7/28/93

I guess that's the gun fighters where once you get any kind of a reputation you had to take on everything. When it came down to the ad-lib songs. I was great. Since then, I've never did that. I've learned my lesson. Oh yeah, I was doing alot of work with Glen Spreen. He knew some guys from his home town in Texas. They had a group called Navasoto. They were trying to get a record contract so they asked Glen Spreen to help them. so Glen asked me to help to help them. So, I said yeah. I met the leader King Cotton, we got a talkin' I said I'll take you to my house and introduce you to my then wife and kids. We did that. I introduced him to my then wife she said hello. I introduced him to my then son he said hello. I introduced him to my little girl, she took one look at him. She was one of those kids. She called it like she saw it. She said "Daddy, he's wild".

(194)

7/28/93

I didn't know what to say. Here was this skinny guy with a long beard standing there. Of course, I apologized for her. To this day, she all grown up, she's not changed. Greg Mathison used to work with Larry Carlton playing piano for him. That's how I met him. Then, he started to work for Georgio Maroda arranging for him. So he was working with Donna Summer doing the song "Heaven Knows", so he recommended me to do sound effects on

117

the song. I got there, I had my album with me. I played it for Georgio. I asked him how did he like it? He said great. Now, could you do some sound effects for me on this album? I said yeah. He said do some sound effects when Donna sings the verse to Heaven Knows. So we did that. We listened to the play back. I suggested: why don't I just answer Donna when she sings on the verse? Georgia said great idea. So, I got my 260 dollars and was glad to get the work. I think she put Joe Esposito on that song, she didn't use that version.

(195)

7/28/93

Just think, I got a chance for 200 dollars to work with Donna Summer. I got a chance for Georgio Moroda to hear my album. Oh boy, great business. I think the song made about 1 million dollars. I made 200 dollars. At that time, I was doing alot of background sessions. The great Venetta Fields was working with me. She's so talented. What a great person. What a great lady. Boy, she used to give some great parties at her house. It was at her house I met Booker T. Jones, Kris Kristofferson and alot of stars. I remember when my then wife left town to visit, Venetta cooked enough food to last me for two weeks. Boy, could she cook. My then wife couldn't come close to her cooking. Around that time, around 1980 Eddie Wynrick introduced me to Cecelia and Kapono. They asked me would I like to produce them? I said yes. In those days, I said yes to everything. Anything to get money to get high. A hippie junkie that's what I was.

(196)

7/28/93

I remember those guys. They never spoke to each other.
If one wanted to speak to the other, they would talk
through me. And I would talk to the other guy for him. I
was not only hired to produce them, but I was also hired
to baby-sit them too! It was around that time that Eddie
Wynrick re-introduced me to Larry Carlton. Man, we hit
it off good. He was doing an album called 335. He asked
me did I have any songs? I said yes. But, I didn't have
any instrumentals. He said that's all right. Let me hear
what you got. So, I played him two songs. I had co-
written with Eric Mercury called "Where did you Come
From?" and "I Apologize". He liked them. I asked him
was he going to do the song instrumental? He said no.
He was going to sing them. I showed him how to sing
them. He sung them. It's on his album. Eddie Wynrick,
thank you.

(197)

                    7/28/93
It was around that time when the trustee of benefit took
me to his house. That's when I met his then wife. He
introduced me to her. The first thing he did was tell me
her name. The second thing he said was we have an open
relationship. Man, what's that? I said to myself I said that
only happens on T.V. or some crazy movie. I said to
myself I said an open relationship is when you can be with
anybody. I said to myself wait a minute. I'm just here to
make music with you. I'm not interested in being with
your wife I said to myself. Turns out I found out that was
his idea. She didn't want to have a relationship like that.
Anyway, she ended up having an affair with his best
friend. He got mad at her. I don't understand. I didn't
know there were rules to having an open relationship. I

thought you could be with anybody you wanted to be with.

(198)

7/28/93

Back to Larry Carlton. Larry and I were hittin it off great. Him and his-ex-wife would take turns going to dinner. I turned him on to sushi. Things were going great. My then wife was jealous of them, 'cause Larry made more money than I did. Larry and I had a great musical relationship. My ex-wife would threaten me by saying if you don't stop yelling at me, I won't go to Larry's for dinner with you. To this day, I still can't figure out why I married her. My first wife, it broke me up when we got divorced! But her, I couldn't wait to leave. I don't care how bad! I've had it. It is better than being with her. Thank you God for letting me see the light. The only thing I got out of that marriage was two beautiful kids. I got a great kid from my first marriage, the only difference is I loved her. We treated each other like human beings. To this day, one thing I learned you pay for mistakes.

(199)

7/29/93

Let me reiterate by stating this book is not in chronological order. Being that I was an antsy person, I moved all the time. But, I do remember time with which house we lived in. So, I'll tell you the event that took place at the time I lived there. For example, I lived on Dumont Avenue in Woodland Hills, CA. From 1978 to about 1982. I'll tell you the events that happened around that time in that house. Once again were talking about alot of big names in this book. I don't want to get to graphic or not get graphic

at all. Go to your local supermarket and get a tabloid.
They make people look like animals. I don't want to do
that. I merely want to write the positive things about
people. And to tell people how and why I'm like this.
And young people don't be this way. Anyway it was
around 1979 I was in the music room practicing when my
ex came in and said "Smitty, just in case something
happens to you, why don't you sign over your half of
everything to me." I said "You get half anyway. This is
L.A." I wonder what she was going do to me?

(200)

7/29/93

I remember around that time, I met a guy named Brook
"Bubba" Shields through the group Navasoto. I was
supposed to produce him and the money I made from him
I was going to take it and give it to her and leave. But,
Bubba never got the financial end of it together. Around
that time lets see around '79 Ry Cooder introduced me to
some guys that resided in Hawaii. Their names were
Baird Brittingham and Steve Smith. They wanted me to
play for their artist that they were producing called Peter
Moon. That was fun. I got a chance to go to Hawaii. I
had been there before to play a job for Graham Nash.
When I arrived from Hawaii, I got a call from Glenn
Spreen. He told me that Bob Dylan's office had called
looking for me. They wanted you to audition for him to
go and work with him. So, I met him and told him that I
didn't do auditions. That I would play for him for three
hours and he could pay me as if I was doing a record
session. So, I played. He liked what he heard. I said what
about the pay? He said "do I have to pay you if I like
what I heard?"

(201)

7/29/93

I said no Bob. He said I would like for you to play on my
tour with me. I said okay. So, I went back the next day
and I met everybody that worked with him. Oh, by the
way, Ian Wallace, the drummer that did the Rolling
Thunder Tour with him recommended me, I met him with
David Lindley. On drums was Jim Keltner, bass Tim
Drummond, guitar Fred Tackett presently with Little Feet.
Singers backgrounds: Carol Dennis formally with
everybody. Madlyn Qubec formally one of the Rayettes,
Regina McCreary formally with Donna Fargo and Clydie
King. She was one of the original black background
singers who started backgrounds on records in L.A.
Those people were something else. Bob always had
plenty of food for us to eat. Everything was fine. Bob was
very spiritual. So, I went on top of the roof to smoke my
dope. I had never seen anything like him. You wouldn't
believe the fans that man had. He would always come to
rehearsal late 'cause he was always busy.

(202)

7/29/93

So I would just sit around and play. Then, Carol Dennis
would sing along with me. Boy, can she sing. She can
sing anything. I fell in love with her voice. I asked her
why aren't you a star? She said, "this man honey, I had
this man, because of him I didn't pursue my career". I
said to her what's a man got to do with you pursuing your
career? Just do it. She said I don't know honey. It
seemed like every time I get involved with a man, he tries
to stop me. I said leave him then. So, I wrote a song about

it called "I Had This Man". Bette Midler heard it and
liked it. I remember talking to Bette, what a smart
woman. Now I see why she is so successful. She recorded
that song. She sat me down and made me tell her what
the song was about. She wanted to know everything
about the lyrics inside and out. I'm glad I know
something about the lyrics. Kathy Wakefield my partner
wrote the lyrics. I just gave Kathy the idea.

(203)

7/29/93

I learned one thing about Bette Midler. She's nobody's
dummy. Carol, good luck with your record deal. Bob
Dylan is the strangest person that I have ever met. For
example, we were on the road, after rehearsal he would
play backgammon with me. I don't know why, but he
would always play with me. I used to beat him everyday.
It didn't matter. He would play anyway. We would talk
about events that took place that day. I remember one
time we were in Europe, London England to be exact. I
had never been to London. He had plenty of times. I was
so excited. I did all the things I wanted to do in London,
like go to the British Museum, ride a double decker bus,
visit Buckingham Palace. So, when I got to Earls Court,
that's where we were playing, we rehearsed. After the
rehearsal, Bob and I played backgammon. We got to
talking. He asked me what did you do today? I told him I
went out on the town. Steve Merritot's wife took me to
the British Museum. I went on a double decker bus, I had
tea at Harrods.

(204)

7/29/93

And I told him I went to Buckingham Palace, then Bob
asked me he said " Do you know somebody at
Buckingham Palace?" I said no Bob. I said do you know
somebody there? He said no. Then I asked him were you
invited there would you go? He said nah. I said why? He
said, "I don't have a thing to wear". With him I always
ended up scratchin my head. Half the time I didn't know
what he was talking about. To show you how cocky I was
in those days, I was making about 5 thousand dollars a
week with Bob. Having lots of fun. We were in Europe.
The band members were bugging me to play like Spooner
Oldham, the piano player that used to play before me. So
I got mad at the band members. I went and smoked a
joint and went to Bob and told him that I was mad at
them. that I didn't want to ride on the same plane or sleep
in the same hotel with them. Bob told me I don't agree
with you. But, if that's what you want to do okay. The
only difference is you'll have to pay the expenses. To pay
my own expenses in Europe cost me about 3 thousand
dollars a week.

(205)

7/29/93

On top of paying for my oldest daughter's expenses, she
was living in Holland with her mother. And I wanted her
on the road with me, so I paid for Jeneanne's expenses all
over Europe. Besides, I had to have my dope. So, every
town we would go to, I would get a new supply. For
example, if I was in London, I wouldn't go to France with
drugs on me. I would throw the drugs away in London
and get some more in France. The tour lasted for six
weeks. I was making 5 thousand a week. When I came
home I owed Bob Dylan 4 thousand dollars. Talking

about money management, I was the king. When I
arrived home, I decided that I was going to record some of
my songs that I had written. My ex decided that we or I
should have a family reunion. Great I said. So her, Amani
and Sala went ahead. She visited her mother in Canada
for two weeks. I had my own bank account then. 'Cause I
was careless then. I had to have some sessions at my
house.

(206)

7/29/93

I couldn't pay the musicians money for all the songs that I
wanted to record. It was about 20 songs. So, I called them
and told them that I didn't have no money to pay them,
but I could get some drugs. Man, I had 4 bands. No
problem. I mentioned the magic word. Being that I was
the only one home, I had a recording engineer to come
and live in. I had two weeks of fun. I had plenty of
women. Plenty of music. What more could you ask for?
To ask God to relieve the pain that you were in. In those
days, I couldn't stand being alone. I was always looking
to fill that void. So, if this book sounds like its about me,
you're right. I'm adamant about people doing what I did
to reach their goals. Don't do it, its a nowhere street.
You're always looking fast and standing still. Always
looking for that thrill. Always wanting to see what's over
that hill.

(207)

7/29/93

I remember talking to Bob Dylan after we arrived from
Europe. You see, he wanted to dress real slick like. So, I
said "Bob we shouldn't dress like that. We look like a

cheap night club act. We should be or dress a little more conservative." So the next night, I went to the wardrobe mistress to ask for my favorite shirt, Bob had it on. He wore it every night. Man, that guy is so off beat. He said he said he liked it. So, he wore it every night. He asked me where I got my clothes. I told him In Woodland Hills. I was telling him that my little boy rode bike professionally, that a guy by the name of Bruce McConnell makes his bikes for him. So, Bob said "great, we'll go to the mall where you get your clothes and we'll go over to Bruce's house to go and get some bikes for my kids." So, I told Bruce's' wife Dee McConnell about this. I told her that Bob Dylan wanted to come over to her house and if he does come, please be cool. You see, Dee was like Lucy on the I Love Lucy Show. So, I reiterated again. Please, conserve your energy.

(208)

7/29/93

So, Dee and Bruce lived in Woodland Hills. They or she owned about 4 dogs, maybe 3 cats. So, Bob came to my house first. We went to the mall to get the clothes at the store where I shopped. The name of the store was called Apropos. Gary owned it. I can't think of his last name. Dylan walked in the store he saw a complete outfit hangin on the wall. He would say I want that outfit. There was an imported sweater that I always would try on when I would go there. I would never think of buying the sweater. It cost one thousand dollars. I would dream about having it. So, I tried it on. Bob saw me with it on. So, Bob bought it for me. Wow! In the end, Bob spent ten thousand dollars on clothes. Gary got a little nervous. So, when Bob went to pay for it, he just signed for it. So, Gary said to him "are you good for the money?" Bob looked at him and said "call the bank". So when Gary called the bank, he asked the person on the phone was Bob good for ten thousand dollars. The person at the bank just fell out laughing. They laughed so hard at him that Gary knew he had made a mistake calling the bank.

(209)

7/29/93

So Gary gave Bob the clothes. Or, Bob's personal valet or bodyguard came to pick them up. Then, we went to Bruce and Dee's house to get the bikes. When we arrived at their house, I reiterated to her again. Please don't blow your cool. She said O.K. So, I introduced both of them to Bob. She was very cool. They took care of the business of buying the bikes. I think Bob bought about 5 bikes. So, Dee calmly asked Bob would you like to have a cup of tea? Bob said yes. So, Bob sat at the kitchen table. While he was drinking his tea, Dee said the animals would like to sing you a song. So you had Dee and her dogs and 3 cats singing jingle bells. If you could have seen the look on Bob's face when 7 animals started to sing. When they finished I said to Dee, I thought you said you were going to be cool. She said "I was, I just wanted to show Bob that my animals could sing." So, we left and went back to my house. We went to my music room and started to play music. We had a good time. Finally, he left.

(210)

7/29/93

When he left, my ex called me into the living room. She said to me I just heard on the T.V. that John Lennon got shot. I didn't want to say anything to you while Dylan

was here. When Dylan found out, he doubled the security
around rehearsal. He took Lennon's death very hard.
You see, him and Lennon was very close. Then there was
the time when I got a call from Waddy Watchel. He's the
guitar player that plays with Keith Richards of the Rolling
Stones. He plays in Keith's band. Waddy does alot of
other things, like he has played with James Taylor, Linda
Rondstadt, Crosby, Stills and Nash. He's produced a
number of artists. He called and said I'm down in
Hollywood playing guitar for the Pointer Sisters Album
and they needed a ballad. So, I recommended your song
"Dreamin as One". Would you like to come down and
play on it? I said yes. Wow! The pointer sisters doing
one of my songs. They recorded "Dreamin as One" on the
Priority Album. Produced by Richard Perry. Associated
producer Trevor Lawrence.

(211)

7/29/93

When they finished recording the song, I listened to the
song. I heard them singing the song, I started crying.
They sounded so good. I couldn't stop crying. I've never
done that. The only time that I've ever cried over an artist
was Oscar Peterson and John Coltrane. I don't know what
got into me. Anyway, I knew Trevor for a long time and I
had worked with Richard Perry on the Martha Reeves
Album. So, Trevor called me and said he wanted me to
collaborate on a song. So I said okay, come on over to my
house. I listen to the song, I couldn't come up with
nothing. You see, Trevor knew I was a songwriter, so he
took for granted that I could write lyrics. Boy, I tried to
come up with something, cause he was co-producing the
Pointer Sisters. I wanted to write a song with him so he

could use it for the Pointer Sisters' album but it didn't work. So he went to the Pointer Sisters for lyrics. So he said if you can't come up with no lyrics could you play keyboards on the song.

(212)

7/29/93

I said yes so I went to the studio in Hollywood to play on the song. The Pointer Sisters were really gong strong then. So I said Oh, well, at least I'll get a chance to play on their album. The song came out and it did well. The name of the song was "I'm So Excited". It did so well that Trevor called me back to play on another song of theirs called "Slowhand". Trevor, thanks for the call. I'm just sitting here at the park writing this book listening to some tapes on the cassette player. I'm just sitting writing and listening to a demo that Carol Dennis made. Damn, can she sing. Carol, you are too much. I remember when we were living in Woodland Hills, we had a neighbor. His name was Uncle Joe. I don't know his full name. We used to call him that. He was the guy who invented credits when you see them at the end of the T.V. show. Uncle Joe I'll miss you wherever you are.

(213)

7/29/93

I remember when we arrived in Woodland Hills. My ex-wife and I enrolled Amani and Sala into the local school there. I remember going to the plays they had in the auditorium. Man, that piano was out of tune. It was so bad that when I had to go to see them in a play, I would hold my ears. That was the time when Jeneanne came from Europe to visit me, Helen and her ex-husband were

ex-change teachers. They were in Holland at the time
teaching. They came back for the holidays, so while they
were in Canada, Helen let Jeneanne come visit me. I
remember having Jeneanne in the car with me. I took her
to my dope dealer's house when I was purchasing dope.
Boy, was I cocky in those days. Anyway, thank you Helen
for being so understanding. You see my little girl,
Jeneanne, is very special. The doctor told Helen that she
would never be able to have children because she had
rheumatic heart trouble. Helen had her in spite of what
the doctor said. Helen's been married for about 18 years
since. No children.

(214)

7/29/93

You see, I told you that Jeneanne was special. Even
though Jeneanne really cares for me, sometimes towards
me she's a little standoffish towards me. Because, I was an
irresponsible person when she was coming up. But, one
day as she gets older, she'll learn to forgive and forget. I
remember having large barbecues at my house on
Sundays. People like Rita Coolidge, Bonnie Raitt, Bob
Dylan, people like that would show up. Rosemary Butler
came. I use to write with her. She sings background for
people like James Taylor, Roseanne Cash, Jackson Browne,
etc. We used to have such a good time. It was about that
time Harry Neilson recorded an album. He worked hard
on the album. When he finished with the finished
product, he took the album and played it for the record
company. They heard the album. They didn't like the
album. Harry was very disappointed in them. So, Harry
asked the record company how much did you spend on

130

my album? The guy at the record company said 175
thousand dollars. So, Harry took out his check book

(215)
7/29/93
and wrote RCA a check for 175 thousand dollars. I had
never seen nothing like that in my life. Boy, was he ever
rich. He was a teller at a bank in New York in the 1960's.
There was a little company starting up, so he bought some
shares in that company. The company rocketed he made a
fortune. The name of the company was IBM. I remember
in those days when Quincy Jones introduced me to James
Ingram. We used to work alot in those days together.
That was around 1980. That's when he was doing
background sessions then. Surprisingly enough, he knew
who I was. Then, it was around that time David Foster's
career was taking off. Maurice White the leader of Earth,
Wind & Fire had approached

(216)
8/2/93
David Paich. Maurice White arranged and produced for
Earth, Wind & Fire. I think Maurice offered Paich about a
quarter of a million dollars to do this. Paich turned it
down. I said to Paich, man you're crazy. Why did you do
that? He told me that I wanted to get my own group
together. I know I've been working with alot of acts.
Now, it's time to do my own thing. I said man get that
money. It's nothing wrong with doing your own thing I
said. But, a bird in the hand is better than a bird in the
bush. He said, I know , but I want to try it anyway. So, he
did that. He got his group together, they put out a record.
It was a hit. The group was called Toto. The rest is

history. David Foster went on to write, arrange, and produce for Earth, Wind & Fire. He co-wrote a song with Jay Grayden and Bill Chaplin called "After the love has Gone". Also, the rest is history. I was wrong all the way around. Foster, I've not seen since then. He's gone on to make millions. He worked with just about every big name in the music business. David Foster, good luck.

(217)

8/2/93

And David Paich? What can I say? The guy is a great keyboard player. He's the keyboard player with Toto. Paich, play on. Venetta's so great she's worked with a lot of big names: Steely Dan, Bob Seagar, Aretha Franklin. If in this book it sounds like I'm name dropping? I am. They are some great people. I'm proud to have been associated with or to know them. It was around that time around the latter part of 1980 that I went to a club called Josephina's with Chuck Rainey, the famous bass player. We just went to hear the music. That's where people like Rick James, Al Jarreau, actors and all kinds of entertainers hang out. Eric Johnson ran the jam session. When Chuck and I left, he had a handful of tapes that young wannabes gave him. It's a wonder if Chuck's not crazy. Not only does he play all day, but when he goes out to relax, he's bombarded by fans. Hang in there Chuck.

(218)

8/2/93

I remember after coming back from the Bob Dylan tour I decided to write some songs. I couldn't pay the musicians, so I paid them with drugs. I purchased about 2 thousand dollars worth of drugs. Hell, it was cheaper to pay the guys. But, I couldn't do that. I would have enough money to buy drugs. My ex had gone. It took me two weeks to record those songs. It took me two weeks to go through the two thousand dollars. Boy, was I cocky then the money I blew. Once again, I'll reiterate by saying this book is about how I spent a fortune on drugs. This book is not meant to demean anyone. The reason why I'm not looking outside my problems is that I think It's necessary to show you what can happen with an individual when he doesn't take care of business. Oh yeah, I had the pleasure of working with Love Lace Watkins. He's American born, but his fame is in Europe. Love Lace, nice knowing you.

(219)

8/2/93

While working with Bob Dylan, Clydie King, his background vocalist 's son had a little friend named Holly Robinson, she wanted to do a demo. So, Clydie asked me would I do it for her? I said yes. We did Blue Bayou by Linda Ronstadt. And one of my songs "Saved by the Grace of Your Love". Since then, she's a little older, she did a show called 21 Jump Street. Holly, it was great working with you. You had talent even when you were a little girl. Good luck with your career. Once again, I'll reiterate and say this book is not chronologically in order. I'm doing this book from memory. I'm telling you the events that happened from the places that I lived in. I remember doing so many things, a multi-talented person. Unlike Tina Turners' book. She left Tennessee, went to St. Louis , married Ike Turner. Sang for him, he abused her, she left him and started her own career. And you know the rest. Even though I did alot of things, and worked with alot of people, I'm not a household name.

(220)

8/2/93

You see, in those days, I had an indefeatable attitude. I was young, I really thought I was indestructible. I played on alot of hit records. Nothing can happen to me I said. You get that way when you're on a roll. But sooner or later, that kind of living will get next to you like Eric Mercury putting me down for not selling my end of the song outright to the producer. And me, not having the stamina to talk to him and say no. Instead, I smoke a joint and told him no. To me, drugs always made it feel better. What an unnatural feeling. Once again, my apologies for not including the hundreds of people in my life. If I was to do that, this book would be about 10 thousand pages long. So, I mentioned their names at the back of the book. Sorry guys, if I can't remember your first or last names. It's only been about 20 years since I've talked to you. So, I didn't put your name down. But, you can rest assured I remember the times, good and bad.

(221)

8/2/93

I had the pleasure in those days to work with Dusty Springfield. The great Jay Grayden who now produces Al Jerrau played guitar on the record session. Sonny Burke, the piano player with Smokey Robinson was the producer. I had to be strong from working with Dusty, Jay Grayden and Sonny Burke. Also, around that time, I had the pleasure of working with Jimmy Weatherspoon. Chuck Rainy was playing bass. Cornell Dupree was playing

guitar. Richard Tee was playing piano. Bernard Purdie
was playing drums. Boy, can Jimmy Weatherspoon sing
the blues. Boy, he's good. That is one of the times I felt
like a super star when I played with those guys. It was
around that time when Dianne Brooks went back to
Toronto. Being that she was a shy person, she didn't do as
well as she did in Toronto. You know how L.A. is. You
have to be aggressive here. You're as good as your last hit
here.

(222)

8/2/93

It was around that time when I got a call again from a
drummer who used to work with Bob Dylan. He said to
me would I like to work with Chuck Berry? I said yes. So,
I worked with Chuck Berry. I'll say this for Chuck. He's
the most dynamic musician that I've worked with. I did
the T.V. show Solid Gold with him. I did an H.B.O special
with him. Tina Turner sang with him. My compendium
of Chuck Berry? He's a bitter man. I remember when I
was a kid, Chuck Berry used to have a couple of songs on
the top ten charts at all times. But by Americans? No
recognition. He would tell me that in his heyday, he
would do a concert and play before hundreds of
thousands of people. When he would finish, the promoter
of that concert would get the money and leave. The
record company would take his royalties. They would put
their names on the songs that he wrote, so they could get
paid . Elvis Presley gets all the recognition, not him.

(223)

8/2/93

And you wonder why the man's so bitter. He's one of the founders of rock n' roll as we know it today. Let alone saying something to him, it's never mentioned in America. We should have a shrine built in his honor thanking him. Chuck Berry, thank you so much for making it possible for me to have a career in rock n' roll. I remember Marsha calling me to come to New York. That's Ritchie Havens' manager. He needed some songs for his new album. So, they called me to come to New York to pitch songs to Ritchie Havens. I remembered going to New York. I think that was the fall of 1979. I got there, checked in the hotel, went to Ritchies office. There was his publishers there. They were these two hot shot publishers there. They listened to my songs. They said that they liked two songs. I remember them telling me right up front, if we do the songs we want 50%. I wasn't used to people being that up front. I was used to L.A. where people would wine and dine you, smile in your face, and then they would tell you.

(224)

8/2/93

Just then Ritchie intervened and said fellows, no. He's not like that. Boy, I'm glad he said something. Or I wouldn't know what to do. So, I left his office and went with Eric Mercury, he had just moved there. He was staying in this loft. This famous lady who owned it had her instruments, gold records and all of her situations stored there. I said, Eric this is nice, where is your girlfriend? Meaning the star who owned it. He said This isn't where she lives. This is a place where she keeps her trophies. I said oh. That's what she treated him like. A trophy. Like a music

colleague of mine wrote for Anne Murry, my highly
prized possession.

(225)

8/4/93

It was around that time it took so much coke to have sex
with my ex, that I used to have sex with her and think
about this one girl that I used to have sex with. Her name
was Delores Murry. That's the only time then, I got
rejected. At that time. I don't know, I would always think
about her alot when things wasn't going right. I said to
myself, memories I'll never see her again. She had great
sex, but she was a little slow. I'll get past that I said and
just have the sex. You see, I mistook slowness for
dumbness. In those days, being that I was the big fish in
town. Live and learn now is what I say. It was about that
time around 1980. I got a phone call from an engineer I
knew named James Armstrong and Richard Baskin, son of
Basnkin & Robins (ice cream). Barbara Streidands -ex.
They asked me if I wanted to play with Lilly Tomlin on
her album. I said yes. I went to the studio. It was in
Hollywood. It was called Silvery Moon.

(226)

8/4/93

I remember meeting Lilly Tomlin. She said hello. She
said I want you to play on this song for me called The
Honky Tonk Preacher. She said that guy was a honky
tonk preacher, and when he started preaching the holy
ghost, you start playing honky tonk piano. She started to
make a face like Ernestine the telephone operator. Man, it
took me so long to do the song. 'cause I was falling out so
much. She was so funny. I laughed so hard that my

stomach was hurting. She kept looking at me so funny.
She kept wondering what was wrong with me. The more
she would try to explain the song to me, the more I would
break up laughing. Man, that woman is a riot. Then, it
was about that time, I got a phone call from Ry Cooder.
He asked me did I want to do a European Tour with him.
Being that I was an impecunious person at that time, I said
yes. Not only that the guy can play. So, I went to Europe
with him. I was real laid-back then. I only drank wine
and smoked joints on that tour. None of that hard stuff for
me. You see, I cut back on that tour.

(227)

8/4/93

I really honestly and truly thought I was cutting back. I
didn't do as many drugs as I did on the Bob Dylan tour.
Ry Cooder had some good musicians on tour with him.
Jim Keltner on drums, Jim Dickinson on piano, Chris
Ethridge on bass, me on organ, Bobby King on
backgrounds, Pico Paine on backgrounds, Willie Green on
backgrounds. The unit was nice. I had fun with those
guys. I played good music with Cooder, got to see
Jeneanne. She lived in Holland with her mother. They
came to see me when I was in Amsterdam. I went to see
her in her hometown. A place in Holland called
Hornsbrooke. Things were going good. We went to
England. George Harrison came to the gig. Ringo Starr
was there. The place was called The Odeon
Hammersmith. It was nice talking to Ringo and George. I
knew Ringo from the Bob Dylan album. We played
together on that album along with Ron Wood. Then,
while in England, I got a call from a guy named Dick
Allen. He was Chuck Berry's agent. Dick Allen worked

for the William Morris Agency. He asked me to work for Chuck Berry in Tahoe at Ceasars Palace. Once again, I said yes.

(228)

8/4/93

So when I arrived from England, I drove up to Tahoe with Eric Johnson. He was the drummer. I remember being on stage with Chuck Berry. He was playing his guitar. Then the string on his guitar broke. So he gave the guitar to the bass player to re-string it. While the bass player was stringing the guitar for him, Chuck Berry started to recite some poetry. I had never heard nothing like that before. Boy, he's great! What a poet. What a writer. Man he's good, since then I've done a radio commercial, a movie, and various night clubs with him. I'll reiterate and say that Chuck is a great player, writer, and an originator of rock n' roll guitar. Chuck, it was an honor to have worked with you. Once again, the impecunious person that I was in those days, we had to move again. We found a place in Woodland Hills. It was on a street called Glendoren. It was a nice house. It set on the side of the hill. When I would take the kids to school, white kids would call me nigger. When will they ever learn.

(229)

8/5/93

Around that time, I know it was after the tour with Bob Dylan. I got a phone call from Mike Finnegan. He asked me to do a T.V. show with him. Basically we were the house band consisting of Reggie McBride bass, the late Jim Krieger on guitar, Marty Grebb on sax, Mike Finnegan on keyboards and me on keyboards and Nick Jaegger on drums. I said yeah, but why do you want me, I asked? He said basically we don't have to have you, but the producer of the show said we needed two blacks, that way they won't have Jessie Jackson on their backs. Great feeling huh? To know you're there because of your color. Anyway, I did the show. I needed the money. Hell, I always needed the money. Hell, I basically in those days was an impecunious person. Anyway, the gig was great. We were the house band. We backed all kinds of groups like Boy George, Etta James, Graham Nash, Ted Nugent and etc. We were sort of responsible sort of for recommending artists. So, everybody on the show knew I had worked with Bob Dylan. So they asked me, why don't you call Bob Dylan and ask him to be on the show. I said, Man, I don't know Dylan that well to get his business. They kept bugging me to call him.

(230)

8/5/93

So I said Okay. I'll just ask him and be very honest with him. Hell, what do I have to lose. All he can do is say yes or no. So, I put in a call to his office. He got back to me in a couple of days. He said hello. What can I do for you? he said. I told him I just said "Bob, were doing a television show for NBC it's called Rock&Roll Tonight" and I said I'm in the house band. And we have to get a guest to appear on the show. Would you be interested I said. He said what's in it for me? I said anything you want you're Bob Dylan they'll give you anything and besides it would be nice for you to do it. The ratings would go up and besides it would be a feather in my cap if you could do it for me. He said, "I can't make you no promises that I can do the show, but I can get you a feather for your cap."

Man, that cat, I don't know. I remember around that time 1981. It was about 1981, I was to make a sub-publishing deal in England. I can't remember the name of the company. But, the guy who owned the company his name was Paul Rich. He wanted to publish my songs in England. He offered me 10 thousand dollars for the rights to publish my songs in England. I agreed. He said meet at the Polo Lounge in Beverly Hills. The transaction will take place there he said.

(231)

8/5/93

I said to myself, yeah. I can pay some bills. So, my ex-lawyer advised me. He said Smith, he's a nice guy and a gentleman, try not to be high or get high. I said okay I won't be high. So what I did is get up at 7:00 a.m., smoked a joint. Took a shower. After I had finished taking a shower, I smoked a joint. Made my phone calls then smoked a joint. Now, being that I lived in Woodland Hills, (that's the suburbs of Hollywood) I didn't smoke any going to the meeting going to Beverly Hills. I call myself being straight. I get there to have breakfast with Paul Rich. We do our business, I leave, I get home and I realize I was so stoned, I forgot the contract. I left it on the table. Anyway, I got the money. We were so much in debt that I couldn't buy a $50 bag of smoke. Boy, was I mad. I owed so many dealers that I couldn't out of that 10 thousand I couldn't take $50 for myself. In those days, money came and it was gone. I think about those days now and I don't even laugh at that person who did that. I feel sorry for him. About a couple of weeks later, Paul Rich called me from England. Just then, I got an emergency phone call. I said Okay, Paul, I'll talk to you later. This was before call waiting. So I had to hang up. I said operator who is it? The operator said it was for Amani Smith, my son. He was ten.

(232)

8/5/93

That's when I got them their own phone. That's when I realized that they weren't little babies no more. Oh, yeah, I forgot something. When I was in Europe with Ry Cooder, He's mega in Europe, we were in Glasgow, Scotland. We were on this big stage. The place was crowded, people were screaming. I remember going to the bus to go to the hotel. As we were going out of the hall, a bunch of girls grabbed me and starting ripping off my clothes. The security guard started pulling them off of me. As he was pulling these girls off of me, I was pulling the security guard off them. I told him to leave them alone. I've never had that happen I said. I got to the hotel I was raggedy, but I was happy. Around that time around 1981, I wrote some songs with Eric Mercury. We didn't even argue. There's one song he wrote the lyrics. It's called "Trust Happiness". Nice set of lyrics. Also, Buzzy Feiten was living down the street from me. He was playing guitar with Neil Larsen. They were with Warner Bros. Records. They needed songs for the album. So, Buzzy got together and wrote some songs. We came up with a song for the album. It was called "Danger Zone". Once again, there was a guy who didn't know I wrote lyrics. Thanks Buzzy.

(233)

8/6/93

It was around that time Reggie McBride was playing bass
with the Hodge Bros. Now the organ player for that
group, Skip Van Winkle was playing organ bass, but,
Reggie McBride! Well, Skip had to let Reggie play. It was
Reggie that introduced me to Skip. Even though I played
organ too, Skip and I hit it off so well that I played electric
piano in the group. Let's see, the guitar player in the
group is the guitar player that plays with Little Feet. I
can't remember his name. Skip Van Winkle played organ.
Tony Braunagel played drums. He used to play with
Bonnie Raitt. Dallas Hodge played guitar and sang.
Catfish Hodge also played guitar and sang. And I played
electric piano. The jobs were nice 'cause they were in
Woodland Hills, where I was living at the time. That was
some good times then. Oh, time to move again the
impecunious person that I am it was time to go. So, we
moved to a place in Woodland Hills called Oakwood
Garden Apartments. Things were pretty crazy then. I had
been on two major tours. I had no money so I had to take
a day job. Mixing concrete for a living. Boy, that was
awful. I was working at a place where the made airplane
parts. I had to wake up at 5 a.m. in the morning to get a
ride with the other guys cause we only had one car. And
my ex had to take the kids.

(234)

8/6/93

It was at that place I was talking to a guy I was telling him
how bad it was that they had to make an F14 plane to fight
and kill other people. He said yeah, but look at how many
people it keeps working. How can you argue with a
person like that? My motto. Live and let live. Of
yourself, always give and you won't end up making

fighter planes. Around that time, Jeneanne, my oldest daughter came to visit. She was getting bigger. I remember I let her drive my car. Lucille also came to visit, the late Joe Riley's wife. I wondered what they must have thought. We only had two bedrooms. The both of them slept in the kids' room. I slept in the living room. By this time, I hadn't slept with my ex in some time now. All of my loving I was getting at various places. I don't know when I was with her last. Maybe a year? Anyway, I was coming home from work one day and I got a phone call from a girl named Mary Unobsky. It was around Christmas of 1983. She introduced herself on the phone. She told me that she had gotten my number from Andre' Fisher, Natalie Cole's husband. I said okay. She said I'm a songwriter and I know you are too. She said Andre' had given her a tape of the record I did with the Pointer Sisters.

(236)

8/6/93

She kept reiterating on the fact that I was a good writer. I said oh yeah. But, when she said that she had given her girlfriend Priscilla Coolidge my tape and a gold chain for a Christmas present, I said wait you know Priscilla Coolidge? I said I'll get together with you. I always had a crush on her ever since she was married to Booker T. Of Booker T. and the M.G's. You mean Priscilla Coolidge likes my stuff? She said yeah. So I said to Mary, " When can we get together?" She said "Next week." I said "fine". So Mary and I met at a studio in Hollywood where Andre' Fisher was producing this album called Body By Jake. I can't remember the guys name, but Mary's boyfriend Danny Ironstone was arranging a song I wrote called

Hard Work. I was excited. I went down to the studio. I walked in the door and there she was. Just standing there nothing but legs. Man, I was elated. She knocked me off my feet. She kept telling me what great writer I was. I kept saying yeah, yeah, yeah. I didn't know what else to say but adulate about her and about her looks. The more she kept adulating about my writing, the more breathless about her I was.

(237)

8/9/93

She was so feminine. I remember one time I took her earring. It had a smell on it just like she smelled. Boy, was she a knock out. After talking to her for a while, I asked her to do a record session for me. A song I wrote with Kathy Wakefield called Choose Your Love. That was an old song I had written with Kathy. But, I pulled it out anyway. Anything to see her again. Anyway, it was on a Thursday May 10, 1984. So, I told her that I had to go to the studio that Sunday. She said okay. She got there just when she was singing, she stopped and took a break. We were sitting outside on a break. Andre' Fischer was producing it for me. I just said to her, I don't know to this day what made me say it but I said, "Priscilla I want you". She looked at me and said "Smitty, you're married". I said "in name only". I said to her I don't care what it takes. I'm gonna get you. Man, she's a knock out. So she told me that she didn't date married men. So, I asked her if she would sing on my songs and write with me. She said, oh yeah I can do that I think you're great. So I said I need your number to call you when I'm ready for you. She said okay. You see, I knew she liked my talent. So I played on that.

(238)

8/9/93

So, I kept calling her. I called and called. The more she adulated about my talent, the more I adulated to her about her. Finally, she broke. I remember the first time we got together we spent 3 days together. Man she mesmerized me. I didn't care if I was married. That woman got to me. She always did get to me. After the third day, I went home. I went to put the key in the door. The lock had been changed to the apt. I called out my ex-wife's name, but she wouldn't let me in. Finally, I went around the side of the building to talk to her. As I was climbing, I fell. When I hit the ground, I broke my ribs. I told her I couldn't move. She said serves you right. You should have not stayed away like that. I told her I had to go to the hospital. She said " Get somebody else to take you". So being that I was living in Woodland Hills, Dicky Sony, a guy I knew and used to produce, lived there as well. So I asked her to let me in please, so I could use the phone.

(239)

8/9/93

So I called Dicky Sony. He said he would take me to the Hospital. So with the help of Dicky, I went to the hospital. Thanks Dicky. I arrived at the hospital. I told the doctor what was the trouble, so he x-rayed me. He told me to go in the other room the nurse will be with you in a moment, and I'll be back with a compendium of the test . I said okay. So while I was waiting the nurse took my blood pressure. She took my pressure, she looked at me all funny and then told me that she would be back. The doctor and her arrived back to the room. The doctor said to me "Mr. Smith, the compendium of your test is that you have broken ribs, that's not your problem. If you tape them up and be careful, they'll heal. That's not the problem. The problem is you have dangerous high blood pressure. He said if you don't attend to it right away, you're gonna die. He said high blood pressure is caused by too much salt, stress, and drinking too much. I was a victim of all three. So, they released me. I went back to the apartment and begged my ex to let me in, even though I knew it was over with, her and I.

(240)

8/9/93

I remember talking to Mary Unobsky alot. She didn't think it was healthy for Priscilla, her friend, seeing a married man. Rita didn't think it was cool either. You see, Rita and my ex know each other well. Now I'm with her sister? Mary you were right, it wasn't healthy. I broke my damn ribs. Anyway we slipped around and saw each other. Finally, I couldn't live like that anymore. So, I suggested to my ex maybe we should separate. She said I think we should seek help. I knew then that the marriage was over. I wasn't in love. What she didn't have as a woman, Priscilla had. So, what I did was call the other women I had and told them this is it. Although, I would miss the kids they were 12 and 13. They were at the age where they were noticing things like the house rolodex. Them and their friends would sit up and go through it. They would see numbers like Quincy Jones, Michael Jackson, Neil Sadaka, Michael McDonald's phone number in it. They would say to me, you know these people? I would say to them how do you think we eat? Like one time they saw Buzzy Feiten on Dance Fever one night. He

was playing guitar with the Larsen and Feiten Band.
Amani ran in the other room to get me. He said daddy
daddy, Buzzy Feiten is on Dance Fever playing guitar.

(241)

8/9/93

You see, Buzzy used to come to my house all the time and
go to my music room and play the piano all the time. My
two kids thought that Buzzy was a mediocre piano player.
So when they saw him playing guitar they were surprised.
Things like that is what I miss. Anyway, I saw Priscilla
alot even though I lived in Woodland Hills and she stayed
in Hollywood close to Beverly Hills. It was being with
Priscilla, that with my ex, she made me see the light. I
couldn't be with Priscilla and then go home and be with
my ex. So, I said I've got to go. I've got to get out of here.
I said what do I do? I've got no money. I can't leave.
Then I said to myself, If you don't you're gonna have that
hunger in your stomach. Always having that looking for
love look about you. And going out with a bunch of
women looking for it. Get out now, no matter what I said.
So, I pawned my organ to Skip Van Winkle for $1,000 and
left. I didn't leave my ex to move in with Priscilla. I
moved in with a musician colleague of mine. The rent
was $250 a month. Out of the thousand dollars, I gave
him $500. That was for two months rent. For that, he let
me sleep on his couch. Hell, I didn't mind, I was sleeping
on my couch at home anyway. That worked out fine.

(242)

8/9/93

Except for one thing, he did alot of coke. He sold alot of
coke too! I remember he was the first and only guy I

knew who used to use a roll of toilet tissue a day for his
nose. I did coke too, but that was another league. Being
that he sold coke, people were coming by all times of the
night. Being that I slept in the living room on the couch, I
had to get up and let them in. He took care of business
right there in the living room. Man, that was some crazy
times in those days. Being that he and I had done up all
the profits, he didn't pay the rent. Guess what? The
landlord didn't like that. So with my rent I had given him
in advance, he was evicted. So there I was with $500. to
my name. So Priscilla said, hey come live with me. I
didn't want to leave one woman and move in with
another. So, I told her no. I'm going to try some other
avenues. I couldn't find any so I said to her reluctantly,
okay. Even though I didn't want to move in with her, I
did it anyway. The first month I moved in with her, we
got along great. No fussing or fighting. She had a great
sense of humor. I would walk in the room, and I could tell
she had been there by the way it smelled. We hugged and
kissed all the time. She was too much.

(243)

8/10/93

Man, I really like that girl. Then I got a call from Hawaii.
It was Biard Brittingham. He asked me if I could do a
session for him. He said he didn't have alot of money but
he could give me some and you could vacation in Hawaii
with your family if you want to on my fathers' estate.
Reluctantly, I said yes. You see, that was just before I was
to split up with my ex and I didn't want to go to Hawaii
with my ex, I might have to sleep with her, God forbid.
So, when my ex and I split, I told Priscilla about the offer,
she said she would go with me. So, all I had was that little

bit of money that I got from Skip Van Winkle. So I called some people I knew like Jim Horn, Leah Kunkle, and Eric Mercury to borrow money. They gave it to me. Biard kept his promise. We could have the house as long as we wanted it. Man, we had a ball. Her and I wrote songs. We wrote songs with Baird, we slept on the beach. The house came with a 4-wheel drive truck. I went snorkeling. Things were going great.

(244)

8/10/93

Then it was time to leave. Man, I hated that. It could have been a worst situation. I could have been over here with my ex. Man, I don't even want to think like that. I'll get sick. I remember when me and my ex split up, and I went to take her some money. The kids let me in. She was in the bedroom so she told the kids she would be right there, as if I wanted to go in the bedroom or something. Man, to this day I don't know why I married this person. I won't say woman or lady 'cause no woman or lady would do to another human being what she did. Anyway, the phone call was from Maurice White, the lead singer from Earth, Wind & Fire. He said he was looking for some songs, he was doing a solo album. He said I hear you're a writer, Andre' Fischer told me you're good, so I told Priscilla. I said great we can make some money 'cause when we arrived from Hawaii we were broke. So, I got together with Maurice White. I played him some songs, he said yeah. Then I played him this song that had no lyrics, he said "I like that one". "If you put some lyrics to that music, I'll do it". I said okay. So I went to Priscilla and told her what he said, boy was I excited.

(245)

8/10/93

I played Priscilla the song. I had the name of the song.
All of a sudden, she became intimidated with my song. I
couldn't understand it. The only other time I had heard
that was when Eric Mercury's girlfriend, who was a star,
who used to call me in the middle of the night and cry on
my shoulder about Eric Mercury, I was so in awe of that
lady, I would listen to her stories about Eric Mercury.
Later on, I got one of my songs on her record. Wait a
minute, it was two songs. A song in a movie she did the
music to. I thought we had some kind of a relationship
with her. So I wrote her to thank her. She never
responded. I would call her. She would never return my
call. So, finally I called Eric Mercury and asked him. I said
" Hey man, did I do something wrong to her? Why won't
she talk to me?" Eric Mercury said that she was
intimidated by my talent. Folks, if you knew who this
lady was, you know this was untrue. Not, putting myself
down or nothing like that, but that lady holds her own.
She could stand up against anyone on this planet.
Anyway, like I said Priscilla was intimidated by my talent.
I was intimidated by her looks.

(246)

8/10/93

Nice house Heh? Perfect harmony. So, she called in her
friend to help her with the lyrics. We finished the song,
Maurice White recorded it. The name of the song was
called "I Need You". Maurice White did a good job. He
did it just like the demo. Now, between these two great
friends, Priscilla Collidge and Mary Unobsky, there was
some discrepancy over who wrote the most lyrics. You

see, I wasn't around when they wrote the lyrics. Mary said she wrote more, so she sould get more money. Priscilla said she wrote more, I said that I didn't want a third party to write with. Whenever I write with somebody, I write with one other person. I think it was nice of Priscilla to bring Mary into the project. Even if Mary did write most of the lyrics, Priscilla and I had our first argument over that. She wanted her friend. I wanted just Priscilla. Priscilla insisted on Mary. After the song was finished, that's when the argument started. Out of all that arguing, neither one of them came to me and said being that you wrote all of the music, came up with a title, and Maurice was your connection, and you got the song to him, you keep 50% of the song. And, we'll argue over who did what. That's when I learned that when it gets down

(247)

8/10/93

to the get down, every man's for himself. So to this day, I get 33% of the song. Well, my ex gets 33% of the song. After that, Priscilla and I started to argue about all kinds of things. I was frustrated and she was frustrated, she had just gotten out of a bad marriage. I remember taking some money over to my ex and she told me that not only am I going to get half of everything you make, but I'm going to get all of your royalties. It went in one ear and out the other. That woman was serious. That person to this day gets every penny I make, whatsoever. It's not that I hate that person, to this day but I have no feeling for that person. You know, I thought the mob was bad. But they don't hold a finger to her. She's got so many bad scams going, it's not funny. Sure you have all of my income and you have all of your scams. But, one day it's gonna catch up to you. Mark my word. You see, I learned from first hand experience. The Lord don't like ugly.

(248)

8/11/93

To my first wife Helen. Thank you so much for being a decent human being.   The only thing I blame you for is not leaving me earlier. Even though I was an insensate person then, I was a little gauh, fractious. You still managed to be a decent human being. You went your way, and I went mine. I thank you so much for not being a vaxatious litigate. For you could have taken me for everything. One day, I don't know when, I'm gonna repay you for that, so you and your friend can have a happier life. Not like you're not having a happy life now, but I hope I can improve on your happiness. And as far as my second wife, I you took, me being a jocund person, a gamutlish person, a person of alacrity. People and things that I see and like I would adulate about your thought that was wrong. You mistook all of that and you thought that was wrong. You know when I was a child me and two more guys used to chase this cat through the alley with sticks and throw stones at him while he was going through the garbage cans looking for food. Then one day we cornered that same cat. Then I said "I got him let's get him". As we were about to hit him, the cat stuck straight out. The cat made a grimace face.

(249)

8/11/93

That cat made a grimace face of which to this day, I've never seen before. He made a growling sound his eyes

turned blood shot red. He snapped at us. Man, to this
day, I've never backed nothing in a corner. So what I'm
trying to tell you is never back nothing human or animal
into a corner. You never know what might happen. Like
one time when I was 12 years old, I was visiting my
cousins' house in Toledo Ohio. We were seeing this lake.
The lake was about 235 feet deep. His name's Howard
McNeil. He said to me Danny can you swim? I told him
no. He jokingly said man everybody can swim. And he
threw me in. Now even though I couldn't swim I got out
of that water. To this day, I don't know how, but I got the
hell out of that water. What I'm trying to tell you is
maybe you have the upper hand now you can beat the
system with your druggin, drinking and your scaming.
But one day, all of that's gonna come back on you. It's not
that I hate you or nothing like that, but in this case, you'll
have to answer to a higher authority. When I say to other
people about our dilemma, people say yeah it's just a
family quarrel. Yeah, tell that to the Lord. I said before,
It'll all come out in the wash.

(250)

8/11/93

Anyway, as I was saying after Priscilla and I got back from
Hawaii and that whole thing went down with the three of
us the song that was written for Maurice White, we were
constantly arguing, Priscilla and I. Like I said before, the
both of us had come from bad marriages. She was seeing
a therapist by the name of Zanwil Sperber. After seeing
him for a while, she convinced me to see him, maybe he
could solve our problems she said. So I went. Man, he's
an intuitive person. We had a session with him and he
said to me I can help the both of you. But, I don't think

the two of you belong together. Professionally, you might have something there, but as a couple, I can't see it. You guys break up and I can help you. You know, he was right. I've learned so much from that man. The first thing I learned from him is how to be a man. You can learn from just being around him. He doesn't have to say nothing. Priscilla and I kept fussing. Finally, we both agreed that if we could split up, we wouldn't have so many problems. You know, Priscilla and I could have had a beautiful friendship, if I didn't pursue a personal relationship. It seems like every week I was moving to Jimmy Roberts' house.

(251)

8/11/93

Seems like every week I was moving to Jimmy Roberts' place. Jimmy thank you so much for being there for me. It was around that time I went to a club in Hollywood to see a group play. It was Bernie Larsen's group. He was the guitar player/piano player that took my place when I was going to go on the road with David Lindley. But, I went with Bob Dylan instead. The name of the club was called "The Central"(now the Viper Room). I was there with yet another woman I was seeing. While I was there, I ran into this guitar player named Brian Wray. At the time, he was playing with Etta James' Band. He wrote a song for Smokey Robinson. He's good, he said hello. And he said that Ettta James is looking for a piano player. I said yeah. I used to play with Etta James in the 1970's. So I had worked with Etta James before, so I knew what she was like. So I told her that I wasn't busy, and that I would work with her. Hell I was out of work. Then she was working at a place in Hollywood called the Vine Street Bar

and Grill. Reggie McBride was on bass, Leo Noceutelli
was on guitar, Man the group was nice. I remember I had
to sing a 4 bar duet with Etta James on "Something is
Wrong With My Baby ". I would choke every time, man
she used to make me nervous.

(252)

8/11/93

Man can Etta sing. She's so powerful. I would play with
her some nights and I would cry. Etta, you're so bad.
Being that I knew Andre' Fischer he was the drummer
then for Rufus. He introduced me to Maurice White, the
lead singer for Earth, Wind & Fire. I said "Andre', I'm
playing with Etta James in Hollywood at the Vine Street
Bar and Grill., you should come down there one night. I'll
introduce you to Etta James." So I introduced him to Etta
James. She knew who he was because of him playing with
Rufus. So she asked him to sit in. He played. The rest is
history. He started to play with us. Man, that was a great
band. Andre' Fischer on drums, Reggie McBride on bass,
Leo Nocentelli on guitar and I played piano. I learned so
much from Etta James. One of the things I learned from
Etta is less is more. That woman could take anything and
make a groove out of it. I would sit there on the stage and
play behind her and say to myself I used to listen to her
when I was a teenager, and now I'm playing behind her?
Man, I couldn't believe it. I played in San Diego, all over
L.A. with her. I remember the drummer didn't show up
one night. So she grabbed her little boy he was about 17
years old and told him to play. She just has a way of
getting things out of you.

(253)

8/12/93

Now, I'll tell you why I almost titled my book "A Nowhere Place to Live". Onetime, it was 1985 or '84. Etta James called me to work at the Watts Tower Festival in L.A. That's the Afro-American district of L.A. So, Leo Nocentelli the Afro-American guitar player in her group called her and said he couldn't make it. So she called her guitar player that used to work with her before Leo joined the group. He said yes. His name's Brian Wray. So Brian called me, and being that we lived so far from Watt's let's take one car. So I rode in his car to Watt's. He was white. So when we got there, we pulled in the parking lot. Across from the parking lot on a hill stood and Afro-American gang screaming out, "Hey nigger, what are you doing with that white boy?" They kept saying that, and getting closer. You see, I had that happen to me in Virginia. So I didn't want that to happen to me again, so we ran. We were there only to make music. The frustrations on that gangs' face. They looked at us with a brimace face. You know I heard the President said he was going to put more police on the streets to stop the violence. Forget it, that's not going to help. Clean up your own back yard first.

(254)

8/12/93

Around that time, I was still working with Etta James and still living with Priscilla Coolidge, when I got a call from Ritchie Havens. He said that he was doing a job in L.A. The Beverly Theater was the place. That was in Beverly Hills. Priscilla and I lived only about a mile from the theater. No, it wasn't Beverly Hills that we lived in, it was outside Beverly Hills. So I told Ritchie Havens that I

would get a band for him. I got the band I was working
with Etta James' band. Leo Nocentelli on guitar, Reggie
McBride on bass, Andre' Fischer on drums, me on
keyboards. And his Ritchies' guitar player Dino. I don't
or can't remember his last name. Man that was fun.
Phoebe Snow opened the show for us. Damn, I've met
and played with some great people in my life. I just wish I
could have been drug free so I could have been able to
appreciate them more. I just want to reiterate again and
say that this book was not written to look for pity, I'm not
that kind of a person. It's written so somebody who's a
multi-talented such as me, won't make the same mistake
that I did. If only somebody had written a book like this
when I was a kid, maybe this wouldn't have happened to
me.

(255)

8/12/93

Anyway, Priscilla and I were having our usual stomp-
down argument. Basically we both were just frustrated
people. Man, if only I hadn't pursued that kind of
relationship, today we would have been close. Anyway
once again I moved out. Mainly in those days, I was an
impecunious person. Just because I was working with
those big names, that doesn't make me a person of alot of
money. When for an example, when I did that job with
Ritchie Havens, that was one time, I hadn't worked with
Ritchie Havens in two years. That was in New York at the
Bottom Line and that didn't pay much. Well, not enough
to raise a family and buy dope. And Etta James? Man I
learned so much from her but as you well know, Etta
James doesn't make alot of money. Well in those days she
didn't, now she does. So In those days I had to work alot

to keep up. I didn't know how to manage money well, hell I didn't know in those days how to manage money at all. All talent and no brains, that's me. Anyway, after fighting all the time, I moved in with a guitar player named Bernie Larsen. I used to play with him at a club in Hollywood called The Central. He took me in with open arms.

(256)

8/12/93

He treated me like I was family. We wrote alot of songs together, his sister and his brother-in-law had a place in Lake Arrowhead. It's a resort town outside of L.A. We would go there and write. I would tell him how hard it was for Afro-American to make it in the U.S. I will never ever forget this. He was white and young and talented. He said it's open here. Anybody today can make it here all you have to do is try. Well I could go on and on about that but, I don't think they've printed enough paper to write about my feelings on that subject. Anyway, this was at a time in my life when I was frustrated. I was at a place in my life when I was being neplusultra. So I went to the dope dealers' house 'cause I needed dope in order to get work, 'cause I wasn't working, and I didn't have the self-esteem to do my own thing. So I needed dope to get the courage to look for work with other people. So, I said man, I haven't worked in a month, so I asked the dope dealer to trust me, he said yes. You see, in spite of everything to the dope dealer I was a person of my word, he knew I was good for the money.

(257)

8/13/93

So I was sitting there drinking some Cognac I had a can of beer, three joints, and a gram of coke. Boy, I was partying back. The all of a sudden, I started to get heartburn, so I asked the dealer for some Pepto Bismol, I took some of that stuff I felt fine for a while, then it came back. I took some more. It stopped for a while. Then it came back. I took some more and some more and it didn't go away, so I took the whole bottle I still had the chest pains. So, I told the dealer that I feel funny. He said, man if you're having a heart attack, don't have it here. Go out on the porch he said. I said it's nothing like that, I said I'll be all right in a minute I said. So, I got up and went to the corner and sat there. Finally, I went to Bernie Larsen's house, that's where I was staying, I was sleeping on his couch. I was used to sleeping on a couch. I was doing that with my second wife. So all day that day it was May 14, 1985 I'll never forget that day, I kept telling Bernie that my chest was hurting. He said, maybe you should go to the hospital to get checked out. I said okay. So Bernie and I, we drove to the hospital. We went to Cedars Sinai that's a hospital in Hollywood.

(258)

8/13/93

So we arrived at the hospital that at around 8:00 p.m. May 14, 1985. I told the doctor what was wrong, he said let's do some x-rays of your chest. I said okay. So the doctor took x-rays of my chest. After he did that, he told me to wait in the waiting room, that he would be in later to give me the compendium of the x-ray. Later on, he came to the waiting room with a gurney, and said, Mr. Smith, I've come to give you the compendium. You are having a heart attack. I said what!! He said please get up on the

table now please. I said oh no not me. That happens to
other people not me. He said we are out of beds for about
3 days, so we'll have to put you in intensive care for right
now. Man, me with a heart attack, I don't do that much
drugs, I only drink a little, I don't smoke pot that much. I
only smoke about 10 joints a day. 1 beer a day. A little
small bottle of Cognac a day. Man, it can't be the drugs I
said to myself. So, the doctor put me on the gurney, up
the elevator he rolled me. Man, I was so shocked I
couldn't believe it. Me in a hospital with a heart attack.
By the next day, the word was out all over town all over, I
got a call from Vancouver, from a guy I haven't

(259)

8/13/93

seen in about 17 years. He's an organ player, his name is
Robbie King. The word in Vancouver was that I was
dying. I said to myself, "the grapevine". Now the people
who came to see me in intensive care. Just the word
intensive care is serious. And when they walk in and see
a tube sticking out of you, the first thing they think, he's
going to die. My ex came to see me in the hospital. She
filed for a divorce while I was in there. Being that I
couldn't appear in court the judge signed for me. The
bottom line she gets my royalties for life. Now it's no way
I could contest the divorce papers cause I was in the
hospital. Good ole America. Once again I'll say I'm not
mad that she's got my royalties for life, I'm mad at myself
for being with a person like that. On a good note there
were many people there to visit me. The thing that got me
was Etta James came to visit me. Etta James don't go
nowhere. She doesn't even come out of her dressing room
for nothing. Not even to see other acts that appear with

her. Even though I was sick I was honored to see her. I got a card from Greg Ladanyi, Jackson Browne's producer. People came though for me at the time. Even though Priscilla and I didn't see eye to eye she came up to visit me. Just the visitors alone made me happy to see them.

(260)
8/16/93

I couldn't believe it's' still a heart attack. I stayed on the phone alot, talking to different people. I stayed in the hospital 9 days. The final day, I had a long talk with the doctor, I asked him I said "Doctor, is this heart attack serious?' He said it's a serious warning. You can't do drugs anymore, if you do you'll die. You have a scar on your heart from doing drugs, you have a scar on your lungs from drinking too much. Take it easy and don't lift heavy objects. Take those pills and you'll be all right. Oh boy I said I have to go cold turkey. That does it, I'm going to stop doing drugs. No matter what it takes, I'm going to stop. So, before I was sick, I was living at Bernie Larsen's house. Eddie Wynrick was staying in Studio City. He was managing Wylie Coyote recording artist David Small. So I stayed with Eddie Wynrick for 2 weeks. Everything went well. Steve Lukather lived down the street, he's the guitar player with Toto. He had a swimming pool in his yard. I splashed around in the water. I couldn't swim then. I had to move slowly, I couldn't move fast at that time. I sat in the pool thinking, what am I going to do? I can't do drugs no more I can't hide no more. I've got to look the world straight in the eye.

(261)
8/16/93

Man, I said I've got to change my life around. No more
drugs. I kept repeating that over and over again. At the
middle of the second week, I got a call from Etta James to
go to St. Paul Minn. with her. I said, yea, I can go. The
doctor said I can work as long as I don't lift anything
heavy. So I said to myself, okay on the road I'm gonna
meet up with someone with drugs. At all cost, I've got to
say no, so I left Eddie's house for St. Paul Minn. But,
before I left a drummer colleague of mine knew what I
was going through, so he invited me to an AA meeting.
Man, it was the strangest thing I've ever seen. I arrived
there. There was about 2 hundred people there. Out of 2
hundred, about 190 of them were smoking cigarettes.
Man, it was like a smoke factory in there. The one guy
was saying that his father was a doctor and he had his
practice in his home. So, the doctor moved in town. So
the doctor told the son to clean the office for him. While
the son was cleaning out the office, he gathered a hefty
bag full of pills he found on the floor. Guess what? He
took them all eventually. The rest is history. Upon my
arrival from the hospital, that's what I was supposed to
do. Man, I said I've got to do this on my own. I can't go
back there. Those people are kicking

(262)

8/16/93

one habit and developing another. For me that place is no
good. Well, here goes. All or nothing I said to myself. So,
I went to St. Paul Minn. with Etta James. Reggie McBride
bass, he played with Boz Skaggs, Elton John, Michael
Jackson, etc., Andre' Fischer on drums, he played with
Rufus, produced the Unforgettable album by Natalie Cole.
Leo Nocentelli, guitar player with the Meteors. He wrote

Sissy Strut. The Meteors did that song. And me, what can I say? I have a 25 page resume. The four of us would meet to eat at airports, hotels, etc. One morning, we were at the hotel's restaurant, the three of us, Leo, Reggie and I. Oh, by the way Leo, if you eat too much you'll going to have a pot belly. When this guitar player approached us, he spoke to us and said, I'm the guitar player that opens the show for Etta, and I know who you are. I've seen all three of your names on other folks records. And I would like to come to your room and pick your brains, being that I've never been to Hollywood. So I said, "sure man, after the show tonight, come up to my room. I myself will be glad to talk to you". The other guys Reggie and Leo agreed with me. So, we played that night. They sounded great. Etta James was good as well.

(263)

8/17/93

After the show, I went to my hotel, took a shower and relaxed. I was ready to turn in. When all of a sudden I heard a knock at the door. I said who is it? He said he was the guy that opened the show for us. I said oh, wait a minute. I went to the door to open it. There was the guitar player, the lead singer and his wife. The lead singer said hi man. We came to pick your brain about Hollywood and about the music business, can we come in? I said yes please. So they entered. The lead singer had with him a case of beer, the guitar player had a bag of pot. He went to the other bed and he started to roll joints. The wife had a bag of cocaine, she went to my bathroom and grabbed my mirror. The lead singer said sorry to disturb you, we brought our own stuff, we heard that in order to make it in the music business, you had to first have drugs. Here man, try some. I said to myself here goes. I said no thanks man. I don't do drugs. That sounded weird coming from me. They were rolling joints, doing coke, drinking beer they were having a good time. As they were doing that, they were asking questions about the music business. At no time did I touch anything.

(264)

8/17/93

Man, that's the first time that I've been in that environment and didn't participate in the goings on. That was the first time I said no. I said if I could get past this, I could get past anything. And that was the beginning of my drug free program. All and all I had a good drug free time in St. Paul. Then there was the time in Chicago. About a couple of weeks later, Etta James asked me to play at the Blues Festival there. I said yes. About that myth that black people never on time? Wrong. I remember doing that job at the Blues Festival and there were all black blues artists doing the show. There was one group that was supposed to go on at 2:15 p.m. to 3:00 p.m. At exactly 2:15 p.m. the act went on the stage at exactly 2:15. At 3:00 p.m. the group started up another song. At 3:00pm a clown came on stage and started to politely clown around. The audience started to laugh. The singer stopped singing and they quietly left the stage. The crew needed 15 minuets to break down the stage. Then at exactly 3:15 p.m. Little Milton came on the stage to perform. Man, he was good. He finished exactly 4:00 p.m. He had a guy with him that handled the equipment. His name was Scrap Iron.

(265)

8/17/93

Man, I'm from the south and I've never heard of a name
like that. All and all it was an honor to finally see Little
Milton. That myth about black people not being on time?
Well, I've done alot of festivals in my time, The Greatful
Dead, Edwin Starr, Chicago you name it. I've done it. I've
never seen a festival so organized as that one. Man, those
people were right on. When I came off of the tour, I lived
with Priscilla Collidge. Things were good for about a
week. Then hell broke loose. Here we go again. Arguing
again. Back to a happier time in my life. I remember
when I was apart from my ex and it was the weekend. It
was time to spend time with my kids. Bob Mitchell was in
L.A. He was the tour manager with Motherlode. This
was around 1982. So, the four of us went to an
amusement park called Busch Gardens. That's in Van
Nuys Ca. So Bob, Amani, Sala and I went to Busch
Gardens. So we were walking around the gardens. And
these two little white girls were following us. I couldn't
figure it out. I know they couldn't rob us. They looked
like they were about 9 or 10 years old. Wherever we went,
they followed. Finally, they came up to me and said
"Mister, can we hug your little girl?" I said what? They
repeated the question.

(266)

8/17/93

I've never heard of anything like that. I just looked at the
two little girls. I said they looked innocent enough. So, I
said yeah, go ahead. Man they were too much. They took
turns hugging Sala. The more they hugged Sala, the more
Sala looked at me. You see, Sala just looked that way. She
was a pretty little girl. I just had to break the story up a

little bit. Every time I think about my kids, I get mushy. I know how those little girls feel. I get that way sometimes when I was with Sala. That's why she was a little brat. Anyway, back to the story. Bernie Larsen convinced David Lindley to get me to play organ. You see, I did David's first album back in 1980. So, David agreed. I made the rehearsal. Lets see, Jorge Calderon was on bass, he played with Jackson Brown, Ry Cooder, Warren Zevon and etc. Walfredo Reyes on drums. He's played with Santana, Boz Skaggs, Neil Carter, Doc Severinson and etc. Bernie Larson on guitar. He's played with Melissa Ethridge and etc. And me. Now I'll tell you right now David Lindley's a nice guy and all that. But he's the strangest guy I've ever met in the world. There's nobody, nobody you've ever ever met like that like him. He has a thing for polyester like you wouldn't believe.

(267)

8/18/93

I remember one time David Lindley got disturbed at his wife for not letting him decorate the house. Can you imagine what that house would look if Lindley would decorate it? Lindley's like Pee Wee Herman with long hair. Anyway David Lindley's concept of the group is that we split everything down the middle. In other words, if we made any money on the job, everything went in to his corporation. We pay all expenses such as plane fare, hotels, the road crew and etc. I had never heard of that before. So our first job was after I had arrived from Chicago with Etta James. Now keep in mind that I didn't get alot of money. You have to remember it was a Blues Festival. On top of that, it was Etta James. Hell I was just glad to work with her. So I think the pay from Etta James was about $200.00? So when David made me that offer, I said yeah. I'll try it. So the first job was at the now defunked Golden Bear Club in Huntington Beach, CA. We worked there Friday and Saturday night. In June of 1985 we did 2 shows a night. And Sunday night we worked the Baccanal Club in San Diego, CA. We did one show there. We sold out all the venues. After we pay for expense, road crew etc., we ended up with $2500 a piece. I said wow! I like this.

(268)
8/18/93

Man, I said to myself I hadn't had that much money since the old days. I took $800. and gave it to my ex. I was then living with Priscilla Collidge then, so I gave her $500 and took $800 and bought a Yamaha DX7. That's a synthesizer. A synthesizer is a machine having a simple keyboard and using solid state circuitry to duplicate the sounds of a musical instrument. Now I didn't have one. Hell I didn't even have money to eat much less own an instrument. So Bernie Larsen the keyboard player and guitar player let me use his. Thanks Bernie. Being that they were new on the market then, they were about $1,900 new then, but you could get one in Japan for $800. then. So after I had arrived from Huntington Beach and San Diego with David Lindley, I got a call from a lady named Gabrial Aris. She used to be an executive at Warner Bros. Music. She said that she was doing a charity job in Japan, that she was sponsoring a benefit tour over there and would I like to go with her? I want to take some studio musicians with me such as you, Jim Keltner, David Lindley, Jimmy Roberts and etc. I said yes. You see, I could get a DX7 while I was there. So, I took $800 of the money I made with David Lindley and while I was over there I got one.

(269)

8/18/93

Speaking of money, right after I arrived from the hospital, I was staying at Eddie Wynrick's house in Studio City. Nobody knew where I was living. At least that's what I thought. I was sitting there one day, and I got a phone call from of all people, Rick James. He said Hi! This is Rick James. I hadn't seen Ricky since we were in Toronto, when he was playing with Neil Young's group. He told me his background singer told him that I had a heart attack, so I traced you to this number. Man, he said are you all right? I said as all right as I can be. He said do you need anything? Yes, your best wishes. He said take care of yourself and he hung up. About 45 minuets later, I got a phone call from the Western Union Office. The lady said "Are you William Smith"? I said "yes I am". She said "I have some money here for you." I said "who is it from". Rick James. I said, "oh yeah? How much is it?" She said it's for $1,000. Man I was so shocked. I hung up the phone and started to cry. I took that money and bought my first car. That car was my only means of transportation. You know I see all of this stuff about Rick James on T.V. That's not the Ricky I know. I don't know what happened. The Ricky I know is a kind fervent person. He's a person that felicitates all the time.

(270)

8/19/93

Ricky, when I used to see you in the Village in Toronto we used to sit and talk alot. And while doing that, this is my compendium of you: Even though you're a little neptusultra, you're benign. I remember when you wasn't a capricious person. You were never fallacious. I never thought you were forlorn person. When we talked you were never a garrulous person. You got right to the point. You were a halcyon person. Even though you're a heuristic person you're a very knowledgeable person. You were gregarious. You were never an inimical person. That's why I don't understand what happened? You were never imperious. When I talked to you, you were an irenic person, you were a laborious person. That's how you achieved the success you have achieved. That's my compendium of you. Like I said before, I don't know what happened. Man, you were always good. You had your group with Neil Young, the group was great. But man the success you have achieved startled me, man I'm so proud of you. To Tabbie Johnson, thank you so much for informing Ricky on my whereabouts. When I had a heart attack, Ricky I have this to say, in spite of what's happened to you, you can turn your whole life

(271)

8/19/93

around. All you have to do Ricky, is to give your soul, your life, your whole being to the Lord. Hell, you've got nothing else to lose. Just try it. Just get on your knees and pray hard. Put your faith in the Lord. Cause Ricky, I know you're a good person. You've done alot of good for alot of people. One of them being me. You came to my rescue when I was down on my back. I saw a fervent side of you then and way back when. Ricky come on man, you can do it. If you have the gift to become a household name, you have the gift to get out of this horrible

situation. Ricky, may God bless and keep you always.
Now back to the story. To reiterate I went to Japan with
Gabrial Aris. I purchased a Yamaha DX-7. I hadn't had
no money in so long. All the time I was a impecunious
person. So after I paid everybody, I had $400. I kept that
and bought little things for myself, hair cream, food, gas,
etc. I know some people could have taken that $2,500. and
made a mountain out of it. Boy, if I could have managed
money in those days like I could manage my talent. Boy
what a hell of a person

(272)

8/19/93

from the start I could have turned out to be. In those days,
1982, 83, 84, synthesizers were getting very popular. So all
the instruments I had in storage were obsolete. So when I
arrived in L.A. from Japan, with Gabrial Aris, I continued
to play with David Lindley. I tried to have a personal
relationship with Priscilla Collidge but at each other we
fulminated so much that we both agreed mutually that we
no longer could do this. It was about that time around the
fall of 1985, I got a call from Eddie Wynrick. He said he
was managing a group in Las Vegas, the name of the
group was Santa Fe. He said they were great, would I go
and have a listen to them? In Vegas? I said yes. I went to
Vegas, heard the group, I liked them. Man, they were
good. The leader of the group was Jerome Lopez. He's
the guitar player. Not only could he play, but he could
sing. We got along great. I agreed to work with them.
Man, it was apropos. Priscilla and I were just breaking up.
So I went back to Las Vegas to produce Santa Fe. I liked
the way they did my songs. They recorded 4 of my songs.

(273)

8/20/93

One song was "Mercedes" co-written by Eric Mercury.
The other song was "I Don't Mind Waiting". Co-written
by Bernie Larson. The other song was called "Something
About Your Love". Co-written by Kathy Wakefield. The
last song I can't remember. The tape is in storage and I
can't remember off hand being that I'm doing this book
from off the top of my head. Like I said before, the record
was nice. The only thing is they were working that Vegas
circuit work. Working all the time. They couldn't afford
to take the time off to promote the project. That's why it
didn't sell. The one good thing about living in Las Vegas
producing Santa Fe, was that when they would play their
jobs at night, not only could I see them perform, but there
was The Four Freshmen playing in the lounge at Ballys.
Man, I got to see The Four Freshmen perform almost
every night. What a learning experience. Not only did
they sing, but each of them played an instrument. Man,
could they perform. And so could Santa Fe. Also, thank
you Jerome for putting me up and treating me like a
human being. I stayed at Jerome's house for a month
doing their album, man were they strong. I guess working
in Vegas all the time builds up your chops. Then I got to
thinking, I have to have some place to go when I get back
to L.A. the album will be finished in a month.

(274)

8/20/93

So I said to myself I've got to do something quick. So I
called this brother I knew in L.A. An Afro-American that
I met when I used to live in San Francisco. Being that he
had an extra room, I could rent it from him monthly. Man

there was no way I could go back to live with Priscilla
Coolidge. We personally did not get along. Besides, I had
business moving from my ex and moving in with her I
liked her but we never should have moved in together.
Nor was she ready. Anyway this guy was what you call a
hippy pimp. He had two girls working for him. This was
when he was in Frisco. And he sold drugs, all in the name
of hippy love. I guess I didn't condemn him. 'Cause
when I was living in San Francisco, I used to get drugs
from him and besides he would take his pimp and drug
money and put it into music. That is all the money he
didn't spend on his two houses, his two B.M.W's, his two
of everything. Being that he had two women working for
him a mile apart he was always on the go all the time.
Finally one of the girls said I want out of this life it's not
for me. So he moved to L.A. to pursue his music career.
The other girl worked alot in Japan alot, until she gave
him an ultimatum. She said I don't want

(275)

8/20/93

to do this anymore. Either you get a job and I quit being a
call girl or we're through. Being that he had a drug habit
and devil worshiper, he had to do something to
supplement his income. He didn't know how to do
nothing else but be a hippy pimp and sing a little bit.
Man, was he awful. So he got a job as a security guard. A
BMW to a Toyota. I can't tell you how frustrated he was.
In spite of how he was feeling he said yes to letting me
stay with them. In spite of my situation, I was just
beginning to work alot with David Lindley. It didn't
make it all that easy me getting all of those phone calls in
his home regarding music. I used to work locally with

David Lindley and I would bring to his house the leftover
beer we would have in the David Lindley dressing room.
He liked that, but that still frustrated him alot as he sat
there drinking my beer that I had for him. That I was
playing music as he was sitting there drinking beer in his
security suit. The bottom line is he had a love hate
relationship with me that dated back to 1971. We were
talking about 1985, I got a phone call from Trevor
Lawrence. The associate producer with the Pointer
Sisters. He said he was doing another album on the
Pointers, and being that he was so successful

(276)

8/23/93

as a writer, he co-wrote "I'm so excited". I missed that
when he offered it to me. I figured that he had heard my
songs before and he admired the lyrics. So, he just took
for granted that I wrote the lyrics but I didn't write them.
I had great lyricists to write the lyrics for me such as
David Palmer, Kathy Wakefield, Eric Mercury, Harriet
Schock, and etc. They all knew I had a hang up about
writing lyrics. So, when Trevor Lawrence called me to
write lyrics for him 'cause he was going to submit that
song to the Pointer Sisters. I said that does it, I'm going to
get some help over here and get somebody to show me
how to write lyrics. All I was thinking about was getting
another song on the Pointer Sisters' album. So I called
Kathy Wakefield over to help me. So she came over to
help me do the songs. We were in the room writing and
this vaxatious litigate was in the other room talking to the
landlord. So when Kathy left my room man I was so
excited. I was telling him about the meeting. He got mad
at me he betrated me and told me I shouldn't have Kathy

up here. The landlord was here and he doesn't know you're staying here. I said what!!! I paid my rent, you see he was putting my rent money in his pocket.

(277)

8/23/93

You see, he had a scam going. And I didn't know it. If only he had told the landlord, it would have been easier on me. That's why he acted so funny when I brought people over. I don't know if him and his wife's together today. He tried to molest his step daughter. Nice guy. He should talk to Woody Allen. Woody Allen can give some pointers on how to make love to your daughter. So we mutually agreed that I should leave. It's no way that I'm going to live in a place where I have to hide from the landlord especially when I'm paying rent. I guess he figured he was doing me a favor by taking me in. It doesn't count that I was paying rent. It was what he was doing for me. Being that it was a duplex, the guy down stairs disputed with him over parking. So being that he didn't like the guy down stairs, when he would come down stairs and the down stairs tenant was parked in the debatable space, he would take his keys and run it alongside of the car. Boy was he an evil and frustrated person. That doesn't say that much for me being associated with a person like that. Priscilla Coolidge never liked him. Every time I would bring him around, the hair on her neck would stand up. Man, she just didn't like him.

(278)

8/23/93

As much as Priscilla and I argued she had the gift of
seeing through people. My compendium of our
relationship is that she worshipped my talent. But she
saw the unorganized part of my personal life, and got love
confused with talent. That's just my compendium and
you know what they say about compendiums.
Compendiums are like assholes, everybody has one. On a
mushy note, this dating back to 1979. I had a big boyle on
my inner thigh. I thought it was cancerous. I went to the
doctor. The doctor took x-rays of the boyle. The result
came back negative but he said you have to get that boyle
cut off. So I went to see the same doctor that handled
Richard Pryor's drug burn. He looked at it and said he
had to operate. So I said okay. I went to the same hospital
that Richard Pryor went to. The doctor set up the
appointment for me to go in the hospital for the operation.
I arrived at the hospital, went to the front desk. The lady
asked me my name, address, I gave her that. She asked
my age, religion, she asked me all of the necessary
questions. Then she said okay William take this pill. This
pill will relax you. We will be with you in a moment to
amputate your left thumb. I said What!!! No, my thigh it's
a boyle she said oops, sorry.

(279)
8/25/93
So the lady at the front desk finally figured out that it
wasn't my thumb but it was my thigh that needed
operated on. I took the pills, went into a trance the guy
that operated on Richard Pryor operated on me. The
operation was a success. I had people like Lovelace
Walkins and his wife. Thank you so much Love and wife
for the visit. The reason why I wrote about this is to get to

this part. I stayed in the hospital for three days. And arrived home my son Amani, he was about 8 years old. He made me breakfast for me. He cooked eggs, sausages, bread and juice. I'll never forget that. That was a great jester. Amani, thank you so much. Now back to David Lindley. Like I said before, Lindley was and is an honorable person. By this time I had been with David for about 6 months. There was some pride about me. I was getting back on my feet so when this guy did what he did to me, I looked in the want ads for another room. This guy answered my call. He asked me to fill out a credit application. I told him my credit was shot. So he one look at my resume' and said wow! You can move in. So I got away from him, the guy I was living with. In the meantime, I had started on a weight reduction program. I was at the Y.M.C.A. everyday working out. I had lost 50 lbs. Man I was doing great when I was on the road with David Lindley.

(280)

8/25/93

I must admit I was doing great at the Y. I remember I had to go to the Y early because I had to explain to my colleague how I was loosing weight so fast. Man was I feeling great. I had a membership at the Y where I could work out all over the world. I would work out in Vancouver, New York, Utah, Colorado, everywhere. For those few months I was doing great. I was on the road with the great David Lindley working out everyday and before I would go to the Y.M.C.A. in the mornings, I would go to Mike Post's house, the T.V. composer he has a gym at his house. He's a fitness fanatic. I would work out with him, before I would go to the Y. I was really in shape

then. One day I was working out and I got tired. So, I had
a personal trainer Tim Britt was his name. I said Tim, I'm
tired I've got to rest. I woke up the next day I felt a little
drowsy. So I said to myself, I said I've been working out
too much. I won't go to the gym today. So I started to go
to the gym every other day. Then when I did go, I would
work out half the time. Then I would go to the lounge and
rest. I couldn't figure out what was wrong. So I said
maybe going to Mike Posts' house is too much for me. So
I stopped going over there. I felt drowsy all the time. But
I was looking good.

(281)

8/25/93

Then the Summer of 1986 I was on a David Lindley tour I
remember sitting in a restaurant in Vancouver I had asked
David Lindley's road manager, David Wells for an
advance so I could send some money for my ex. He said
okay. I don't know for sure I think we took home after
expenses $2000, out of that I paid rent, phone, food and
sent my ex $700. I was feeling great. Then we arrived in
L.A. around August of 1985. I was sitting back resting up.
Feeling a little queasy, when I got a phone call from David
Lindley he wanted me to come to his house. He wanted to
talk to me. I thought I had done something wrong. I got
there and David Lindley was pissed. Turned out that my
ex had garnished his corporation. In other words,
anything that I made with David Lindley the courts would
take half of my pay. If I would end up with $2,000 after a
tour, I would pay the hotel, plane, food and whatever was
left out of the $2,000 half of that would go to her. Man he
was getting sick, making about a third of what the other
guys in the band was making. It was so humiliating.

Here I was doing the best I could to send money to her. It wasn't like I was hoarding money from her or I was staying in a mansion. If it wasn't for Rick James, I wouldn't even had a car. I was doing the best I could. I would ask for an advance. The road manager in David Lindley's band,

(282)

8/26/93

his name is Ray Woodbury. Ray would have to check his computer to make sure I hadn't overdrawn my limit, 'cause if I overdraw more than 50% of my wages that's my ex's money and if they do that, by law they or David Lindley would go to jail. I would hear that every time I would get money to eat, If we did a tour I would never make money. So I had to rely on what little session work I could get my hands on. In other words, after being on the road for about 6 weeks, I would get off of the plane and look for work. Just once I would have liked to have come home and took a week or two off. Do like Danny Kortchmar the guitar then for James Taylor. He would do a hard tour with James Taylor then at the end of the tour he would take a two week vacation in Hawaii. Relax then get ready for the L.A. grind. But, I wouldn't even think of that. I didn't even make enough money to pay my electric bill. My next door neighbor ran an extension cord from her house to mine one weekend just so I could have some electricity. To Joanne Albert, Thank You. One of the reasons for this unfortunate mishap was money management on my part. The other was my ex taking money from me. It would be something different if I had a bunch of property or a bunch of money.

(283)

8/26/93

But I had nothing. And what little I had, she tried to take that. And the time she was doing this, I wasn't taking it seriously. Cause I said nobody's that cold. Maybe she's just mad. That's just the way she is. Anyway around the winter of 1986, we were in the recording studio with David Lindley's band putting down an idea for a Levi's commercial to submit to them. In other words, an audition. So while we were doing that David said we would break for dinner. Walfredo Reyes and I didn't break Walfredo's a great drummer. He can play anything. I'm a John Coltrane fanatic. My favorite song is Giant Steps from John Coltrane. So when the rest of the fellas broke for dinner, Walfedo and I stayed. Him and I started to jam on Giant Steps. You see, David Lindley's group was more a rock band. We never played music like that. So while Walfredo and I were playing, this guy walked in the wrong studio. There were two studios at this place. It was called Amigo Sound. It is located in Burbank Ca. His name is Rosco Beck. Man he freaked out over what I was doing. Or should I say Walfredo and myself. He introduced himself to us. He said "Smitty, I would like to use you on whatever I do". I said "Great! call me." Figuring he just liked the music.

(284)

8/26/93

Man I really thought he was shucking and jivin. Sure enough Rosco called me. He said hey man, I'm Rosco Beck, the bass player you met at Amigo Sound. I said yeah man how are you doing? He said fine. He said I'm producing an album on Jennifer Warrens. She's doing an album on songs of Leonard Cohen. He said I would like it if you would play on it for me. I said great. I said Jennifer Warrens and I used to do backups in the 1970's. I remember one session Jennifer and I did. It was for Etta James. I enjoyed working with her. She's good. I said yeah. I'll do the session. I was doing the session for Jennifer, Leonard was there. It was fun. Except, by this time I was getting flatulent. We finished the album. I asked Jennifer, what were you going to name the album? She said I'm going to call the Blue Raincoat. We finished that project. Roscoe said to me thanks. I went on tour with David Lindley. My ex took my money as usual. I can remember I was looking good but not feeling good. Rosco Beck called me again this time he wanted me to play live with the guy he was playing with. His name was Robben Ford. This was at a place called Hop Singh's. Now that was unreal. Robben Ford can play some guitar. Michael McDonald sat in with Robben. Man, what a treat. Michael was great.

(285)

8/30/93

That night, Vinnie Caleuta was on drums. Man that cat can play. He's now with Sting. The reason why I can't forget that night is because that was the first time since I've been in L.A. that I have sweated on stage. Man I had a good time. It was around that time let's see April or May of 1986. I was all settled in my room when the landlord let me use his dining room, and Willie Ornelas and I would sit at the dining room table and play backgammon. We would sit and play, discuss current events, tell our utmost secrets to each other. Those things he and I said to each other I won't get into that but one thing he told me is that he had just gotten out of a bumpy marriage and he was never ever getting married again. He and I was playing backgammon one day when I got a phone call from Trevor Lawrence. He said that Gamble and Huff had listened to his production of The Pointer Sisters and wondered if could produce the O'Jays for them. Trevor said yes. So that's what he was calling to ask me. Could I play on the O'Jays record? I said Man, are you kidding? Yes, I said. So I played on their record. That's the second time I cried. The first time was when I played on "I'm So Excited". Man, to play with the O'Jays record.

(286)

8/30/93

When I heard Eddie sing, he's the lead singer of the O'Jays. All of those memories came back. I got so hung up in listening to his voice that I forgot what I was there for. I felt my face and there was a tear there. Don't laugh. You would do the same thing. I wonder what happened to that record. It was called Step By Step. Man, I don't care what anybody says. Musically, I've had a great time. I've worked with some talented people. Now, if only I would have taken care of business. Man I would have been a superstar. Thank you Trevor Lawrence for calling me for that record session. With the little bit of work I was getting I could barely make ends meet, so Reggie McBride, I call him by his nickname Tones, was playing with Nell Carter. So she told him that she wanted an organ player in her group. So Tones recommended me to play in her band. So I talked to Nell and I went to rehearsal. It worked out all right it was a good band. She had Michito Sanchez on percussion, Walfredo Reyes on drums, Carl

Verheyen on Guitar, Devaughn Pershing her conductor on piano and I played organ. With her we played some great rooms. Vegas, Lake Tahoe, Atlantic City, Colorado Springs, Fort Worth TX. We traveled as a rhythm section, but when we arrived in a town, we picked up violins and horns. Devaughn had arranged for her. I remember in Fort Worth, we had 50 pieces.

(287)

8/30/93

I especially remembered the Ft. Worth gig. That's when I was doing both David Lindley and Nell Carter at the same time. In Fort Worth, on a Saturday night, I would be in Fort Worth with my tuxedo on playing with Nell Carter and the very next morning, be on a plane with my rock & roll clothes on, lying in a fetus position on the plane going to San Diego to work with David Lindley. It's not that I was drop dead sick, but my stomach was hurting so bad. Between those two jobs, I made enough money to pay my rent and buy gas and buy food. On my pay I wouldn't dare think about trying to save any money. My ex was taking half of my money that I made with David Lindley. And with Nell Carter, my ex threatened me that she would go after Nell and garnish my wages with her. She went after me like I was making millions. It would be something different if I was making money like Michael Jackson, but, I wasn't making nothing. I remember Michelle Marx, she did publicity for people like Alan Thicke and etc. She invited me to her house for a x-mas party. I went but I couldn't eat nothing, man my stomach hurt so bad. And Priscilla Collidge and I were supposed to get together and write. I had to cancel. She accused me

of being stand offish. Every time she would make an
appointment with me, I would be sick.

(285)

8/31/93

I remember finally getting together with Priscilla Coolidge
to write some music. I remember having to go into my
bedroom and lay on the bed and write on my portable
Casio piano. Man, did I feel bad. Priscilla thought I was a
hypochondriac. At least that's what she told me. At the
time, I wasn't drop dead sick but I had an upset stomach
all the time. The only time I felt good is when I would lay
down or sleep. Anyway, I finished writing with Priscilla, I
don't know how but I finished writing with Priscilla.
Then it was tour time with David Lindley. The tour was
nice. We went to Vancouver, places west. After we
arrived home I relaxed by playing backgammon with
Willie. We had a running tournament going. We had
been playing for years him and I. By this time the girl he
was seeing wanted to get married. He said to me, no way
man, I don't want to ever do that again. She had told him
that she wanted to get married and have a baby. He told
me under no circumstances and he wanted to have
another baby. He told me had had one teenager by his
first marriage and she was a handfull. No man, that's
what he told me. So anyway we played our game. Man it
was halcyon then.

(286)

8/31/93

Then it was time to do another tour with David Lindley.
This time we toured the east coast. Being that I used to
live in Toronto for so long earlier, I was beginning to miss

it. I remember when we would play Toronto, being that
we take turns driving, the guys would let me drive when
we arrived in Toronto cause I knew it so well. So being
that I missed it so much, I wanted to play with some of the
locals up there. So when I was there, I had a meeting with
the great Doug Riley, a great, great, talented piano player.
When I arrived in Toronto to live years prior, I used to
listen to Dougie. Me and everybody else. Now that cat is
Baaaaaad. With a capital B. So I was telling Dougie what I
wanted to do. Who's who? What's what and etc. So
Dougie said to me Man, I'll put a band together for you.
The guys I work with would be glad to work with you. I
said what! You!! Man, I don't want you to do that.
Dougie was so superior. Even though he's so humble. He
said no man I'll do it. You play organ and I'll play piano.
Me with Doug Riley. Damn, he used to be my manager.
Dougie's so good. Man I wanted a band, but not him. In
my wildest dreams I couldn't imagine me playing with the
great Doug Riley. He said he would call me in L.A. when
everything was set up.

(287)
8/31/93

So I figured that Dougie was so busy doing other things he
would forget. He was always busy. He was like that even
when we were teenagers. Sure enough this cat called me.
He said he had everything set up to play at a club called
the Blue Note. In June of 1987. He said we would have a
rehearsal before we went to the Blue Note. I said oh no,
this guy's serious. Man what do I do? He called my bluff.
So what I did was have a rehearsal down here in L.A.
standing up singing. So I rented the Alley rehearsal
studios and got a rhythm section to help me to stand up

and sing. I've never did that before. So I got Tones on
bass, Carl Verheyon on guitar, Tony Braunagel on drums,
and Danny Ironstone on piano. I rehearsed standing up
singing so after I did that (Oh by the way, to Peggy
Sanvig thank you for copying my music for me) I called
Dougie to tell him what I had done. He was disappointed
because he wanted to play with me. I said what?!! He
said the guy up here was looking forward to playing with
you. Man was I nervous you see, Dougie is one of those
musicians that when he plays he sounds like 10 people
playing. David Lindley's like that. Walfredo Reyes is like
that. That's the only thing I tried so hard to get out of.

(288)

9/1/93

He (Dougie) would take no for an answer. So I said yes.
Then it was time to rehearse. I arrived to Toronto that
Sunday. We had a rehearsal. I think the rehearsal studio
was McLeans Sound or Interchange or something.
Anyway, the guys in the band were sitting in the studio
lounge watching T.V. Every commercial that came on the
guys in the band did the music. Every time a commercial
could come on one of the guys in the band would say "I
did that". Another commercial would come on another
guy would say "I did that." They didn't have musicians
like that when I was living there. Man, those guys were
good. I remember the drummer Kevin McKensie. He
could play anything. Then the guys finally took their
places. We had to learn 15 songs to learn. Besides, me,
B.J. Reid was on the show. Those guys were finished in an
hour. Man could they play. My oldest daughter was
living in Toronto. She could sing. So my oldest daughter,
Jeneanne was on the show. She sang backups for B.J.

Reid. So that Monday we opened up the Blue Note. Man,
it was great. Alot of people that I knew when I was living
there showed up. The club's capacity was about 100
people. And out of 100 people, 90 smoked cigarettes.

(289)

9/1/93

The stage was pretty small. You know how those stages
are in nightclubs. Dougie's piano was right next to my
piano. We did two shows a night between the hours of 9
p.m. to 1 a.m. Dougie smoked about a pack of cigarettes a
night. Man, could he play but those cigarettes drove me
crazy.   Then I would take a break and leave the stage
from those cigarettes right to people I knew when I lived
there. Maybe there would be a family there to see the
show. They would have a table and maybe there would
be 9 or 10 of them at a table and out of 9 or 10 of them,
maybe 6 or 7 of them would be smoking. The whole club
would be like that. That would only make my stomach
hurt more. So after the third or fourth day, I would leave
the stage and go directly to the dressing room. I would
only speak to people I knew so the people I knew that
came to see me thought that I was trying to be stand offish. But I was trying to get to the dressing room fast.
Most of the people I knew there had coke breath. You mix
that with cigarettes, and Wow! You have a smell that will
make your stomach turn. On one hand I was glad to see
everybody. But on the other hand, that smell was killing
me.

(290)

9/1/93

You see, I've been where they were before. I knew that smell. The whole cub smelled of that alcohol, cigarettes, coke and pot. So by my hurrying to the dressing room people thought I had an attitude. To this day Dougie never knew it but those cigarettes drove me crazy. But I was afraid to say anything to him for fear he would be upset. But as far as the show, I got a chance to do some songs I co-wrote. I got a chance to work with Jeneanne and I got a chance to work with Dougie. I guess the way I was thinking my health and Dougie smoking cigarettes didn't bother me. I never dreamed that I would be working with Doug Riley. If I may say so, I'm not exactly chop liver. But you would only would have to hear Dougie, and you would see what I mean. He's so great, that he doesn't have to leave Toronto. I've known Dougie for 30 years. And for 30 year Dougie's been working every time I see him. I remember one time when he was producing Motherlode when we were younger, he was producing us and doing T.V commercials and records and etc. Right in the middle of producing us, he fainted. It was from exhaustion. That's the way it's been with him his whole life.

(291)

9/2/93

While I was in Toronto playing among many people I met from long ago was this girl. She's the ex-wife of this big big star in L.A. I told her that when she was married, I had my eye on her. She responded. The last night that I played Toronto we hit it off. As Skip Van Winkle would say, we became an item. He said that to me one time when I was with Priscilla Coolidge, you have to just imagine this guy with his ten gallon hat on with a

Oklahoma accent say that. So as I was saying we hit it off.
For six weeks we had a whirlwind relationship. Being
that she was a professional writer, we wrote some songs
together. She's a wise woman. I remember Eric Mercury
use to call her alot. She would hear my side of the
argument and she would hear Eric Mercury's side of the
argument. She told me you know Smitty, I think the both
of you have a point (what ever we were arguing about).
My opinion she said you know what it is. You and Eric
are old friends, just because you are old friends, that
doesn't make you now good friends. She said that I
couldn't believe what she had said no way, I said to her
I've known Eric at that time I knew him for 25 years. She
said, yeah I know but that doesn't make you good friends.

(291)

9/2/93

Just because you know somebody for 25 years, that
doesn't make them your best friend. She said a friendship
is something you have to work at. Sure you guys write
nice songs and all that but most of the time, you don't
speak. You've known him for 25 years and out of those 25
years half of them you end up not speaking. I didn't want
to believe her so I forgot about what she was saying. She
was a white girl. She had sex with alot of black guys as
long as nobody knew about it. Deep down inside she was
prejudice. The relationship I had was getting too much
out in the open. It made her nervous so she broke the
relationship off. Even though she was street-wise and
liked being wth black people, she was a racist. While I
was playing in Toronto, Eric Mercury was living there
with his second wife. He was producing a group called
the Age of Reason. He was trying to get that off the

ground. While he was doing that, he was doing a couple
of commercials that Donny Troiano had gotten him.
Donny did alot of commercials and he did or was the
musical director of alot of T.V. shows such as Night Heat,
Diamonds. etc. So Eric said to me being that I was raised
here and it's so prejudice here I'm moving to Chicago.

(292)

9/2/93

So against my advice, he moved to Chicago. He kept
saying to me Man, it's so prejudice here. That's like a man
jumping out of the frying pan into the fire. Anyway was I
ever wrong. Eric and his second wife moved to Chicago
to look for work. Boy did he ever get work. Now he does
the Coors' commercials, The Coors Cutter commercials,
Cool Whip and etc. You see, that goes to show you when
you have a dream and follow it you never know you just
might win. Oh, while I was in Toronto Eric and I tried to
get together and write but our schedule's prevented us
from getting together. Anyway, to Eric Mercury, in spite
of all of the arguments, I wish you all of the luck in the
world. Anyway, I arrived in L.A. and I got a message
from Nell Carter. She was having a birthday party for
Marium Makeba and you are invited to come. So I got off
of the plane and headed for Nell's House in Beverly Hills.
What a party. I met Marium Makeba, Jackee of Room 27
and etc. And the food? Well, Nell Carter what can I say?
She had a disc jockey. The music was great. I couldn't
believe it. I danced all night. Me dancing.

(293)

9/3/93

Then when I went back to my room the landlord told me he had met this girl. You see, he been auditioning girls to get married. He wanted to get married bad. Girls were turning him down left and right. You see, he was a nerd. Then he met this one girl. She's a pretty girl. She did catering for a living. That means she had to cook and drive a van for a living. But being that she had retinitis pigmentosis, in simple English, that's the deterioration of the eyes, in other words, you slowly loose your eye sight. Now she had to quit her job cause she couldn't drive. So she had to go back to college and learn another trade. The college is in Santa Monica Ca. The landlord and I lived in North Hollywood CA. The college was about 20 miles from N. Hollywood. Being that they were getting married they had to be closer to college. Taking a bus from N. Hollywood to Santa Monica took about 4 hours. Any of you that know the L.A. transit system? It's a joke. So they had to move closer that meant buying a house in Santa Monica and renting the house in N. Hollywood. So he told me that he was going to put the house up for rent. So he put a For Rent sign out front. The house went for $1,700 a month, mind you it was two bedroom house.

(294)

9/3/93

Man, I didn't have that kind of money. I had to move, so my housekeeper then, Jo Jean Ruper, suggested that I move to an apt. So I inquired about a place in N. Hollywood. I found a nice 2 bedroom apt. in N. Hollywood. It was nice, 2 bedrooms 2 baths security building, for $750 a month. Now I could do that with the two jobs I had working with Lindley and Nell Carter. So I filled out the credit papers and gave the lady the deposit.

Then the lady called me and said "sorry mister Smith, your credit didn't go through".. My credit was still bad ever since I got a divorce. It was like that everywhere I called. So I said what am I going to do? So I told the landlord about what happened. Being that we had been burglarized that week. Man, they took alot of stuff. You see, he had open house when he was trying to rent the house. Somebody came in and cased the joint and broke in the place. After that had happened, he got nervous and realized that he was asking too much for that place. He got no bites for what he was asking for. So he wanted somebody in the place. So he dropped the rent from $1700 to $1200 per month. He asked me did I want the place? I had no choice. I had to take it. No place else I could rent because of credit complications.

(295)

9/3/93

So the deal was I stay there pay $1200. a month for the first year. $1300 a month the second year and 7% of the rent the next year. Then I said to myself where the hell am I going to get that kind of money? Then I said to myself, where there's a will there's a way. So on top of working with David Lindley and Nell Carter, I got a job working locally with this girl named Ty Parr. I met her through her brother Bob Parr. He used to substitute on bass for Tones with Nell Carter. I worked at a little night club in N. Hollywood called Josephina's. She's a good singer and a good song writer. She did alot of movies and record sessions. Boy, was I pinching pennies in those days. Between my stomach cramping and working so hard, I didn't have time to rest. When I did, I was nursing my stomach. Even if I did go to the doctors, I couldn't afford to go anyway. I remember I used to come home from work with my stomach hurting. At the end of the month, my bills were $3200. a month. I would make $2000. pay $1300. rent, buy food, pay the phone the rest would be bounced checks. That's the way it was every month. And when I was late, I listened to the landlord cry.

(296)

9/6/93

Now I'll go way back for this one. The guy's name is John Peter Brandford. He's from somewhere in Connecticut. I don't exactly know where about in Connecticut. All I know is his father owned a radio station and the late Allen Freed used to work for his father. He was a disc jockey there, John's father's radio station. John grew up went to college in Toronto. He majored in psychology. While he was in school, he was classmates with the girl then I was dating a singer psychologist by the name of Stephanie Taylor. I met him through her. I remember we used to have alot of group discussions, him and the group the Soul Searchers. After he graduated from college, he became the President of Rochdale College. Man, we use to have some fun there. I did alot of gigs there. Being that he was the President, I did alot of trust fund gigs there. Oh, Rochdale College was located on Bloor Street in Toronto Canada. I remember about 2 years later when Stephanie and I parted ways I got the girl I was going with at the time her name's Carol Shannon with John as his secretary. Things were looking good then. Then, the Canadian government didn't like the way he was running the college. So the government closed down the college.

193

(297)

9/6/93

You see, he opened the college based on the idea that the students should take what ever subjects they wanted to take when they wanted to take it for whatever they wanted to take. For example if a kid wanted to know what reaction you'd get when you did drugs. Man, we stayed wasted all the time. That place was like a drug emporium. The government didn't like that, so they closed the college down. Then John moved to Ottawa Ont. We sorta drifted apart. Then my oldest little girl who wasn't so little anymore went to college in Ottawa. Her name's Jeneanne she ran into John at a lecture. They hit it off real nice. He found out that I was her father from my first marriage and they put 2 and 2 together and presto, they became good friends. So when I talked to Jeneanne on the phone, she told me that she had met John Bradford in Ottawa. He had his practice up there. She gave me his phone number, I called him, I hadn't talked to John in near 20 years. It was so good to talk to him. We went down memory lane. He asked me what was I doing now. I told him I was now playing with David Lindley. He knew who he was. I told him that I was coming to Ottawa to play with David Lindley.

(298)

9/6/93

I said lets get together and talk over old times. So I went to Ottawa with David Lindley. Saw John Bradford. We went out to dinner. We talked over old times. My former manager that managed me when I was with the Soul Searchers 20 years ago was Harvey Glatt. We went to his house. He still had the original organ that I had with the

soul searchers 20 years ago. Man, that brought back some
memories. After we left, Harvey Glatt's house, I was
telling him what Doug Riley had done for me and I was
going to play in Toronto in a few months. I was going to
play my own music in Toronto. I said John, would you
like to come he said yeah. So 3 months later, I went to
Toronto to do my own thing and on my show Jeneannie
my daughter was on the show. She sang two songs. I
finished the show then went to John's table. He was there
with his girlfriend and his assistant. His assistant had two
cousins with her. One girl's name was Lark. The other's
name was Christine Midler. Man, that Christine's a
knockout. I said to myself. So I talked to both of them,
Lark and Christine. So after the second show, John and
company dropped me off at the hotel.

(299)

9/6/93

Man, I laid there in my hotel room and thought about
Christine all night. I said to myself oh well, I'll probably
never see that girl again. Man she was pretty. Christine
was half Barbadian and half Czechoslovakian. She was
almond color. She had natural red hair. She had beautiful
red lips. She had ginger colored eyes. She spoke soft.
Man, what a beauty. So the next day, the bellboy came to
my door. He said Mr. Smith, I have some flowers for you.
I said ME?!! I wonder who they're from. The flowers
were beautiful. They were roses. I opened up the card it
was from Christine. She said something to the effect of
lets get together. Man, I really hit the floor. That girl sent
me flowers wow! We got together after the show that
night. She told me that her cousin Lark and her were
going to take a chance and come on to you and which ever

one of us was successful, the other one would step back.
Man I couldn't believe that this was happening to me.
Two beautiful cousins wow! I'll never forget that woman.
She was so soft. She smelled like milk. Boy was she
strong hearted too. But that's all right she was pretty. I
called all the time.

(300)   Living in L.A.
9/7/93

Now I will attempt to explain to you why North America
is not a nice place to live. I was playing at a place in New
York called The Bottom Line. For those of you that don't
know that place, that place is a night club that features top
artists. I played there with David Lindley. John
Hammond opened the show for us. Now that we have a
standard contract stipulating that the promoter must
provide: a deli tray, a fruit tray, some water and a case of
beer. The reason why the contract stipulates that is
because we're doing one night concerts everyday, and we
don't have time to get in a town to do a rehearsal, then try
and find a restaurant in that town. So, we get to the
Bottom Line. Not only do they not provide food for you,
but when David Lindley was on stage performing in the
middle of the show he asked the waitress for a cup of
coffee. He had to stop the show and give the waitress
$3.00 for a cup of coffee. Walfedo Reyes ordered a
hamburger for dinner. He had to pay $7.00 for the
hamburger, so he said I'll fix them. I'll bring in my own
food to the club so he did that. They wouldn't let him
bring the food in the club. I ordered a diet coke. I had to
pay $2.00 for the diet coke. So I mean, this is too much.

(301)

9/7/93

So I said I'll take care of this situation being that I don't know any restaurants in New York, I'll order from the Hilton. That's the hotel I was staying at in New York. I ordered from the room service menu: a tossed salad and a glass of non-fat milk. The bill came to just for these two items $22.00! I wasn't surprised, this was 1988. In 1976 I was there with Mike Finnegan this was a bus tour . The bus driver was staying at the same hotel. He ordered from his room: a hamburger, an order of french fries, and a coke. The bill for those 3 items were $32.00. That's the reason why I say this is a nowhere place to live. I'm not saying this out of anger or nothing. I'm merely observing. You see, that is nothing but greed. What does the song say, in New York if I can make it here, I can make it anywhere. You damn right you can make it anywhere, cause there's no place like it anywhere. That's an inhuman place to live. It's like going to a movie. It's a nice place to visit but I wouldn't want to live there. Man I'd hate to think now a days what it would cost now for a cup of coffee at the Bottom Line. Just to think everybody wants to go to New York to be a star.

(302)

9/7/93

Anyway, back to something pleasant. We played the Bottom Line two nights. Christine Miller came to visit me while I was there with David Lindley. I remember after the job that night, we were trying to get a cab, her and I so we started to walk uptown to the Hilton. The Hilton was around 52nd or 53rd around there somewhere. The Bottom Line was in the village. It was around 22nd or

23rd around there somewhere. So we started to walk. We walked about 6 blocks, we got a cab we got to the hotel we got to my room we sat down. In the hotel room there was flowers. Christine and I started talking about flowers. I said those flowers reminds me of my grandmother's flower garden. Just then for no reason, I started to break down, and I started to cry. You see at that time my grandmother had passed away in '77. When I went to her funeral and saw her just lying there I was in shock. That was the lady that showed me how to write, sing, spin a top use a yo- yo shoot marbles and most of all, my friend. I just looked at her I couldn't cry. When I was little, I use to work in her flower garden I use to hum hymns. Man I miss her. So I guess when I saw those flowers I lost it. Viva La Grandma.

(303)

9/8/93

Now we're going to go even further back in time. Let's see, this took place around 1974. I'm only mentioning this incident to show you how people can get gratitude with lust, and how you can get so disillusioned about music. About 1974, I was in a recording studio with Kenny Rankin the studio was called Devonshire Studios. It's now and was located in North Hollywood, CA on Magnolia Street. It's owned by Dave Mancini. No he's not related to Henry Mancini. Michael Stewart was the producer. The album was called Silver Morning by Kenny Rankin. It was on Little David Records. It was owned (the record co. that is) by Flip Wilson. He had artists on his label like George Carlin, Flanklin Ajai, Dianne Carrol's ex-husband Monte Kay was the president. Anyway we did the album we had some good players on the album. Wilton Feldon

on bass, he's the player with the Crusaders. James
Gadson on drums he the drummer on the Temptation's
record Standing on Shaky Ground, Bill Withers
Grandma's Hands. Wendy Hoss she married to Martin
Mull. Man there was some good players on that record.
So after we finished the album Kenny had to go on a road
tour to promote the album. You know how it is when
you're promoting something.

(304)

9/8/93

The record goes all out. Kenny was opening the show for
George Carlin. He was doing then the Johnny Carson
show, he was doing everything. Then we did a road tour.
We went to a place outside of Conn. Being that Kenny
Rankin played acoustic guitar, we traveled very light I
played piano he had Roy McCurdy on drums and a bass
player I can't remember his name. All I know that Roy the
drummer use to play with my hero the late Cannonball
Adderly. We would fly back to east to New York, rent a
station wagon and put the two instruments in the back
with the rest of the stuff. We had one guy that handled
the equipment that's called a roadie. His name's Hal
Cooper I see his name now on T.V. He's directing and
producing T.V. shows. Kenny and the rest of the guys
went inside of the club when the car stopped. So that left
me in the car alone. Even though in those days I was
laviathan and even I was a lascivious person I was
incurious when it came to this one particular girl. She
came up to me and said hi. I said hello. She said are you
with the band? I said yes, I'm the piano player. I said are
you coming in to see the show? She said yes.

(305)

9/8/93

She said I'm a college student from New York, and I saved
my money for two months to take a train to Conn. to see
Kenny Rankin. She said I'm a Kenny Rankin junky. She
said after the concert, I'm going to save my money to buy
a Kenny Rankin album. She said that won't take me long.
I'll only take me about 2 months. I said to her you don't
have to do that. Take one of these albums, being that this
was a promotional tour, we have some promotional
albums. Here, I said take one that's what they're for. To
give to the club owners, the promoters, and fans. She was
beside herself she thanked me so much, I got tired of
saying you're welcome. So we went in, did the show, we
got finished, I was on my way back to the dressing room
to change my clothes and I saw her again. Once again she
thanked me for the record. She said can I repay you for
the record? I said no I don't want no money for it. Then
she said can I have oral sex with you for the record. Man
what can I say. All I can say is Kenny please lets hurry up
and do another record together. To Roy McCurdy I hear
you alot on radio with Cannonball Aderley. Man You're
great.

(306)

9/9/93

Speaking of going down memory lane. This was in 1965 I
was married to my first wife Helen. You see, I can say her
name, by nature she's not a vaxasious litigate. Anyway,
Helen was teaching school when I was married to her. We
had a little girl. Her name's Jeneanne. She was about 14
months old then. You know how it is with little kids.
They pull and nag at you all the time. This one morning

Helen had gone to school to teach. I said good-bye to her.
She said could I handle things here? I said to her yes. She
went off to teach I fixed Jeneanne's breakfast. Changed
her diaper, and went back to bed. You see I was playing
to one in the morning. So I thought I would get some rest.
So I put out some toys for her to play with. We stayed at
this two bedroom apartment on Davenport Road on the
west end of Toronto. It was small, the bathroom was off
of the side of the kitchen, so I went back to bed, left
Jeneanne in the kitchen to play with her toys. About
every half an hour I would wake up and say "Jeneanne?"
She would say "Yes, I'm all right". I said okay just
checking. You see, she just learned to walk and talk. So
she was into everything.

(307)

9/9/93

So I was there in my bedroom just relaxing getting some
Z's. Every now and then, I was dozing cause I know I had
little girl in the apartment. So subcontiously I was half
sleeping and half awake. So after being like that for a
couple of hours, I had to go to the bathroom to take a leak.
Being that the bathroom was off of the kitchen, I had to
pass Jeneanne for about two hours she was quiet is a
church mouse. I walked in the kitchen, she was setting in
the middle of the kitchen floor with a box of oatmeal, a
box of cream of wheat, a box of flour, sugar, salt, pepper
all of the boxes of cereal and etc. everything from the
kitchen cupboard. I looked at her and said
JENEANNE!!!!!! what are you doing with that stuff???!!!
She at me with those pretty little dark eyes and said to me
Oh, I'm just playing with this stuff . When she said that,
and looked at me I melted inside. Now I'm not just saying

this because she was mine. But damn she was a pretty little baby. If you were to see her, you couldn't spank her. Not that's she's not pretty now but then? Wow! Just goes to show you I can make some pretty babys.

(308)

9/9/93

Now back to 1988. I was going with Christine Miller then. I was calling her everyday. Sometimes two and three times a day from LA to Toronto. Being that she was a very economic person, that bothered her alot so she ask me not keep calling like that, as a matter of fact she said stop calling period. You see at that time, it didn't matter to me about the phone bill, I just wanted to see her. So it was time for me to get on a David Lindley Tour, and I noticed on the itinerary we were going to Toronto. So I didn't call Christine, I sent her my itinerary so she'll know that I was coming to Toronto. You see, I thought she was seeing someone else. It never occurred to me about the phone bill. When I got to the club in Toronto, there she was, she cursed me out for not calling and telling her that I was coming to Toronto. But, I said, "Christine, you told me not to call you ". Anyway, I never saw her again, except one time when I was playing in Toronto. She came to see me. She was with her boyfriend. I can use Christine's real name. You see I don't have to worry about her suing me. She's to strong headed and too independent to do that. That's just not her style. I remember when she came to New York to see me. She had her own room. Even though she didn't sleep in the room. She had it just in case.

(309)
9/9/93

Just in case anything would happen between her and I.
Man that woman's independent. Anyway I never saw her
again. She told me not to bother her no more, and I didn't
and that's the end of that chapter. Anyway I came back to
L.A. and the trustee of my benefit (Willie) was having a
party. His then girlfriend was giving him a surprise party.
That party was an introduction to their marriage. The
party was nice, she owns a bardering co.

(310)   Working with Chuck Berry
9/10/93

Now in this chapter, I will attempt to show you how
excruciating as a minority I live in the United States as a
multi-talented person. I have go back further in time.
About July 1982 I was working with Chuck Berry. We
were working at a club called the Roxy. That club is
located in Hollywood, CA on Sunset Boulevard. We had
some incredible people working with us at the time. I'll
name a couple of the guys in the band. The great Jim
Horn on tenor sax. Man he's played with everybody. He
played solo sax on Laughter in the Rain with Neil Sadaka.
He played with Toto man he's played with everybody.
Then there was Ritchie Zito on guitar. He use to be in the
Elton John Band, among other things. Now the both of
them are now great producers. Willie Ornelas on drums.
Then there was Ingram Berry singing. She opened the
show for us. Then there was the main feature Tina
Turner, you can still see that show on the T.V. show Arts
and Entertainment, the Chuck Berry Show it's called.
Anyway, we were all ready to go on stage, it was a packed
crowd. The host of the show said now ladies and

203

gentlemen we present to you Chuck Berry. The crowd
went crazy. Just then Chuck Berry went to the promoter
and said "man, I can't go on" the promoter asked why?

(311)
                    9/10/93
Then Chuck said " man, I can't go on unless you give me
$5,000 more dollars. The promoter hit the roof. He said
"Chuck, I can't do that, I've already gave you $25,000.
Chuck said "I know man but I changed my mind. I want
$30,000." You had a house full of screaming people out
there what would you do if you was in the promoters
shoes? The promoter paid him. Then there was the time I
was working with Chuck Berry in Lake Tahoe in one of
those gambling casinos Chuck was to appear there. In his
contract, it stipulated that he must have a Fender Twin
Reverb amplifier. So we got there and they had a Ampeg
amplifier there for him to play thru. Chuck looked the
amplifier and said "man I can't play through that Ampeg
amplifier, the contract said that I have a Fender Twin
Reverb amp." So the promoter had to drive all the way to
San Francisco to S.I.R. to rent a Fender Twin Reverb
amplifier. Now for those of you who knows that area you
know that's a good distance about 200 mile or so. The
promoter got the amp for Chuck. He sat the amp on stage
for Chuck. Then Chuck look at the Fender and said " I
think I'll use the Ampeg I like the way the Ampeg sound.

(312)
                    9/10/93
My compendium of Chuck Berry is that the guy's a bitter
man. I use set by him on the plane. That's how he learned
my name. And I would ask him why he did that. You see

he said when I was coming up I didn't have the freedom, if you're a minority in this country, man it's hell. He said, You think it's hell now you should have seen this country when I was younger. I would go to a city and play a big arena and I would pack the house. When I would finish playing, the promoter was gone with the money then all of those records I had in the 50's. I said all those records I was weaned on that you made. He said yea, He said in order to get those songs on record I had to give half of my songs to the president of the record co. He said to me as long as I live I'll never forget it that's why I get all of my money in front in cash. He said to me you'll never know what it's like to be stripped of your dignity like that. Then I said I know what it's like. The only thing that's changed is they polish it up a little bit these days. Then he said to me that's why it's hard for me to change. That's why my compendium of Chuck Berry is that he's a bitter man.

(313)   Working with Etta James
9/10/93

To show you further why I don't think this country's not a nice place to be. I was working with Etta James at the Vine Street Bar & Grill. I believe it was 1984. We had done one show and Jesse Jackson was in the dressing room, and Etta James was sitting in the dressing room talking and I was telling her about my record deal I got in the 70's and manager Ken Fritz got me $35,000. She said wow! She said you know all those hit records I had? I said yea. She said I've never received a check for $10,000. I said what! She said in those days people were ripping off black artists left and right even though we had the talent you couldn't do nothing without the white man. Those people that are from the 50's that I've worked with have a whole different approach to music. They have a bitterness that I've never seen before. Even though I'm a black man and I have experienced racism in this country. But, not like they have experienced. It hurts, what makes it so bad, if I have had problem with racism you can imagine what they must have gone through.

(314)   Working with Soloman Burke
9/10/93
While I'm down memory lane, I might as well mention the time I did an album with Soloman Burke. This was around 1977 or '78 I can't remember the exact date. Anyway, it was late at night and all the restaurants was closed. You didn't have 24 hour places like you do now. So Soloman Burke called his wife. They lived in Beverly Hills, they lived close to the studio. He ask her to bring some pots and pans and food to the studio. In the '50's when Jackie Wilson , Lloyd Price and us black artists couldn't go in the white restaurants then. I would cook up a lot of hamburgers and sell them on the bus. I would do that then some time we would send the white bus driver in the restaurant to get food for us or we might know a black cook in a town and they would sneak us in the kitchen and let us eat before we went on stage. You know, the way us and our four fathers been treated in this country? I would never even think of treating an animal the way some people in this country have been treated. And you wonder why there's so much hatred going on. Soloman, hope in your lifetime you see a change.

(315)   Wondering
9/13/93

I was just sitting here under a tree at the park just
wondering, why is it so much hatred in North America?
Why the whites have so much prejudice for the blacks.
For example, you have Bill Robinson. This man showed
Shirley Temple everything she knows about tap dancing.
And she was a millionaire. Yet, and still, when they went
to Palm Springs, CA to shoot a movie, she stayed in a
hotel. He stayed in the coach house with the servants.
Let's not forget he was a millionaire. Lena Horne was the
main attraction at a Las Vegas Casino. Her daughter
decided to go for a swim at the casino's pool she went,
and the casino's owner drained the pool 'cause Lena's
daughter was there. Nat King Cole decided to live in
Hancock Park. That was a white place where white
people lived. They burned a cross on his front lawn. Art
Tatum was and is greatest piano player that's ever been
on this planet. But, yet and still I've never heard of him
until I was 25 years old by a drummer by the name of
Philip Wilson. Michael Jackson's the greatest entertainer
that's ever been on this planet, but he's still a second class
citizen. These are some of the things I simply don't
understand.

(316)

9/13/93

Just please tell me what did these people do but be the
best they could be at what they do what do black people
have that makes white people hate us so much? I don't
want to go and get a gun or nothing like that then I'll be
just like them. I merely want to understand. Please write
and give me the answer at P.O. Box 298 N. Hollywood CA
91603. A black and white couple moves into a white
project the white people don't like it, so they kill the black

guy. If God would have made me different, I wouldn't
have a white girlfriend. You see, she turned me on . I
don't know she was a girl that was nice, she's opposite of
what I am and being that she's a girl not only a white girl,
she just turned me on. I don't know why she does. You
have alot of these hate groups saying that your group is
superior that this your country. You say you believe in
God if you do believe in God. God doesn't believe in hate.
He says love your brothers and sisters. How could you
believe in his sayings and not believe in that saying. I'm a
brother why don't you love me? What did I do? In the
words of John Lennon Give Peace A Chance. You just
might find you may like it. Now that I've said what I
thought should be said I'll move on with my book.

(317)   Working with Rod Stewart
9/13/93

Let's see, I had been in L.A. for a while and I got this call
from Rod Stewart's office. They wanted to know could I
do a record session for Rod Stewart? I said yeah. She said
there are no overdubs. Wait a minute it wasn't his office
that called me, it was Chas Sanford who called me. I had
done record sessions with Chas Sanford when he was
playing guitar on recording sessions. Now he producing,
just finished working on Stevie Nicks album he's
produced alot of people's records. This was 1988. I got
there, the session was big time. Rod had rented the studio
for a year. He was trying out different ideas with
different bands. This band was really nice. Nile Rodger's
drummer, Tony Thompson was on drums. Nile Rodgers
and him was in the group Chic. Nile played guitar. Now
Nile produces people like Madonna "Like a Virgin" that's
Niles production he's done Diana Ross and etc. On guitar

Michael Landau, Martin Landau's son on Mission Impossible. Bob Glaub on bass. He use to play with Jackson Brown, Linda Ronstadt, etc. Andy Taylor wrote songs for Rod. Andy wrote all the Duran Duran hits. I remember asking Andy I said " Andy, how old were you and how big was your first royalty check from Duran Duran?" He told me that he was 18 years old.

(318)
                    9/13/93
He said my first royalty check was for 3 million dollars. I said man what did you do with all of that money? He said in an english accent "man, I bought 5 of everything". At the time he was 28 years old then. Anyway the record session went great. I'll say this about Rod Stewart. Not only is he talented but he's a hell of a business man. Rod Stewart didn't get where he is now just by talent alone. He's made some nice investments . Rod, Good luck in everything you do.

(319)   Working on the movie Bull Durum
                    9/14/93
Now this was around April of 1988. One day I got a call from this recording engineer Paul Brown, anyway he said hi. I hadn't seen or talked to him since the Ry Cooder days. When I recorded with Ry Cooder, he was the engineer. He said man I've been trying to get your number 3 months. I said all you had to do is call local 47 I'm with the Union. He said man I never thought about that, he said I thought you were an obscure person like Ry Cooder or David Lindley. Maybe I said there's only one difference between them and I. They're rich. I'm not, that's why you'll find me in the book. Then I said what's

happening. He said I'm engineering this movie score with
this musical director named Bill Convertino. The name of
the move is Bull Durum. I said isn't that some kind of
tobacco? He said no it's about a North Carolina baseball
team. It's about a baseball groupie. I said who's playing
her. He said Susan Sarandon. He said Kevin Costner's
playing a baseball player. I said I've heard of Susan
Sarandon. I did a score for one of her movies, she was
with Don Johnson, the guy on Miami Vice, I said yeah this
should be interesting. So I got to the studio. The studio
was in Hollywood on Santa Monica Boulevard. It was
called WestLake Studios. That's where Quincy Jones
recorded some of the thriller album with Michael Jackson.

(320)
                    9/14/93
So I got to the studio, and I met Bill Convertino. He
explained to me what the movie was about. He was
telling me that Susan played a groupie. He said every
time a baseball player would get an average, she would go
to bed with them. I would start to laugh. So he said play
at the opening of the film. I said okay where's the music?
He said I didn't write anything for the opening. He said
watch the movie and make some music as the movie play
along. So I said Okay. The movie started Susan started to
talk. Just that accent broke me up. It took me so long to
do that opening every time she would talk I would
breakup laughing. Then he wanted me to play at the part
where every time a baseball player would do good that
night at the game. Susan would bring the player home to
her baseball shrine then the baseball player would do a
ritual in front of the shrine. She would go to bed with
him, that's when I would come in and play some spiritual

music. That was the funniest movie I've ever done. It took me so long to get through that movie it was so funny. The only other thing that I worked on, but it wasn't a movie score was the Honky Tonk Piano Man with Lilly Thomlin. That was my introduction to Kevin Costner on the Bull Durham movie.

(321)   Meeting Parlishka
9/14/93

Moving right along, this was in November 1988. I was playing keyboards for David Lindley at The Palace in Hollywood, CA on Vine Street. Any of you have been there you know The Palace is downtown Hollywood. You have to park around the back of the place. The parking lot was full, so I found a space in front of the place. I did the show with David Lindley. We did our usual encores, the show was over. Now what I normally do when I play The Palace is go out of the side door to the back parking lot to get to my car. But, this time being that my car was in front of The Palace, I had to walk thru the front door. That means walking thru all of those people to get to my car. So our road manager David Wells helped me to get thru the crowd. Then when I got to the back of the club, David said to me . He said this girl wants to talk to you. I said okay. Then, she said hey Smitty. I looked around and I saw her and I almost fainted. She said hi. I couldn't even speak. Man what a knock out. She said my name is Parlishka Navatlova. She's Czechoslovakian. She looked like a young Bridget Bardot. I couldn't believe it. I thought I had died and gone to heaven. She said to me I like the way you play. I could hardly keep my mind on what she was saying.

(322)

9/14/93

She said I manage some groups she said as I was looking
at her legs, she would like it if you could play some of
artists records. I said yeah, yeah, yeah when do you want
me to start? Do you want me to start tonight? She said
lets talk about it over lunch tomorrow. I said yeah, yeah,
yeah, figuring I had really made a score this time. So, I
met her the next day at Jerry's Deli on Ventura Blvd in
Studio City, CA I got all prettied up and everything. Got
there and found out she was dead serious about
management. There was no playing around with this girl.
She played me a tape of her artists. The guys tape
sounded like early Paul McCartney's music. It was nice so
I said when could I meet this guy? Figuring I could get
over there. Then I met the guy at her house in Sherman
Oaks. His name is Chris Hyde. He sang and played
guitar he was serious too! That guy could fix anything.
Before he moved to United States, he was a trouble
shooter for the RAF in Australia. There, he fixed anything
from refrigerators to jets. Perishka insisted that I worked
with him and they didn't have enough money to pay me.
So I said Chris lets enter a bartering system.

(323)

9/14/93

So I said to Chris, I produce your record if you fix my old
jalopy for me. I had a '76 Oldsmobile Cutlass Supreme.
My mechanic would let me use it sometimes to let me
drive it. When I brought the car in 1986 for $1,000. that's
the $1,000. Rick James gave me . The guy I bought it from
said to me that the car would last maybe a year. Man did I
stretch that car and I made it last almost three years. Then

Chris got a hold of the car. He took the motor completely apart. He showed me the stuff that was in the motor. Man, you should have seen the dirt and grime that came out of that motor. When Chris got finished with that car, it was like brand knew. If I would have gotten that car done up like Chris did, the mechanic would have charged me about $5,000. I had a V8 engine in the car. Even though it drank alot of gas, I didn't have to make no car payments. Chris and I had a nice arrangement. I did his music, he fixed my car. He also brought an old Peugeot and fixed it up and I gave that to my son. Perlishka thank you so much for believing in me. I'm honored you're more than just another pretty face.

(324)   Working with David Lindley
9/15/93

Now this was before Perlishka. Just before I met Perlishka, this was in August of '88 I get a call from David Lindley. He told me that the band was going to do an album with him or he ask me to do an album with him. He said that Linda Ronstadt was going to produce it. I said what are you going to call the album David? He said I'm going to call the album Very Greasy. That's what we would say to David when he would have on at work 2 or 3 polyester shirts in the summer when David would have on those shirts he would get greasy. So we, the guys in the band would say David was very greasy. So that's why he named the album Very Greasy. Anyway, we rehearsed for the album . We recorded the album at a studio called the Complex Studios. It is located in Santa Monica. It was owned by Maurice White of Earth Wind and Fire. It was a nice environment to make a record. Toto was in the other studio recording. They were putting horns on there record. They had Tom Scott and Jim Horn on sax. He's now producing Delbert McClinton and Bonnie Raitt together. Even though the album didn't sell, I think that Linda Ronstadt did a wonderful job producing . The record company didn't promote the record properly.

(325)
>   9/15/93

At that time Linda was dating George Lucas. Now I don't have to tell you who he is. Everybody should know who he is. Being that he was dating Linda at the time and he's a David Lindley fan, he was at the studio all the time. While David Lindley was at the studio recording, George Lucas asked David to play at his Christmas party for him. So David agreed. And while David was at the Complex, Toto ask David Lindley to play on their album. Man, that was an unbelievable sound David and Steve Lukather playing guitar together that sound was like something else. We would stop recording when those two were in the room recording together. Not only is Toto a great group, but all of those guys came up as studio musicians: David Paich, Lukather, Mike Pocaro, the late great Jeff Pocaro. God Bless you Jeff. It's just a pleasure just sitting and listening to those guys. The only thing you miss when you're listening to those guys, is a box of popcorn. Other than that, you're going to enjoy yourself. As far as I'm concerned, they are commercial geniuses. Viva la Toto

(326)   Working at Skywalker Ranch`
>   9/15/93

David Lindley took George Lucas up on his offer. It was on Christmas Eve 1988. We arrived at the Skywalker

Ranch. It's located in Marin County where else? Lucas
Road. It's on about 6000 acres. To this day I've never seen
nothing like that place. Being that he had to build
everything to code. All of his buildings and studios were
built in the Victorian style. We stayed at the one house or
building. There were 5 of us guys in the band and five
assistants. In our party each one of us had our own suite.
Not room but suite. Being that the Sky Walker Ranch was
away from everything, we had our own cook. He came
with the suites. Man I've been in some pretty swanky
places, but I've never seen a place like that or I've never
eaten food like that chef cooked. Eventually I got to see
the office building. He had computers in the bathroom.
That building took 5 years to build. The hallway was solid
oak all the way thru. That place is something you see in a
fairy tale book. When I played there, on the intermission,
I got a chance to meet Francis Ford Coppala. Man when I
met him and his daughter, I was thinking the first time I
saw his daughter was in God Father I. She was a little
baby.

(327)
                              9/15/93
The things that I'm writing is things that happened to me.
A lot of things that happen in my life, I'm leaving out I'm
not going to say I'm going to write about the important
part cause everything that happened to me was important.
I'm just trying to capture the main events in my life. The
musical events the drug events, what it's like to be a
minority in America and be in the music profession. Even
though I left out a lot of events I've given credit to people
that played a crucial part in my life. No research was
done on my life. I did not have a ghost writer to write

about my life. I'm not proclaiming to be Shakespeare or a
Robert Burns or Maya Angelo or nothing like that. I
figure I went to public school and learned how to read and
write. And learned how to read a dictionary. I figure I
would try and write this book myself. Hell, I figure you'll
either like the book or you won't like the book. I don't
understand why writers get a ghost writer who write's
about people's life history. Hell, you the person has to do
is sit down and get a dictionary and let you the people
judge whether it's good or bad. Man you pay somebody
to tell you what you did in your life??

(328)   Working with Robben Ford
9/16/93

Now we're going to go back a few months to April of 1988
when I received a phone call from Robben Ford. He told
me that he had a job here in L.A. I said Oh Yea? Where
about in L.A.? He said well it's not exactly in L.A. It's in a
place outside of L.A. its in Santa Monica. It's a club called
At My Place. It's on Wilshire Boulevard and 11th. Would
you like to do it with me? he said. I said yeah, to work
with Robben Ford, and play some jazz you're damn right
I'll work with Robben Ford I said to myself. Roscoe Beck
on bass, Tom Brechtlein on drums, Vence Denum on sax,
Wow! What a band. So that night, we played the club At
My Place. It's owned by Matt Creamer. I remember
coming off of the stage soak and wet. The time I sweated
on stage when I played with Sam & Dave and Robben
Ford. Every time I play with Robben Ford, I sweat.
Robben is so fluent. When Robben plays, it flows like
water. Damn that guy is good. I just have this to say
regarding Robben. I hope he gets to you one day like he's
got to me. Once again Robben, thanks for calling me.

(329)   Working with David Lindley

9/16/93

Now, this was June 1988. I went out on a short tour with
David Lindley about a week. Being that Lindley didn't
get paid every night when we were with him. I didn't
have no money, hell in those days, I was an impecunious
person. Anyway, so when I got back to L.A. and arrived
home, my electricity was cut off. My next door neighbor
then was JoAnn Alpert. Being that the house that I lived
in was about two feet from hers, she ran an extension
chord through my window so I could have heat and I
could eat for two days. You see, I arrived home on a
Friday night and the DWP didn't open for business until
Monday, so I had to go all the way to Claremont CA.
That's about 30 miles from the place where I lived and ask
Ray Woodbury for an advance. So he gave me the money
to turn on the electricity. I got about $500 from him. That
money was to come out my pay from being on the road
with David Lindley. By the time they took out expense
money for the road crew air fares, Hotel, food rental,
truck. All of this was on a computer. Even though David
Lindley was weird, he's an honest person. They sent the
check less expenses and the advance I made, the check
came to $1.39, that was what I had to live on.

(330)

9/16/93

My compendium of that situation is that Hell hath no fury
like a woman scorn. While we were on that tour that
August of "88, we played a place called the Coach House
in San Juan Capastrano, CA. Owned by Gary Folgner. We
were playing one night. Man that song was sounding

good the song was called Brother John has gone. I must
admit we were sounding extra good that night. In the
middle of the song, Walfredo Reyes, the drummer takes a
solo in the middle of the song. He sounded like 10
drummers when he took his solo. After he finished his
solo, he got a standing ovation. After he took his solo, all
of us came in playing. So we came in. And while we were
playing, this lady came up to the stage. (later I found out
that her name was Sandra Campbell) being that I was
surrounded by keyboards and they were all flat surfaced,
she walked up to the stage while I was singing and placed
a $100.00 bill on the organ. Then she said this is from me
and my husband. This $100.00 bill is for all of you, you
guys are great. I was startled, I couldn't believe what she
had done. The only time somebody did that was when we
were playing in Northern CA. and they use to throw pot
at us on stage. So when we finished playing, we left the
stage. People were still clapping. While we were in the
dressing room, people were in a frenzy.

(331)
9/16/93

I told the guys in the band what had happened. We were
to divide the money evenly. The guys in the band
simultaneously said to me that's all right, you keep it. I
said "no, man you don't understand, it's for all of us".
They repeated the same answer. Man inside I felt so bad.
You see, everybody in the band knew I was being
garnished. That's why I felt so bad. By that time, I had
been in Lindley's band for 3 years, and we would get to a
town in Canada or U.S. and being that all of the guys had
traveled before, they knew all of the antique music stores.
They would all go and buy things . Not once did I go with

them. I never had no money. When we would have a day
off on the road, the guys would unwind by going to a
movie or all of the guys would go out for dinner. I could
never do that with them. I was like the second class poor
boy of the group. Even though the guys respected my
talent, when it came to business and money management,
I was a lunatic. One day in life, I'm going to show each
one of those guys I'm more than just a keyboard player.

(332)   Going to Jail
9/17/93

Now this was when I arrived from the David Lindley tour.
I believe it was in October of 1988. I was sitting at home
one day, and I heard a knock on the door. I went to the
door and answered it and said hello. I said yes, can I help
you? There were two detectives at the door. They said
are you William Smith? I said yes. They said "Mr. Smith,
you are under arrest for child support." I said what! Then
I started to laugh. The two detectives said to me " what
are you laughing about?' I said child support? My two
kids live with me here. The two detectives started to
laugh along with me. Then they said to me, even though
this is ridiculous, we're going to take you downtown. So
they hand cuffed me, read me my rites and took me
downtown. They took me to a holding tank. I got so mad
I started to cry. Then all of a sudden, I got real quiet.
Then I said to myself, this lady's real serious. I really got
myself together. I stop freaking out. Then I said even
though I'm in a holding tank, business must go on, so I
called the girl that was helping me to do my taxes. Her
name's Lana Harris. I was very calm, I ask her how she
was doing. She said great. I said I have some papers at
the house you have to sign.

(333)

9/17/93

Some papers for me. She said okay. She said are you
home now? I said no I'm downtown L.A. She said good,
you can drop the paper at my house. I said I can't, I'm in
jail. Lana said WHAT!!!? You're where? I said I'm in jail
for child support. Then she said how could you be in jail
for child support when the court has been garnishing your
wages for 3 years? I said you know the American court
system. Lana was more freaked out than I was. She was
doing my books so she knew what was going on with my
personal business. That's why she got so freaked out. So I
cooled her out and after I had cooled her out I hung up the
phone and got real haleyon. Then I called a lawyer. I
can't remember his name off hand. He went through my
books with a fine tooth comb. He called the royalty
companies. We got everything straight. We went to court
for child support. After paying 3 years of alimony. I
owed her the judge said $13,000. To this day I don't know
why she's doing this to me. She knows I don't owe her
any money. Like I said before, hell hath no fury like a
woman scorn. Maybe I should be punished for falling out
of love. I really believe in my heart that woman should
get some help.

(334) Working with David Lindley

9/17/93

After I got out Jail in October of 1982, Ray Woodbury
called me. He's the guitar player and saw over things,
and booked the David Lindley group. He said we had a
gig opening the show for Jimmy Cliff at the Wiltern
Theater. That's on Wilshire Boulevard in L.A. I said what

does that job pay? He said $2,000 for that show. I said
great. I can pay back that $100. I borrowed from this
person I know. So we got there and did the show, the
show was great. I ask Ray for a $100. advance. Ray said
okay let me check the computer and see approximately
what you're going to make. I said to him I know we're
going to get $100. I said we're playing home. We don't
have no hotel bills, airfare, or nothing like that. Ray said
okay. So Ray gave me the money. While Jimmy Cliff was
on stage performing, I took off to pay my debt to this
person that I owed. I got back to the Wiltern. I was sitting
in the dressing room Just then Ray came to the dressing
room and he said to me "Smitty! Smitty! I got to get that
$100. back" I said "why?' He said The money I gave you
went into your ex-wife's money and If I mess up your ex-
wife can put us in jail. I said "Ray, I took the $100. and
paid this person that I owed.

(335)
                    9/17/93
Ray said to me that man we're in trouble. We went into
your ex-wife's money. Being that at the time it was an
unpretentious person, I ask Ray, man you have to loan me
some money so Lindley won't have to go to jail. That's
what kind of pressure we were under the whole time I
was with David Lindley.

(336)
                    9/20/93
Then there was this time I was with David Lindley, it was
August of 1988 and I received a call from Ray Woodbury.
He said the group was called to play at the W.E.A.
convention. That's a record corp. Warner, Electra, Atlantic

Groups. Being that we had just finished a record for Electra Asylum Records, we had to play the convention. It was held for a week long in New Orleans. The WEA Convention was just like any other big company convention. You have your record executives there, secretaries, disc jockeys, etc. They rented the whole Hyatt Regency Hotel for a week. I said to one representative, man that must be expensive to rent that hotel for a week. The rep said yea, the hotel cost to rent the whole place for a week about 1 million a week. Then I said wow! That's alot of money. The record representative said they grossed so much for this year a billion dollars. I said oh, now I don't feel so bad for those people.

(337)
                    9/20/93
Being that this was on all expense paid trip to the convention, the hotel, food, you could order in your room anything you want. I did just that. Once again, I'll say being that I was an impecunious person I couldn't order alot of food when I was with David Lindley. This time I could order anything I wanted to order. So that I did. I ordered soup, salad, gumbo that is lobster and dessert. The bell boy came to my room with alot of food. Even though I was flatulent I said what the hell, this food is not going to kill me. So I ate all the food. I finished the food, I was sitting back watching T.V. when all of a sudden, I threw up. I threw up all of the food I had eaten. That was the day I realized that lobster and crab didn't set too well with me. Still, I didn't go and see a doctor, cause after I threw up, I felt normal again. I just only had my usual pain in my stomach.

(338)

9/20/93

Then there was this time it was Christmas of 1988. We
were playing a gig at the Skywalker Ranch. That's George
Lucas's place. We were having a good time. I look up
from the keyboards and there stood Linda Ronstadt with
her secretaries sister, Jennifer. She just stood there staring
at me. I said oh, no. I'm messing up. She didn't smile at
me or nothing. We finished the song and she came up to
me at the keyboards and said I like the way you play. I'm
going to use you on my next record. I didn't know what
to say to her all this time while I was playing, I thought
she didn't like my playing. Anyway, I had a nice time that
night. Clarence Clemmons the sax player who use to be
with Bruce Springsteen was at the party. He just lived
down the road. I saw and met alot of movie stars there. I
think we had played there before. Like I said before the
place is something else. I would like to go there one day
and just sit there on one of those hills.

(339)

9/20/93

Then there was New Years Eve of 1988. We had a job
outside of San Francisco the hall was called Henry J.
Kissenger Auditorium. We were on the show with Little
Feet and Ivan Neville, Aaron Neville's son. So we had to
fly from L.A. to San Francisco to the job. On the way up
there, on the plane I was sitting besides the bass in the
group Jorge Calderone. I was saying to him, as soon as I
get my pay from David, I'm going to pay this person and
that person. Then Jorge told me that we had gotten paid a
month ago. I said What! why didn't I get paid. He said I
don't know. Why don't you go to the back of the plane

and ask David. So I did that. And David said yeah, the
rest of the guys got paid but we had to hold your pay
because your ex-wife said you were ordering too much
room service, so she threatened us if we didn't send her
all of the money. Man, I hit the roof. The reason why I
was ordering room service 'cause my stomach was so
flatulent all of the time. And a lot of the times I would eat,
I would throw up and I didn't want David to know I was
real sick, I might get fired. With David, I was
embarrassed, he didn't know what to do. All he knew, he
like the way I played. In order to have me, that's what he
had to.

(340)

9/20/93

So right then and there, I gave David my notice. I told
him that I had another offer. But, I didn't. I just couldn't
take the humiliation any more. So, I played just one last
job with David Lindley in San Francisco. Rock Deadrick
was our drummer. Walfredo had another offer to go with
Jim Barnes. He's an Australian artist. Walfredo took the
offer. I don't blame him the offer was for $4000 a week.
Man, was I steamed at my ex-wife for doing this to me.
The girl I was with helped me to calm down. So like I said
before, we played that night. This other girl I knew up in
the Bay Area came up to me and said, "That was a good
show, what are you doing tonight?" I said I'm with this
other girl we are going to spend the night together, and
she's going to catch a plane early in the morning to
Mexico to see her boyfriend. She said to me can I come
over to your hotel room after she leaves? I said yeah. So I
had sex with one girl all night, and sex with another girl
New Year's day. I'm too old for this kind of stuff. Hell,

I'm 44 years old this has to got to stop. When I got back to L.A. the next day when I woke up, I had a charlie horse in my leg. I had to use a cane for about a week.

(341)   Living in L.A.
          9/20/93

My leg was cramped then, all of a sudden it just went away. I said to myself I don't need to see a doctor. This came from just positioning myself the wrong way when I was having sex with these girls. Then a month later it came back. It stayed like that for again about a week. Then, it went away again. I was getting this cramped in my leg along a flatulent stomach. All of this was happening to me, and I didn't see a doctor. I don't know why I didn't see a doctor. I guess all of the working out at the YMCA I did, justified to me that there wasn't nothing really serious wrong with me. The cramp would come and go. This is not a sex book. If I wanted to go that way with this book, I could have. I merely told you about this incident to show you how stupid it is for a grown man my age to be with two women sexually in 24 hours. My self personally I don't think in any profession you should abuse your powers. If you do, eventually it will catch up to you. For example you take Al Capone, even though he was a crook, he was a powerful man. He didn't die from robbing a bank, or killing somebody. He died of a social disease. Why? Because he abused his power.

(342)
          9/20/93

And just to think, all I wanted to do is play music. With AIDS going around the way it is going. Man, I was watching a talk show and a musician from heavy metal band was on. He was bragging that he's been with 3,000 women. That's nothing to brag about. All he's doing is showing you how lonely he is. I know, I've been there. I haven't been with 3,000 women, but I've been with enough women to know, that the more you get the more you want. You get to the point where you like a gun slinger. You just want to shoot somebody so you'll have more notches on your gun. In the end, You'll end up with nothing. So please if you're in a position or in a powerful position to have those little girls screaming at you, scream back at them. Don't make love to them, you can have only so many women. That's the bottom line. Learn all you can learn about your profession. Spend your whole life learning. Cause messing with alot of girls is not right. Pardon the pun, but you won't end up on top, you'll end up a flop. Fellas, just keep your pants zipped up and play your music and you'll be all right.

(343)   Working in L.A.
9/22/93

Well, moving right along. I left the David Lindley band Dec. 31, 1988. After that, I didn't work for a couple of months. When I did, Ray O'Hara called me. He's a Japanese bass player who's a star in Japan. He's a liaison for the United States and Japan. In other words he gets American musicians to play on Japanese records. He called me to play this record. I can't think of the Japanese artist name, but I played keyboards on the record. Kenny Arnoff played drums on the record. He's the drummer for John Cougar Melloncamp. I nicknamed him "Max" cause every time he would play, he would max out. Man, can that boy play. I remember I use to sit and watch Max play. He did so many record sessions out here that he

always kept an extra set of drums out here on the West
Coast. You see him and Melloncamp lived in Indiana.
Anyway those sessions with Ray O'Hara were fun.

(344)   Doing the Tonight Show
           9/22/93

Now this took place in February 28, 1989 Jo Jean Rapier
my ex-bookkeeper and tax organizer was now working for
this guy he's a producer he produced Dwight Yokum.
Anyway, he was the producer for Michelle Schock. They
had finished the album, and they wanted or should I say
she wanted to do some promotional spots on television.
So, she wanted to do the tonight show, but the organ
player that did the record couldn't do the Tonight Show
'cause he was busy with another job. So being that, JoJean
use to work for me she suggested to the producer that I do
it. So Jo Jean called me. She ask me to play with Michelle.
I said yes. I did the rehearsal. It was then, my eyes got
blurry on top of white stuff coming out of my mouth.
Being flatulent, my leg cramping up, my eyes was going
on me. I said that does it. I'm gong to see a doctor. So on
the day of the taping of the Tonight Show, after the
rehearsal, I told Michelle that I was going to see a doctor.
So I went from Burbank to the Wilshire District that's
about 15 miles to see this doctor that Grace Eisenstein
turned me on to his name's Doctor Plotkins. I saw Doctor
Plotkins, and told him what was wrong with me. He's a
Jewish doctor. Everything I said to him , he said let me
take your blood.

(345)
           9/22/93

So he took my blood. Then after he took my blood, he came back into the room where I was, and he said to me in his Jewish accent "Mister Smith, you have sugar diabetes" I said "what??!"   But he said we can control it if you follow my instructions. He said take these pills, these pills will clear up your eyes and mouth, also, if you take this other pill, it will stop your leg from cramping. And you can't eat no salt or sugar. He said to me in his Jewish accent as long as you follow these rules, you'll be all right. You'll still have diabetes, but it will be controlled. I said to him okay. By then it was rush hour. I had to hurry and get back to the Tonight Show. I was driving like a bat out of hell. Boy I had to hurry. When I got back to the Tonight Show, I arrived 2 minutes before we were to go on. I was in shock. I couldn't believe it . I had sugar diabetes. Man, my mouth was white, anyway, I did the Tonight Show. Jay Leno was the host. Johnny Carson was the regular host, but it was Johnny's night off. Needless to say, I never heard from Michelle again. So I did what the doctor told me to do. He was right the pills worked great as long as I did what he said. I would prepare diabetes food at the house and I was losing weight and everything.

(346)   Getting Sick
9/22/93
Then I had my two kids living with me. They started to complain about the food. Not enough or no salt or sugar. So I started fixing food so they would eat. Slowly but surely I started to develop my old way of eating. Then I started to feel weird again. Oh by the way, for the Michelle Schock for doing that show with on The Tonight Show, the money I made for doing that was $295 gross $265 net.

(347) Working with Bruce Willis
9/23/93

This was about March 12, 1988 I received a phone call
from Rosco Beck, the bass player with Robben Ford. He
ask did I want to play on Bruce Willis' album? I said yes.
Does Bruce Willis play an instrument? He say yeah, Bruce
plays the harmonica and sings blues. I said yeah, who's
doing the album? Rosco said Robben Ford will play
guitar, Tom Brecthlien playing drums, Joe Sublett's
playing saxophone, and you are playing organ, and I 'm
playing bass. I said great what's involved. He said it's a
weeks work Robert Kraft producing the album and for the
album you'll get pay $4,000 for doing it. I said great. I got
to the studio the name of the studio was Ocean Way.
That's on Sunset Boulevard. Damn it's amazing how
somethings you can remember and somethings you can't
remember. Anyway, I got to talking to Robert Kraft and
found out that both of us at one time had the same
manager. Ken Fritz. Bruce Willis wife was there with
there first little baby. She was holding the baby in her
arms. Her name is Demi Moore. We finished the album
in a week. Robben Ford played great. On the $4,000 for
the album, after hassling Motown for the money, I finally
got paid September of 1988. What's that saying? The rich
get richer the poor gets poorer. The compendium of the
music business.

(348) Working with Irie
9/23/93

By this time, I had reached a point in my life where I was
fed up with doing record sessions. Even though I was in
with some of the stars on the records, but it took so long

when you did a record to get paid. You couldn't get mad
at the record co. cause if you did that. You didn't work no
more. So the record company's late paying you. The
record company don't care. They have to pay the union a
penalty for being late. So a record company might owe 15
or 20 musicians 15 or 20 thousand dollars in late penalties.
The record company don't care cause the interest they
make off of that is something else. That's been going on
for years. The union law says you are supposed to get
paid 2 weeks after you do a record. Man that never
happens. So when Jimmy Dale called me and said would I
play the Red Onion with him in Costa Mesa, first I said no,
then he said the job paid $90, and you get paid after the
job. I said great. Then I said at last I'll have some money
in my pocket. We did the job, he paid me. Jokingly, I said
to him I said if you have more of these little jobs call me
cause I didn't want him to know that I was impecunious
person, so the guy started calling me for all of his jobs. I
would ask him where is your regular piano player? He
would tell me he couldn't make it.

(349)
                    9/23/93
I would always say yeah the reason I would say yes, cause
the cash was great and reggae music was new to me. I
know even if you're black, you supposed to know about
reggae music. But I was born in Portsmouth VA and I've
never visited the West Indies. Jimmy Dale's the guitar
player for Irie. He had a lot of $100, $150, $80 jobs. I took
them. You had to drive a hell of a ways to do the jobs, but
at the end of the night I had cash in my pocket. I could go
and pay a bill the next day. Sometimes I would drive
about 2 hours some nights. When I first joined his band, I

had to read music. I could barely see the music. I had to wear glasses. I remember working with Jimmy Dale and he had to take my equipment and load it for me, cause I couldn't lift it cause I was so flatulent. I would play a job with Jimmy and we would take a 15 minute break. Jimmy and the rest of the guys in the band would go and socialize with other people. I would go to my car and go to sleep. As long as I was sitting down, I was all right. But when I stood up, I felt a little dizzy and being that the jobs were so far away. I would fall asleep at the wheel. One night, I almost hit somebody so I took $40 of the $80 I made that night and got a hotel room.

(350)   Writing
         9/24/93

This around the time I was working with Irie. I had been toying around with the idea of putting my classical riffs to rhythm. I had been toying around with this idea for years. So one day I came up with a musical idea. It was this classical piece of music I had in my head. I put it down on a cassette. I sent it to Eric Mercury in Chicago. He sent me back the tape. He didn't have a clue where I was coming from. I'm not saying that he didn't know how to write or nothing like that. But even though we would have disagreements all the time, we would never have any problems writing. But this time we did. That's when Eric and I had a 4 hour long distance conversation. I won't get into what we discussed. The only thing I'll say is his views and my views about things are very very different.

(351)   Working with Keith Edwards
         9/24/93

231

Now this was right after I finished working with Bruce
Willis. About March of 1989 Walfredo the drummer that
use to be with David Lindley had been on the road with
Jim Barnes, Jim Barnes is an Australian super star. I did
his first album. Walfredo wanted to spend some time at
home with his family. So in order to do that, he had to get
work locally. So he started to work for Keith Edward
corporation. Keith has alot of bands for any occasion.
Like one of his bands played for the dance at the
Grammys, his band played for Warner Bros. Christmas
party. So being that Walfredo has a heart that's big as
gold. He recommended me to work with him. I
remember I did a job for him. It was Rose Hills Mortuary.
It was their annual Christmas party. I remember I was on
a 15 minute break, and one of the sales ladies that work
for the mortuary was trying to sell me a cemetery plot.
Boy was she doing a sales pitch on me. I was sitting there
in the corner feeling bad. Anyway, I thought she thought
I was dying or something. Rose Hills Mortuary is the
biggest undertaking service in CA. I remember the first
gig I did for Keith was in Arizona. It was in Scottsdale AZ
the Hyatt House Hotel. It was in one of the convention
rooms for a bunch of lawyers. We were booked to play for
them from 8 p.m. to 2 a.m.

(352)

9/24/93

Man this place was plush. Out in the hallway, you had a
guitar player in the hall playing music before you even
went into the convention hall. As you read this book you
see that I've played alot of gigs with alot of people. But,
the most boring gig I've ever played in my life was that
gig. The lawyers were so boring that instead of playing

from 8 p.m. to 2 a.m. we played from 8 p.m. to 10 p.m.
The only thing that was good about that gig was this guy
on drums. His name is Peter Rivera. Man he could sing
and play drums at the same time. I said man where do
you come from? He said Detroit. But I live in Palos
Verdes CA. I said that song you sang "Celebrate" was
good I said wasn't that by Rare Earth? He said yeah, I'm
the one who sang it on the record. I played drums and
sang on the record. I said wow one day I would like to
work with you man, you're good. Then he said what do
you mean. I said one day I would like to produce you.
Then I said this gig is awful. Then, I said one day we will
work together.

(353)   Chuck Rainy living with me
9/24/93

While working for Keith Edwards and Jimmy Dale and
doing lots of that work and being still an impecunious
person, Chuck Rainey called me from Fort Worth TX.
He's the bass player that played on the Little Rascals
record Groovin. The TV sitcom Sanford and Son, The
Jeffersons and etc. Being that he didn't like staying in
hotels, the guy's been living in hotels all of his life. Like
when Gary Katz would fly him from Ft. Worth to play on
all of the Steely Dan hits. Gary would put Chuck in a
hotel suite. Chuck doesn't like to stay in a hotel. Me? I
like to stay in a hotel room. I like the privacy. I like to be
left alone. That's where him and I are different. Like Sly
Stone said different strokes for different folks. Man, that
cat's unreal. I remember he use to get up in the morning
and play his bass. I would hear him play and go into my
room and cry. Man now that cat can play. I watch
Sanford and Son just to hear him play on the Sanford and

Son's theme song. He was in LA teaching bass and doing record sessions. He's good and tells stories and plays bass at the same time. He does that with so much ease. Chuck it was an honor to have you to live with me.

(354)   Working at the Blue Note in Toronto
9/24/93

While Chuck Rainey was living at the place I was staying at, I had to go to Toronto to play the Blue Note again with Dougie. I didn't have to go. I wanted to go to Toronto. Now this took place while I was working with Irie. Around February of 1989 I arrived in Toronto. Dougie and the band and I had our usual rehearsal. B. J. Reid did her usual three songs. Dougie was right beside me. The stage was so smoky. Dougie smoked about a pack a set. Most of the audience were smoking. I knew most of them in the audience. The club was so smoky. When we finished playing I said hello quickly to everybody, cause not only did I want to get away from them, and I was flatulent, but most of the people I used to know had that lurid look so I started down the hallway to get away from the cigarettes then I heard this little voice say "Smitty?" I looked around and I couldn't believe it. It was Delores Murry. I said "Delores Murry!" We grabbed each other and hugged each other for about ten minutes. Then she said I didn't think you would remember me. Then I said to her "Are you crazy!!! I've been thinking about you for 17 years. Whenever I was with a girl I wasn't comfortable with I would think about you." "I thought I would never see you again." she said.

(355)
9/27/93

She said my last name's not Murry no more, it's Apps. I said are you married now? Yes she said, but I haven't slept with my husband in 7 years. She said, "I sleep on the couch." I said I've been there before. I said what's wrong with your relationship. She said we've grown apart. I said that's what happened to my relationship with my second ex. I said maybe it's meant to be running into you like this again. Afraid of being rejected again by her like she rejected me in 1971, I said to her, Delores, I would like to sleep with you. She said Okay. Man I don't know what it was, but I was so afraid of her rejecting me. Anyway we did have sex. For the first time in five years I reached a climax. You see I had for 5 years been taking high blood pressure pills. The doctor said that the medicine would affect me sexually. But I don't know, I can't explain it, I reached a climax with her. That's the only person I could do that with. I was in Toronto for 2 weeks, and for 2 weeks I played music and spent part of the night with Delores. We would have sex at night then she had to get up and leave cause she was married. Now that part I didn't like cause I didn't like seeing married women. That wasn't my thing. She said to me that she wanted to leave, that's what she was in therapy for, to get up enough nerves to tell her husband. Delores is a layed back person.

(356)

9/27/93

While I was playing the Blue Note, Dougie thought that we should have a Motherlode reunion. I thought that was a good idea. All the original guys were there. Steve Kennedy on sax, Kenny Marco on guitar, Wayne Stone on drums and me on organ. Man that felt great. Then Dougie suggested that Motherlode get together to record

four songs. It was just like old times. Steve Kennedy
came up with some great lyrics, Kenny Marco came up
with some great music. It was called In My Minds Eye. I
came up with the verse. That song that I sent Eric
Mercury months ago, and Eric sent it back to me? I gave
that song to Steve Kennedy. He sat in Bob Aston's living
room (that's where we were staying at the time). Steve sat
there in his B.V.D.'s with his hat on and a candle burning
in his chair and wrote the lyrics to that song in about 2
hours. The name of the song is called "Now That I've
Found You". Steve wrote the lyrics with such ease. That
guy can write anything. As you read this book, you can
see that I've had a lot of musical experience with a lot of
great people. But to me, my greatest musical experience
I've ever had working with a musician is Steve Kennedy.
Now I didn't say that he was the greatest musician I've
heard, I said that I had my greatest experience musically
working with him. There's nothing musically I can't do
that Steve Kennedy can't do. If I can dream about it, Steve
can make it real. Is just one thing though. Man, that's a
strange cat.

(357)
          9/27/93
While working the Blue Note none of us were taking
home any money, so Dougie extended his invitation for
me to stay at his house. Even though it was a 23 room
house, unlike Chuck Rainey, I like my privacy and my
hotel room. Even though it's small, while I'm renting the
room, it's mine. So I nicely said no. He insisted, so I said
Okay. He was trying to save me money. But I didn't care,
I just wanted to be and play in Toronto especially since
I've remet Delores. Now that was a crazy period for me.

Being that Dougie smoked about a pack of cigarettes in shows setting right besides me on stage. Being that he stayed in Mississauga, that's a suburb in Toronto. About 25 minutes outside of Toronto. Being that I lived with him I rode home with him in his BMW. He smoked about 5 or 6 cigarettes in the car then when we got to the house we set and talked for about 2 hours. He smoked cigarettes then. I gently ask him not to smoke. He said to me, Oh man I'm sorry, and he went into his guest bathroom to smoke, and to talk to me. Then I said this is ridicules. Here's a man that paid a half million dollars for his house that he lives in, and he has to go into his guest bathroom and smoke. Now I don't know but I don't think it's against the law in Canada to smoke a cigarette at your kitchen table. That's why I like my own hotel room. As long as I'm paying for that room I can do anything I want to. As long as I don't break the law.

(358)   Being in Toronto
9/28/93

A buddy of mine (who I've known for about 28 years) had become a successful TV composer in Canada. His wife decided that she wanted a house with an indoor swimming pool in it. As cold as it gets in the winter in Canada, you need an indoor swimming pool up there. So she was so excited when the builders were building the house. I was excited for them as well. So when she called I said let's go and see the house. It was close to Ann Murry's house. I don't exactly know where, I think it was Northern Bayview I think. Anyway I was living in another suburb at Dougie's house, about 30 minutes away from her house, so she came and picked me up. Wow! Just think the first time I saw her she was in bobby sox and she was in high school. Now she's driving her own car and having a house built. So on the way to the house she was having built, she was smoking cigarettes like crazy. About 10 or 11. Finally some smoke got down the wrong way down my throat. I started to gag. She said to me, Oh I'm sorry, is the cigarette smoke bothering you? she said. I said, Yeah. She said, I'll put the window down for you. It was 5 below zero outside. So I had to ride in her car for about 40 miles in her car with the window down in 5 below zero weather while she smoked. Smokers will never know what it's like to be in that environment. I've been there before, being that you're a smoker, you justify it. It's a painful thing to being somebody when they are smoking. You see I thought she would put the cigarette out and wait until we get to the house.

(359)   Being in Toronto
9/28/93

Then there was the time I was living at Dougie's house. Now I'll show you why Canada or the USA is not good for minorities. Whites shouldn't be here either, but I'll show or tell why minorities shouldn't be here. Dougie had his own company. His wife was the vice president of an advertisement company. Both of them had gone off to work, which left me alone in the house. Now I'm setting at the kitchen table with my legs cocked up on the table with my house slippers on laughing loudly at a joke, a dirty joke that my buddy for 35 years was telling me on the phone. This white house keeper was cleaning the house. She came in the kitchen and took one look at me and said as I was on the phone laughing, she said are you here to paint the outside of the house? I said no, I'm a house guest of Doug Riliey. I said I'm just setting here having a cup of tea and talking to my buddy on the phone with my pajamas on. She said oh, I'm sorry I thought your pajamas was a painters uniform. My pajamas was sky blue. They were made of cotton, it was 10 below zero outside. You figure it out. My compendium of Toronto? You can never go back no place to recapture nothing nowhere. People everywhere are too busy these days trying to survive. I thought I could go to Toronto to get away from the turmoil of L.A. It's the same up there as here. The only difference up there is it's a little colder and a little more backwards.

(360)   Working with Peter Rivera
9/28/93

It was right after I had arrived from Toronto around the spring of 1989 I was doing some work for the Keith Edwards Corporation. Walfredo Reyes was playing percussion Peter Rivera was playing drums and singing. He was his usual self, good, I said to him I would like to produce you man. Once again he said to me, you're a producer too? I said I'm not established, but I can do you because you're good. He said, man that's great now we need to find some money. Then he said, I know this guy this guy who I used to work with when I was selling stock. I said, you were selling stock? Peter said, yeah, then he said the guy was my boss. Peter said if I even wanted to get back into the music business he would help me. So Peter called him. His name's Kenny. Peter told Kenny the idea, Kenny said yes he would do it. So it took Kenny about 6 months to get the business and the money together. The money was nothing. It was $55,000. I know that may sound like a lot of money to you, but making a record cost a lot of money. I remember Walfredo and I were doing David Lindleys album. Now that album didn't even sell and that album cost $250,000 to do. You see if I was a big named musician, I could have got more money. But I wasn't. Take it or leave it, that's the way it was through my career. But if I have anything to do with it, I'm going to change. That by the way, we finally did the record even though I was sick most of the time.

(361)   Working with Soul Patrol.
9/29/93

While working with Jimmy Dale's Irie, the bass player of that group, Larry Fulcher, was the leader of a group called Soul Patrol. They worked around Orange County CA being that he lived in Santa Ana, CA. It was a 10 piece soul group with a lead singer. They worked in San Diego at the Belly Up Club, and around Santa Ana CA for private parties, weddings and etc. It was fun working with them. I got to play all the old R & B hits. I don't remember the guys names. The full names I remember is the bass player Larry Fulcher and the lead singer's first name Kenny. Man, to have all of those horns blowing off those R & B riffs at you is really nice. Guys, it was nice working with you. That was about 1990....

(362)   Working with the Gary Herbig band.
9/29/93

Around the time I was working with Irie, and the Soul Patrol I got a call from Gary Herbig. Gary Herbig is a sax player who's a studio musician who's worked with people like Michael Jackson to Frank Sinatra. He also has his own albums out. Any way he said he heard me play with Robben Ford's group in 1988 at the club At My Place

in Santa Monica, CA. He asked me if I would like to play
with him at the Baked Potato. That's a club in Studio City,
CA. I said, yes, are you kidding? I said, Gary, I know who
you are I said I'll be glad to play with you. So I played
with Gary. He had people in his band like Paul Jackson,
guitar man . That guy has played on just about every
record that has been made including the Thriller. Pat
Kelly on guitar George Bensons' guitar player Jerry
Brown, drums George Bensons' drummer Joey Heredia
on drums a session player Carl Verheyen guitar, a session
player Jimmy Earl bass a session player. These guys were
the giants among giants. Not only was the gig great, but I
learned a lot from those guys. That was when I could
make the gig when my stomach wasn't cramping or when
my across the street neighbor Joe Sheu could pack my
equipment for me. You see I couldn't lift any thing cause
of the high blood pressure, and the diabetes.

(363)   Chris fixing my car.
       9/29/93
By this time I had a nice relationship with Chris Hyde. I
would do his music. He kept my '76 Olds running for me
like I said before Chris had the car engine in mint
condition. Even though the blue book said that the car was
worth about $1,000. Man did that car run smooth. I was
working with Irie one night and after I got off from
working with them, I stopped to eat breakfast. I had my
equipment in the trunk of the car. I was in a restaurant in
North Hollywood CA. In a restaurant called Sittons,
which is right off the freeway. I parked my car right in
front of the restaurant where I could see it. Then all of a
sudden I heard a bang sound. I looked around and it was
my car. This guy or young kid was coming off the

freeway, and he didn't live in North Hollywood or L.A.
He lived in Valencia CA. So he was driving and looking
at his map at the same time. While he was doing that he
wasn't watching where he was going. He ran right into
my car. He hit my car doing about 30 miles per hour. So
he smashed the back of my car to bits. I ran out there to
see if he was alright. He was alright. Then I tried to get in
my trunk, I couldn't. I towed the car home. I pried the
trunk open. The instruments were damaged. Then the guy
said don't worry, I'll fix every thing.

(364)   People in L.A.
9/29/93
He said I'm insured. He said I'll take care of everything.
So I said to him that my amplifier and synthesizer were in
the trunk. That's damaged I said, that has to be fixed. He
said get it fixed my insurance will take care of it. Then I
said I have to get my car fixed. I told him that even though
the blue book says that the car's only worth $1,000, Chris
put the car in mint condition. He said to me, get the car
fixed and rent a car I'll have my insurance pay for it. So I
had the car towed to the place where I was living. The
next day I had it towed to the body shop. They gave me an
estimate for the car to be repaired. They told me that to fix
the car it would cost $3,000 to fix. He said if I were you I
would junk the car. Then I said you don't understand, the
motor in that car is like brand new. The body shop man
said okay, I'll fix it. So I said I've got to rent a car. I tried to
rent a car but my credit was no good. Then this lady I met
when I was playing the Baked Potato, who used to date a
trumpet player I used to know from Montreal. I hadn't
seen her in about 18 yrs. She said she would sign to get the
rental car for me. The car to rent was $300 a week. I made

the payments on time every week. I kept the car for a
month. Boy did that hurt to make those payments. I at
the time was working with Gary Herbig, Keith Edwards,
and Irie.

(365)

9/29/93

As fast as I was making money from those groups, I was
taking that money and paying for the rental car. I was not
used to making car payments. I would call Javier Gullien
at his house every day to find out what was happening
with the insurance, and to please help me cause $1,200 a
month was killing me. He would assure me that
everything was alright then I got my ex lawyer to check
him out but good. Come to find out, his insurance only
covered his car if he got in an accident. I went, I don't
know what I'm going to do. I said I can't keep renting the
car for $1,200 a month. Then the lady that signed for me
said, why don't you buy an old heap or something; this is
going to kill you making payments like that. I said, yeah,
I'll look in the paper and see what I can find. So I looked
and looked and I couldn't find nothing. So I told her my
situation she said why don't you buy a new car. I said I
don't have the down payment. She said you don't need
one, I'll sign for it. (By then I had written Javier off.) Then
I said to her okay. What could go wrong, whatever the car
payments a month is, It's better than renting a car for
$1,200 a month. Then I thought to myself, I said, being
that I'm indorsing J.B.L. products, and they're going to let
me have this great system for keyboards, I'll get a van. So I
discussed this with the lady that was signing for me.

(366)

9/29/93

After I told her the situation, she agreed with me. So the neighbor across the street from me had a Mazda MPV. I said that would be a nice van to carry my musical equipment in, I said to her where did you buy that van from. She said the local Mazda dealer in North Hollywood. I went there. That place was so expensive. So the dealer told me there was another Mazda dealer in Valencia, CA. That's about 20 miles from North Hollywood, CA. So me and the lady went to Valencia, CA. to look at MPV's. We went up there and sure enough they were cheaper up there. So as I was looking at MPV, I looked to my right and there was this recreational car. I said to the dealer, What it that! He said that's a Mazda Navajo fourwheel drive. I said to the dealer, I like that car. The dealer said it's loaded. It's got everything. I saw that car and fell in love with it. So I told the lady that was co-signing for me, I said that's the one. I asked the dealer, How much? He said $20,000. I told her. She said don't make no never mind, if you wanted a Rolls Royce you can get it, if you can make the payments. The dealer and her worked out the deal. I drove off the lot in that 4 wheel drive playing John Findly's tape. Boy was I happy. I gave that lady $1500 two weeks later for car payments. The car payments was $469 a month. A far cry from $1200 a month.

(367)

10/1/93

Then there was the time, this was around the spring of 1990 that I got a call from Lesley Morris, she was a music contractor. She used to contract movie sound tracks and record sessions. She called me, I had met Lesley on the Ry

Cooder record sessions way back in 1979. She said that
she was booking a movie sound track, would I or could I
do it. I said when, she said next week. I said, Yeah, what's
the movie called, she said "Ford Fairlane". I said, who's in
it, she said Wayne Newton, Priscilla Presley, and Andrew
Dice Clay. I said, That crazy guy Andrew Dice Clay? She
said yeah, can you do it? I said yeah. So we did the sound
track. It came out good. I can't remember the musicians
names that did the sound track cause I didn't know the
guys. The only guy I knew on the session was Jim
Keltner, the drummer. After we had finished, the director
of the film of which I can't remember his name, liked the
sound track so much that he wanted the guys who played
on the sound track to play in the movie. The rest of the
guys couldn't be in the movie, cause they had previous
engagements. The movie was for 20th Century Fox. So I
was the only one that showed up from the original band.
That's when I met the music supervisor of 20th Century
Fox music. His name's Lonnie Sill, of the Sill music
dynasty. His whole family's in the music business.

(368)   Working in L.A.
10/1/93
His father Lester Sill is the president of Jobet music.
That's all the music on Motown Records. His two
brothers, Chuck and Joel own their own publishing
company. Chuck used to head Almo music. That's all the
music at A&M records. His brother Joel used to be a
music supervisor for a lot of the big movies we see today.
His other brother Gregory is the head of Lorimar T.V.
Man, that's quite a family. It was fun doing and being in a
movie, even though I didn't like the movie. Almost
instantly Lonnie and I took a liking to each other. His wife

Niky's a singer. He asked me would I be interested in producing his wife. I said send me a tape and let me hear her. So he did that. I listened to the tape, then I said yeah I'll do it. So William (just can't say no) Smith did the record. I used Jimmy Dale on the record session. I also recommended Jimmy Dale to appear in the movie as well. Instead of charging Lonnie for my services for the record, I told Lonnie to just get my son Amani a plane ticket to Toronto, cause his grandmother, that's my second ex's mother, had terminal cancer. And he had to go there and being that I was a impecunious person, I couldn't afford to send him. So Lonnie put the ticket on his credit card. Amani went to see his grandmother. I was feeling all good and everything. I had figured out how to get Amani to Toronto. I had gotten Jimmy Dale his first movie role.

(369)

10/1/93

When Amani arrived from Toronto, he walked in the house, went into his room, the phone rang. It was my second ex's sister telling him that his grandmother had just died. I went oh no, he just got back from there. Then I said, What do I do now. I said I've got to think. Then I said I know what I'll do, I'll borrow the money from my music colleges. So I borrowed a $100 each from people like Reggie McBride, Tony Braunagel, Mary Unobsky, Rick Wilson and etc. All in all I had about $1000. I gave the money to Amani and told him to get his mother back up there as well. Even though I hadn't spoken to his mother for years, this was different. Amani and her went to the funeral. After Amani had arrived from Toronto, about 3 months later Amani moved out, to go live with his mother.

(370) Being in L.A.

10/4/93

Then there was a time about a year later, Jimmy Dale called me to thank me for getting him in the Ford Fairlane movie. I said you're welcome, I said why are you thanking me now, we did that movie over a year ago. Jimmy said, I know, but I just got a trust fund check for $2000. A trust fund check is when the movie company takes out a certain amount of money and put in a trust fund and distributes it to you over a period of 5 years. They have two trust funds, one is for movies, the other one is for recording records. Anyway, I got excited. I said great. I said to him, if you got a check for $2000 I'll get a check too. Then he said everyone else in the band got a check then I said I'll get one too! I live in North Hollywood, maybe the mail takes longer. So about a month later Jimmy Dale calls again. He said, did you get your check yet? I said no then he said you better call the union and find out what happened. So I did just that. The union said that they mailed me the check over a month ago. I told them that I never received the check. They said they mailed the check to my new address. I said, New address! I said to them that I hadn't moved from this address that I'm at now in 7 years. They said that they mailed me my check to Eureka, CA. I said, Oh no! You've mailed my check to my ex second wife.

(371)   Being in L.A.

10/4/93

Come to find out that my second ex has been getting my trust fund check for 9 years. She has been forging my name on my check for 9 years. I didn't even know I was

getting a check. I thought being that I was working
sparsely I wasn't getting a check. For 9 years she has been
forging my name. What a way to live. I don't understand,
why don't she just go ahead with her own life.

(372) Being in L.A.

10/4/93

Then there was this time in L.A. about after Xmas 1990,
when Doug Rileys wife who's the vice president of an ad
agency in Toronto. They've done Bill Cosbys' Coca Cola
ad, the Smothers Bros ad for Nabisco. She's big time. Her
and her company would come to L.A. to do an ad. I was
excited. That woman, I would treat like she was my sister
let alone a friend. Her ad company would have parties in
the lounge where she stayed. (She stayed at the Westwood
Marque Hotel. She had a suite there.) I used to entertain
them in the lounge. They had a piano there. They had a
private club in L.A. called R&B live. I took her there. I
introduced her to the great Joe Sample, a music colleague
of mine. Man she freaked out. Her and Dougie were so
good to me. Hell ever since I've known Dougie, he's
always treated me nice, hell Dougie's that way with a lot
of people, that's the way he is. Even though she had an
unlimited expense account, I wanted to show her that I
appreciated what she did by putting me up when I was in
Toronto.

(373) Working in L.A.

10/5/93

Now, to give you an example of why North America's not
a good place to be in. Especially if you're an artist. You
take Scott Joplin, I never heard of him until the movie The
Sting came out. I was about 31 years old then. Not only

because he was a black man or nothing like that, but I never learned any thing in school about him. Later on in life I learned about him because it was fashionable to learn about Scott Joplin, and because two great white stars did a movie and used his music for the theme. Being that those stars were big and the movie was good then and only then did I hear about Scott Joplin. You can say that a great singer can make it big here in Hollywood or North America, Jackie Wilson was one of the greatest singers of all times, while he was alive. He was great. Now you very seldom hear of him. James Brown is the godfather of soul. Only in America does this happen which brings to mind a club I was working at it was called the China Club. It was located in Hollywood. The club owner wanted to bring in some famous sidemen who did hit records. For example Bruce Springsteen made hit records with the drummer Gary Malabar. He help to make those records. If some of these famous sidemen went to Europe or Japan or Australia or Brazil and etc. they would be stars but people don't support the arts in North America.

(374)

10/5/93

Now this took place around Oct. of 1990, to March of 1991. The club owner had finally closed the club down because of poor attendance. Some of the people that frequented the place, and I played with, blew my mind. In the Bohemian era, you had people like Picasso, Braque, Robert Craft, T.S. Eliot. Sigmond Freud and etc. All of those guys including Ravel hung in the cafes of Paris. They discussed ideas about things. It was a melting pot for artists. You have nothing like that in North America. Sure Walt Disney said, If you can dream it you can do it. Sure you can do here providing you're white. Oh yeah that kind of stuff goes on to this day. To this day I think of some of the people that I played with and met at that club, and it blows my mind. I'll name who I played with at the China Club. I'll first give you the name, then I'll tell you the instruments they played then I'll name one person they've played with, because if I named everybody they've played with, this book would be 5,000 pages long. The club owner hired Kenny Lewis then Kenny hired myself, and Scott Page as regulars. Man did I have a nice time. Okay here's the list. I guarantee that one of these people you have in your c.d. or album collection, if you own one or more c.d.'s or albums.

(375)   Working in L.A.
10/5/93
**Girls and guys I played with, and met at the
China Club**

Name	Instrument	Played With
Kenny Lewis	Guitar	Steve Miller
Scott Page	Saxophone	Pink Floyd
William Smith	Organ	Bob Dylan
James Gadson	Drums	The Temptations
Rock Dendrick	Drums	Tracy Chapman
Buzzy Feiten	Guitar	Olivia Newton John
Robben Ford	Guitar	Late Miles Davis
Micheal Landau	Guitar	Rod Stewart
The Lead singer with Simply Red		
JIm Keltner	Drums	John Lennon
Bill Sharpe	Bass	Tracy Chapman
Abraham Laborial	Bass	Manhatan Transfer
Reggie Mc Bride	Bass	Michael Jackson
Danny Kortchman	Guitar	Linda Rondstadt
Steve Lukather	Guitar	Toto
David Paich	Keyboards	Toto
David Garfield	Keyboards	George Benson
David Swanson	Keyboards	Lily Thomlin
Alvino Bennett	Drums	Chaka Kan
Mary Russell	Singer	Leon Russell
Laural Satterfield	Singer	Rita Coolidge
Larry Williams	Keyboards/sax	Aretha Franklin
Marlo Henderson	Guitar	Lionel Ritchie
Gary Malabar	Drums	Bruce Springsteen
Phil Chin	Bass	Rod Stewart
Boz Skaggs		
Carol Dennis	Singer	Bob Dylan

Brenda Russell		
Bernie Larsen	Guitar	Melissa Ethridge
Mike Tyson	Customer	
Gary Buss	Owner of the Lakers basketball team	
L.L. Cool J.	Customer	
Prince	Customer	
Cher	Customer	
Christine Reedy	Producer	Night Court
Lou Diamond Phillips	Customer	
Carl Verhyen	Guitar	Cheers
Bob Mann	Guitar	James Taylor
Jimmy Weatherspoon	Blues singer	
Lee Thornburg	Trumpet	Tower of Power
Jerry Jumonville	Sax	Billy Vera

Now this really blows my mind why these people are not popular in the U.S. Oh well, live and learn. You know as long as I've been a melanoid person, I've never learned so much about music as I have learned working with these great talented artists at the China Club. What a great musical experience. Guys thank you so much. May God bless all of you guys. That's the time when I was playing the China Club, Delores came down from Mississauga Canada to see me. Being that she is a nurse, she would rub my back and head every time I would play. The only time I would feel good is when she was around, cause by this time I was feeling pretty bad.

(377)   Working with Ramona
10/6/93

Now this took place after the China Club around the end of March 1991. I got a call from Bob Parr. He was the bass player that would substitute for Tones when Tones couldn't make it when we used to play for Nell Carter. He said he was producing a demonstration record for a girl named Ramona, could I play on it for him. I said yes. It was at Pacific Studios in North Hollywood, CA on Magnolia are literally right around the corner from where I used to live. I got there, did the session. It was good. Bob was a good producer, Ramona was good as well. She sang locally with a three piece all girl pop group. We had a break and on that break I was talking to the drummer who played on that session. Come to find out we had something in common. He was the drummer (I forget his name) that played on the Tracy Chapman hits. The guy that produced those records name's David Kershenbaum. I did the Richie Havens album with David Kershenbaum back in 1976. So I told the drummer say hello to David for me and tell him that I loved what he did on the first Tracy Chapman album. The drummer said to me we're in the studio doing a Tracy Chapman album right now. He said David would be glad to hear from you. Then I said tell David to call me, I would like to say hello to him. The drummer took my number. I had forgotten about that incident. About 2 weeks later I got a call from David Kershenbaum. Man was I surprised to hear from him. He asked me to play on the Tracy Chapman album.

(378)   Working with Tracy Chapman
10/6/93

I arrived at David Kershenbaums' studio in Hollywood. Man that place was nice. The first thing I noticed was all the gold records he had on the wall, 28 of them. Man that guy had produced some hit records. It's probably more now, cause that was 1988. I remember that session so well cause when I arrived at the studio, there was so many keyboards there and Tracy was so hard to please. She knew exactly what she wanted. I remember I was so glad when I did something right. You have a lot of artists like that. When I worked for Joe Cocker, he was like that, Bob Dylan was like that. I could go on and on. But you know what? That's what makes hit records. People being meticulous. Any way I enjoyed playing with Tracy Chapman, even though it was hard.

(379)   Working with Linda Ronstadt
10/6/93

Right after that, not right after that about three weeks later, I got a call from Linda Ronstadt. She asked me if I could do an album with her and Arron Neville. I said yes. I said now that guy is talented I told her. I also told her that his brothers played on my album in New Orleans. Once again I said yes to her. Then I said where is it going to be. She said at the George Lucas Ranch in San Francisco. I said great. Man do I like that place. You know that place is so big that they have their own fire dept. That place is like a little city. I got there, she had Lee Sklar on bass. That guy has played with almost everybody. One person is Phil Collins. Carlos Vega on drums. He played on all the Olivia Newton John hits, and the great great legendary Dean Parks on guitar. Man what can I say about him. Not only has he played with everybody, but he put the "g" in guitar. The session went great. We went overtime, so I had to stay at the ranch over night, cause the session went to about 1:00am in the morning, and there were no planes going to L.A. that time of the morning. So once again, I got to stay in one of those great suites George Lucas had at his ranch. I remember we were taking a lunch break, so Linda and I were having

lunch in the big lunch or dining room George had his own
eating place there because the place was so far away from
everything.

(380)

10/6/93

So while Linda and I were having having lunch one of the
workers on the ranch walked by. There were so many
workers there, cause they were working on so many films
there. So while I was talking politics to Linda, this girl
walked by. For about a third of a second I just glanced at
that girl, and I said to myself hum, nice butt, ugly face.
Just then Linda stopped talking about politics and said to
me, I know what your thinking. I said to her what. She
said you're thinking she's got a nice butt but you don't
like her face. Just then I jumped up and grabbed my head.
I couldn't believe it, she read my mind. That incident and
other things. She did make me realize that she was the
most perceptive person that I have ever met. Not only
does her talent keep her at the top, but being perceptive
keeps her up there as well. I learned a lot from Linda from
her producing the David Lindley album that I was on, and
doing her album as well. I can honestly say that I have
never met a woman like Linda Ronstadt. Coming back
from the ranch, being that all of us in the band was from
L.A. we were all on the plane together. I was sitting beside
Dean Parks. Being that I hadn't seen Dean since the old
days when we were doing sessions, we were catching up
on things. I asked him what's new in your life, he said I
got married about two years ago. I said oh yeah, is she in
the business?

(381)   Working with Ricky Lee Jones
10/6/93

He said she's a music contractor. I said great, you guys
have something in common. If she just booked you she
would be working 24 hours a day, I said. Then I said she is
working on the Ricky Lee Jones album. Then he said do
you know the Bull Durham movie? I said yeah I played
organ in the movie. Then he looked at me and said, what!!!
He said man, my wife and I have been trying to find out
who played organ in that movie. Then I told him the
reason why I didn't get credit, cause I got payed in cash,
cause you know how it is, the record companies, they take
so long to pay you. That's why when it's possible I try to
get my money up front. Then he said, but you lose a lot of
benifits that way. I said yeah, but I also eat that day.
Anyway Ricky wanted that organ player that did that
movie to play on her album. I said here I'll call me Dean's
wife. The sessions were in North Hollywood. The session
was good. Being that was her big comeback, she was
going to do a road tour to promote the album. I get a call
from her office about three weeks after I had done the
album. They asked me if I wanted to go on the road with
Ricky Lee Jones. But first I had to audition. You know,
only in Hollywood does this happen. When Janet Jackson
said in the song What have you done for me lately, she
should have wrote what have you done this morning.
That's the way Hollywood is.

(382)   Working with Robben Ford
10/7/93

Now this took place around the first week in July of 1991. I
got a call from Robben Ford, he asked me to play with him
in San Francisco at Slims. Boz Scags owned that club. So I

agreed, we rehearsed at studio instrument rentals up there. As usual the show was great. After the show I went to the dressing room. It was there that I met Chick Corea's wife. The drummer Tom Bretehlien used to play with Chick Corea being that she was there to catch him, I got a chance to meet her. She must have thought I was crazy, cause when I shook her hand, I kept rubbing my hand against hers, hoping that some of Chick Corea would rub onto my hand. But I guess that doesn't work if you want to be good like Chick, I guess you have to practice. This took place the second weekend on a Saturday night July of 1991.

(383)   Working with Bobby King
10/7/93

The day after Robben Ford called me up to play with him at Slims. Bobby King called me up to play at Slims with him and his partner Terry Evans. Bobby King sang background for Ry Cooder, Bruce Springsteen and etc. Terry Evens sang background for Ry Cooder and etc. They had their own thing they were trying to promote, of which I arranged. Bobby wanted me to play with him at Slims that following Wednesday. I got back from San Francisco with Robben that Saturday before Wednesday. One of the waiters at Slims thought I was the house organist for groups out of L.A. That's the way it was looking. Once again both Saturday and Wednesday I was with two girls. Boy was I a lunatic person back in those days. In spite of that, I had a nice time playing with Bobby King and Terry Evans. Man are they good. To Bobby, good luck with Bruce Springsteen.

(384)   Working with Boz Skags
10/7/93

Now this was in early August of 1991. Walfredo Reyes, the drummer that I used to work with when I was with David Lindley, was now playing with Boz Skags. Boz needed an organ player to play with him. Boz had two gigs, one in Vancouver, B.C., and the other gig in Lake Tahoe. Walfredo Reyes recommended me for the gig. So I got a call from Boz. He asked me to play with him. As usual I said yes. He rehearsed in North Hollywood. David Garfield was on piano. The piano player that plays piano for the TV. show Fame. Man can that guy play. Anyway it was really fun playing all of his hits. And by the way, Boz is a good guitar player. So he played Whistler. That's a ski resort right outside of Vancouver. That place was way up on the ski slope. Being that it was a three day festival, Natalie Cole played the first night, Linda Ronstadt played there the second night, and Boz Scags played there the third night. I remember because it took us half an hour to drive up the ski slope, once you got to Whistler. Even though it was an outdoor stage, and it was summer, it was cold as hell up there. We were way up there in the mountains. they had big heat fans on stage to keep us warm. Once again Walfredo sounded like 10 drummers when he played. That gig was first class all the way. Boz can play some blues on that guitar. He reminded me of back home.

(385)   An Encounter in Vancouver
10/08/93

After we had finished playing with Boz, him and I and the band went back to the dressing room. Well they had a tent for us as a dressing room. I was sitting in the dressing room talking to Walfredo Reyes, the drummer for the group. the road manager came back to the tent and handed me a note. I read it, and it said, Hi!, I saw you play, you sounded great. Then she said I would like to see you. I went outside, and low and behold, it was Wayne Stones ex girlfriend. We hugged and hugged. Naturally, we spoke. I hadn't seen her in 23 years or since Motherlode. We talked over old times. I asked her about Wayne, her old boy friend. I know that he was married. I never understood why he let her get away. Man she's beautiful, she has pretty blonde hair, and a body any woman would die for. Anyway she told me she had a place up in Whistler, and she had a place in Vancouver, and a tile business in Vancouver. She and her 7 girl friends were up here to see Linda Ronstadt, and after she wanted to go back to Vancouver, and her girl friends convinced her to stay and see Boz Scags. She said, I'm really glad I stayed or I would never have run into you. Then I said, how did you know it was me? I've changed so much in 23 years. She said, I recognized your hands on the organ, and also I have your album that you recorded for Warner Bros. records; I've been listening to that record for 16 years. Then she said, I know your sound.

(386)

10/8/93

Then I said, wow! I then said we have so much to talk about. Then I said look over in the ski lodge, in the back room, they've set up a dining room for the artist to eat dinner. Why don't you and your girl friends have dinner with me? Then she said no, I couldn't do that, there's too many of us here. Then I said don't worry about it, I'll take care of it, so I did. Here I was in the back of the ski lodge,

sitting with 8 beautiful women, all of them looking like
they just came from Sweden. Walfredo sitting at the next
table making fun of me, cause he's thinking all these
women are mine. I'm saying no to him, they're not my
girls. The more I say no to him, the more he laughed. Boz
was looking at me all funny as he was sitting at the other
table, as if to say to himself, who is this guy? Finally I got
up from the table and went upstairs where they had a
local dance band from Vancouver. They were playing
what else, dance music. So Wayne's ex and I started to
dance. For once my stomach wasn't hurting. I started to
dance with her other friend, then I started to get lascivious
with her. She responded. Man I said, what a drag, I've
got to go home in the morning. She said I could call you
in L.A. Being that she had a government job, she couldn't
travel much, she didn't have much money. I said oh well,
I guess I just have to wait then.

(387)

10/8/93

Man I was excited. Even though I had a girl in Toronto,
that didn't make no difference. Being at the time, I was
libertine. I had to have a lot of women. So when I arrived
in L.A. I was so excited, that I called Stoney's ex, (that's
Waynes nickname) and told her what had happened. She
said you can't see her. Then I said what! Then I said is
there something wrong with her? She said no. Then I
said, she's married, right? She said no. Then I said what
is it then? She said the reason you can't see her is because
I love you. Then I said what!!!! then I said, no that can't be,
I never looked at you like that. All of us stayed in a house
together. Kenny Marco the guitar player with
Motherlode, Wayne Stone the drummer with Motherlode.

I watched and used to talk to you and Wayne, when you where in bed together. Then she said, I loved you then. I said to her, this is weird. Then she said to me, let me come to L.A. Man, she knocked me off my feet. Even though I liked what she did, I felt kind of weird. I liked her beauty. Her beauty left me breathless.

(388)

10/8/93

Now I got to thinking, I can't live the libertine life I've been living and have her too. She could get on a plane to LA to see me any time she wanted to. So I said to myself, it's time for a change, if I can give up drugs, I can give up being libertine, cause this girl's something else. So I started calling all the girls I knew. Nobody took me serious. Then came the phone call of doom. I took a deep breath, waited a couple of days, and called Delores. She, Delores was really hurt but she understood. You see, at the time, Delores was my main squeeze. Now that I got that out of the way, Waynes ex and I went after a relationship. She would fly to see me about once a month. She would see me, then go to Disneyland, then go to the Chinese Theater in Hollywood, when she wasn't off stealing a chance smoking a cigarette she was shopping for Peppridge farms cookies. She would buy 7 or 8 bags of them she would tell me that it was for her neighbor. I remember she was supposed to come to L.A. but she couldn't come to L.A. because she had to wheel and deal to get this piece of propertyon Vancouver Island. Now even though I was an impecunious person, I lived in a $1,375 dollars a month house. I had a brand new Mazda 4 wheel drive recreational vehicle. I managed. I don't know how but I managed.

(389)

10/8/93

Every time that girl would come to visit in L.A., when she would leave, she would leave me 2 or 3 hundred dollars. I would be so insulted. I felt bad enough as it is that I couldn't pay for her plane ticket every time she came to LA. She could afford to do that. The ticket and her leaving me money, I over looked because she was this pretty blonde who had money. Sure I lived all right but I just managed to get by. I was like the average American, my head barely above water. Even still I wasn't no pimp. Every time she did that to me that's what I felt like. Her and I would sit around and discuss politics and she would tell how she couldn't stand the influx of Orientals in Vancouver. Then I would say to myself, (cause I wouldn't want to upset her) how do you think the Indians felt about the influx of white people in Vancouver? Dumb question, they have it justified. Oh well, I guess she must have thought I was a mellifluous person. She had started a tile shop in Vancouver, and became successful. So she sent for her mother and father, her sister and her brother from London, Ontario, Canada to work in her tile shop. The father, sister and her brother works for her. All of them resent her. She's been trying to get her parents approval all of her life. She plays the role of a placeter in that family.

(390)

10/8/93

We used to debate a lot about how each of us lived. She used to think how bad it was that I worked, and never had no money. I agreed with her, she would say to me, you

take for example (meaning her) I own a tile business, I
don't like the tile business, but that tile business affords
me a life style I didn't have when I knew you in the old
days. Then I would say to her are you happy though? She
would say to me that doesn't matter, I'm working. I knew
right then and there it was over, cause I wasn't used to
that kind of life style. Even though I was backing up
people and not doing what I wanted to do, I was still
doing music. Heck, I was having such a good time backing
up people like the Pointer Sisters, Billy Joel, Bob Dylan,
Nell Carter and etc. that I kept putting my thing off cause
their thing was so mellifluous. That's why I couldn't do
my thing, cause their thing was so comfortable and I loved
their thinking so much. I'll do what I have to do to get by,
except kill or rob somebody or smoke cigarettes and do
drugs. But whatever I do, I'm not going to make a career
out of it, you give me an inch and I'll take a mile. Even if I
was doing something that I didn't like, I would always be
scratching at music. Or by taking $5 out of that $100 a
week I'm making and buy a pencil or pen and paper and
write some music, and play it for somebody until they
liked it. When I was a teenager, we couldn't afford a
piano, so I went to the YMCA every day and practiced.

(391)

10/8/93

You live and learn to do something in life that you like, all
you have to do is want to do it bad enough. That's the
problem with a lot of people in this world today. People
are doing things that they don't like, and it shows through
their work. Now I'm trying to bond with this person when
she comes to LA and she's busy seeing buyers most of the
day. When she gets back to the house, she's beat and I'm

trying to bond with her, and I can't because she's so
fractious from doing something she doesn't like. In my
world, I don't see none of that. Sure people in my world
have problems, but that's not one of them. I'm sure being
that Billy Joel, Donna Summers, Linda Ronstadt, B.B. King,
Bonnie Raitt and etc. have problems, but I don't know,
they look and sound like they like what they're doing.
They got me fooled. So much so that I even went out and
purchased one of their albums. All I can say is that if
you're doing something you don't like, work toward doing
something that you do like. If every body would do that,
this would be a halcyon world. I know what you can say,
you can say those people are different, they're stars. I
remember way back when Linda Ronstadt did her first
tour. She did her first tour to make her payments on her
refrigerator that she owed when she lived in Hollywood,
in her one bedroom apt. Now, if she wanted to, she could
by a fridge factory if she wanted to.

Girl From Vancouver

My compendium of this chapter is that I'm honored and
nervous that to have had a relationship like that with her.
Honored to have had a love affair, nervous that one day I
would be rejected. When I met her in '67, I chose her to be
my buddy and friend, that kind of relationship I could
handle. Boy, we've had some nice times then. I never
dreamed that that kind of a relationship could be rejected.
So when we were lovers and you said let's wait a while, I
got nervous. Presto! It happened. I only hope that one
day it could go back to the way it used to be, cause you're
on hell of a lady. By the way, I don't care what your girl
friends say, keep singing. Once again thanks for

everything, I'm so proud of you at what you've become. Wow! What a giant.

Smitty

(392)   Realizing that I was sick.
10/13/93

It was around Oct. of 1991, I was in the supermarket, doing a little shopping. I went to the refrigerator to get some milk. As I reached for the milk, I got dizzy as if I was going to faint. 3 seconds later I got myself together, got the milk and went home. When I went to use the bathroom, in my stool was blood. I was pissing blood. I'm saying to myself, what's wrong with me? Then I said to myself, even though I have diabetes, it or this thing can't be this serious. then I say to myself, I make hit records, I'm indestructible. Nothing can happen to me, I've had ever so many woman. So around the first of Nov. 1991 that night I went to bed. My stomach was hurting as usual, a little bit. I fell asleep. My stomach started to turn. I went up to the bathroom. I went to the toilet, I threw up. After I threw up I went to the sink to wipe the sweat off my face. As I was washing my face, I passed out. I must have passed out for about half an hour. I came to. I tried to get up, and I felt dizzy. Being that the bathroom in the house was off of the bedroom, I stumbled to the bed. Man was I feeling bad.

(393)   Being Sick
10/13/93

I said to myself, I better call 911 to get myself some help. I went to pick up the phone. I couldn't hear a dial tone. My hearing was bad. Then I threw up again. Boy did I feel bad. The phone was ringing, I couldn't answer it cause I

265

couldn't hear who was on the line. So I said I had better go to the kitchen and get some water. So I went to the kitchen to get some water. I staggered back to the bedroom and I laid down on the bed. Three minutes later, I threw up the water. As a matter of fact, I threw up everything I had in me. My roommate had gone to stay with her girl friend, so nobody else was home but me. I just lay there listening to the phone ring and I couldn't do nothing about it. I was doing that and throwing up. So about the second day I was laying there and somebody was banging on the door cause I couldn't hear the doorbell. It was the lady that signed for the 4 wheel drive for me. I staggered back to my bed after staggering to open the door for her. I fell on the bed. From 2 days of vomit in the bed, the room was sour. She saw me in the bed, she said to me, look, I can't stay long, I have to run, here are the insurance papers for the truck. Here take them. I have to run. Bye. If only she could have dialed 911 for me, that would have helped. Oh well, since she signed for the car for me I guess it made it all right not to call.

(394)

10/13/93

The phone was just ringing. Finally this one lady that I knew, Cathy McBroom, came to my house cause I didn't return her calls after 3 days. I was glad to see her even though I kept passing out. Now that I know what it was, I was going in and out of a diabetic coma. Cathy was very mature. She kept giving me crushed ice. It felt good even though I kept throwing the ice up. Finally she said, I've got to get you to a hospital. Then she asked me, do you have any insurance. I said to her no. By then I was in a coma. I'm going to get you to a hospital, you're dying. I know the symptoms, she said, I've been around diabetic people before.

(395)

10/13/93

So she called the first ambulance. They wouldn't take me cause I didn't have insurance. Then she called another ambulance. She did what she had to do. She lied and told them that I had insurance. Anything to get me to the hospital. She got me in the hospital. St. Joseph Hospital, it was a private hospital. Once again she lied and got me in there. I'm just so glad that Cathy did what she had to do to get me in the hospital. If she didn't, I wouldn't be here today writing this book. I got to the hospital they gave me all kinds of tests, then they told me I was dehydrated, that they had to get fluids into my system immediately. then the doctor said you almost died. I met a wonderful doctor in there, his name is doctor Winn. I stayed there for about a week. When the hospital started to treat me for diabetes, I didn't throw up that much. I didn't feel so dizzy. I was getting much more stable, so they released me Nov. 9, 1991. I made it out of that one okay. Even when I got out I was dizzy. I threw up. but not as much as I used to. I had to walk slow.

(396)

10/14/93

Man was I in shock, even though I was throwing up on a regular basis, I was still throwing up. Joe Sheu, my across the street neighbor had to drive me to my gigs. The cerebellum of my brain (that's the part of the brain that controls balance and speed), was slowly going bad. In other words, I was walking slowly. This one day when I

first got out of the hospital, Eric Mercury's first wife was
in town. By then she had moved to New York city where
there she managed a lot of big named groups. She used to
live in LA but she was in L.A. on business, so she stopped
passed to see me which I thought was a nice gesture. She
helped me in her car, and we went to a restaurant in the
North Hollywood neighborhood. We talked over old
times, we drove home, she helped me to the house I was
living in at the time. Before she said goodbye she gave me
$80. Man, I was so offended. Right then and there my
heart fell to the ground. Please please don't get me
wrong. I really appreciate what she was doing. If that's
all she had that's allright too! But after 30 years of
knowing her (well almost 30 years of knowing her. I met
her the third week of April 1965) I thought she was so
great that I introduced her to Eric Mercury. They got
married then got a divorce. Now she's the god mother of
Eric Mercury's second wife's baby. When do you see that
happening now a days. I didn't make them end up being
the best of friends or cause them to get married, but I did
bring them to the water.

(397)

10/13/93

I just said to myself, is that all 30 years of friendship meant
to her. The thing that would really encourage me to keep
going, is that she could have said, Smitty, being that
you've had all illness, why don't you put your furniture in
storage, and come and live on my couch until you make a
full recovery, Then I would have said to her with my
strong headed self, thank you so much for the suggestion,
but being that I can still walk and play music, I can make
it. It's good to know you're there for me. Steve Kennedy

and Kenny Marco of Motherlode, who lives outside of
Toronto, who are struggling to make ends meet. They're
not poor, but their not rich either. They both said to me,
we're here for what ever it takes to get you back on your
feet, we'll do it . Now that made me feel good. I never ask
them for anything, but it's good to know they're there just
in case. I've known those guys for years. boy did we have
our disagreements through life. But it's good to know you
had an effect on some body's life. The encounter with Eric
Mercury's first wife took place Nov. of 1991. As I'm
writing now, I've not heard from her. This is Oct. 13, 1993.
Like the spiritual song, The love of God says, A friend is
closer than a brother.

(398)   Working at the St. James Hotel
10/14/93

This was around Dec. of 1991. I go t a call from Kenny
Lewis to play the St. James Hotel. That's a hotel located in
Hollywood on Sunset Blvd. I said yes. He then asked me,
was I well enough to play. I said yes I can handle it. So I
got Joe Sheu my across the street neighbor to drive for me.
I got to the St. James Hotel. Kenny Lewis was on guitar,
Scott Page was on horn. We were having a good time,
then they gave the mike to me to sing. I was feeling good,
so I sang a song called Stormy Monday. I got finished
playing and singing. About a minute after I was finished,
I was just sitting there when all of a sudden I threw up all
over the piano. I didn't sing no more that night. The next
day I got in my 4 wheel drive and went to the restaurant
to eat lunch. The restaurant was only about a mile from
my house. I ate my lunch, got in my 4 wheel drive and
drove home. I pulled in the garage. just when I pulled in
the garage, and turned off the car, I threw up all over the

car. You see, I was all right as long as I didn't strain my stomach muscles like sing or eat. So I downed a lot of liquids. That stroke really affecting my cerebellum part of my brain. Every time I would eat something that didn't agree with me, I would throw up. Seems like that's all I ever did.

(399)   The Second Stroke
10/13/93

By this time I was seeing Doctor Winn about once a week. My condition was getting pretty bad. By this time I couldn't drive. Joe Sheu, my across the street neighbor, would have to drive me to work. I had flown to Vancouver to see the girl I was seeing at the time. (well one of them you can say was my main squeeze) On the way up on the plane, I went to the wash room to take a leak, and I threw up, I got there and had to cut my visit short. Came home, on the way home on the plane, I threw up again in the wash room. So I made an appointment with Doctor Winn the third of Jan. 1992. Joe Sheu took me there. I had to hold onto Joe's shoulder, cause I couldn't stand up. Joe took me into the doctors office. The doctor took one look at me and immediately said to me, go to the hospital now. So Joe Sheu took me to the hospital. I went back to St. Joseph hospital. Once again, I don't know how we did it, but we got in. It was easy to see Doctor Winn, I paid cash every time I went there to see him. Once again they took a CAT scan. The doctor at the hospital told me I had another stroke, and this time it had affected the cerebellum part of my brain, but you will make a complete recovery, in a week, a month, or a year. Who knows I said to myself, oh no, what am I going to do, I said to myself.

(400)

10/14/93

Just then the girl I was seeing in Vancouver, who owned property on an island, a tile business in Vancouver, a house in Vancouver, a house in Whistler, and a brand new Jeep Cherokee, I borrowed $2000 to make ends meet. I personally think that was a good gesture. I don't care if I felt like a pimp. Heck I was sick in the hospital. So thank you very much for your help. The late Willie Dixon was down the hall from me, in the room. Willie, rest in peace, you done a good job here. The hospital food not only was bad, but it had no love in it. To Rita Coolidge, thank you so much for the brown rice, the reading glasses of which I still have to this day, The shaving moisture, the beet juice, the apples, and bringing your niece to see me. Being that I had to go straight to the hospital, right from Doctor Winns office, I couldn't return my phone calls, so people were wondering what was wrong with me. So this girl that I was libertine with about twice a year with. (I had my reason which I think is personal) came across the street to Joe Sheu's house to find out what had happened to me, and that I was down and out and I was impecunious. The word got out all over town that I needed help.

(401)

10/14/93

So this one guy had called me to see how I was doing. This girl told him what had happened to me. After she had told him what had happened to me, Willie and Carol thought of this idea of having a benefit for me. They discussed this with me, I thought it was a great idea. All of those people on the benefit man I couldn't believe this. All three of us were excited. Then she spoke to me in the hospital and said to me I got about 14 people committed to do the benefit, Bob Dylan, Michael McDonald and etc. consented to do the benefit. Then she said I booked The Palace for Jan. 30, 1992. It holds a thousand people, then she said I don't know if it's going to sell or not. Then I said, "Are you crazy!!!!!!! Do you know what you just did. I said you just did something that's never happened in this world as I know it. They were Carol and Willie Ornelas.

(402)

10/14/93

Maybe I didn't know enough business like she did but I knew about business that if Jackson Browne played a concert anywhere in the world he would sell out. And you got people like him? Man I mumbled to her I said if you pull that off I don't care how sick I am, I want to see that concert, cause I know that kind of people on one stage will never happen again in my life time. This I've got to see. Anyway the doctors at St. Joseph Hospital said to me that being that you had had your second stroke and that was over, you had to go to a rehabilitation center to recover. Here we have a private hospital across the street or you can go to the county hospital in Downey CA. It's called Rancho los Amigos Medical Center. Being that you don't have any insurance, you'll probably have to go to Rancho los Amigos Medical Center, the doctor said. Then I said I'm having a benefit for me. I'll use some of the money to go to a private hospital I said. Then I mumbled that to the guy who was giving me the benefit. I explained this to him. He said to me trust me we can get in there for free. Then I said man, but it's a county hospital. A private place is better I said. Then he said don't worry about it you won't be there long, and anyway

you can save that money we take up for you at the benefit.
Then I mumbled to him, I said isn't that what's the
benefit's all about? I said.

(403)

10/15/93

Jan 23, 1992 the ambulance came to move me from St.
Joseph Hospital to Rancho los Amigos Medical Center. I
remember arriving there. That place looked to me like a
prison camp. They kept the prisoners in the same ward
where I was. I remember telling my private doctor who
came to see me at St. Joseph Hospital where I was going.
Dr. Winn said to me if you're going to be at Rancho los
Amigos Medical Center, I won't come out there. Then he
said that place is not fit for humans. Man that place was
horrid. How can the President of the US sleep at night
knowing that he gets paid to make sure that places like
that run properly. By the time I got there and did another
CAT skan the cerebellum part of my brain was dead. I
couldn't walk but I could mumble. They would feed me
solid food. The food was horrible but I got it down. Then
one day I got some food that looked like mush. I couldn't
figure it out. Then one day I was rolling my wheel chair
down the hall and the therapist saw me coming down the
hall. I stopped for a cup of water in the hallway. She saw
me drink the water, then she said to me you can drink
water? I said to her yes I can. She said to me, I thought
you had a hard time swallowing, so I order your food
mashed up.

(404)

10/15/93

The day when I first arrived there I went to physical therapy, and I cleared my throat. She thought I was choking. Being that I could only mumble, she ordered my food mashed. That food was horrible anyway. Mashed up it looked like vomit. I remember laying there thinking about this great benefit of mine. So I request to the nurse that even though I was sick I wanted to go to this benefit. This will never happen again in my life time I said. Then I told the nurse I don't care what kind of condition I'm in, I want to go. So they said to me yes on one condition, that the physical therapist had to go with you. Then I said okay. The physical therapist consented to go with me on one condition, that I be given a shower. I hadn't had a shower since I've been there. As a matter of fact I had one shower from the 30th of Jan. to the 10th of March. Boy was I malodorous. They had the benefit for me. I was so grateful for what they had done for me. I would thank them once or twice a week.

(405)   My Second Stroke
10/15/95

Then I said to them, that will make me feel better knowing that my back rent is paid. So before the benefit I had discussed this with them and they had told me this. So when I got to the benefit the landlord was there taking pictures. He's a photographer. He came up to my wheelchair and I explained to him what was going on. They could pay my current rent but they couldn't pay my back rent with the money they collected. The landlord looked me in the eyes and said, Don't worry about it, when you get back on your feet you'll worry about it then, he said. After the benefit was over my daughter Jeannene came from Toronto to see me. She flew down and rented a car. Drove 70 miles a day to see me. I thought that the $55,000 was mine to do with what I wanted to do with. I said to my ex lawyer, Please give Jeannene $5,000 to cover her expenses, cause if you've read this book, you know the strain I've had with Jeannene. Then my ex lawyer humored me by saying to me, we meaning him and the trustees decided that you were too generous. So we don't think it's right. Not one of them said to me, that's too much money, we'll pay for her plane ticket or pay for her rental car or nothing like that, they just said no. They gave a benefit for me it was all right as long as they controlled the money. The ex lawyer was in on it, because the husband and wife gave the money to him, cause my second ex wife was trying to get the money. He put the money in a tax free trust account. Along with that came a forty page contract.

(406)
10/15/93

Now what that 40 page contract said that they had the final say so I couldn't spend a penny of that money without their permission. I really thought that the money was mine. Being that they had thought of and had known me as a pecunivous person, that's the way they thought of me now. The only thing is none of them has never had a stoke. That stroke shocked the heck out of me. Then I was telling them I wanted to renew my membership to the "Y". The guy told me well why don't you let the doctors see what they can do here first and if that doesn't work, you can join the "Y" then. I said to him, you don't understand, I'm not trying to override the doctors, I'm trying to help them. I told him that I had been a member of the "Y" since 1986. I know about exercise. I could help

the doctors out I said. So he humored me and shined me
on by saying we'll see. Then I said can I pay something on
my car cause I was late with a couple of my payments. I
had to cancel a couple of my gigs because of this sickness.
Then they said to me we can only pay your current bills
with this money. Then I said what about getting out of
this county hospital. Then he reiterated by saying to me
that it's free, don't worry about it he said. People, you
think you know about frustration. You want to see some
frustration? Have a stroke like I had. Then you'll know
what frustration's all about.

(407)   Sleep Apnea
10/18/93

Now readers, please try to follow this. Cause this gets
pretty tricky. One night I dosed off to sleep. The nurse
noticed that I wasn't breathing when I was asleep, so she
reported it to the doctor. The doctor reported it to the
sleep center. So they had two guys to pick me up and take
me over to the sleep center. They had me to go to sleep.
They had a nurse to look at me. The nurse reported back
to the doctor after monitoring me all night. The doctor
gave me his compendium of the test. He said that I had
sleep apnea. I then said to him, what is that, he said to me
that's when you stop breathing when you sleep. Then I
said how do you treat that. He said there's a machine that
pumps oxygen into your brainwhile you sleep. Then I
said to him what else. Then he said by losing weight you
can get rid of it. Then I said to him, loosing weight is no
problem, I don't eat that garbage that they give me out
here no way. That seemed to go over his head, or he
didn't take me serious cause people that came to Rancho
los Amigos medical center actually got fat off of that

garbage. He gave me that machine. That machine was so awful, big, and it made so much noise, and besides, when I put it on my face, it hurt so bad, that when they put it on my face, I laid there all night in pain. When they took the mask off, that's when I went to sleep. I told the doctor that I didn't like the machine he said to me that if I didn't use the machine that I would be brain damaged in 2 months.

(408)

10/18/93

That was a year in a half ago. When he told me about the weight lose thing I said to myself yeah, that food was so bad that I would eat that garbage every three days. The other two days I would eat Jell-O and a carton of low fat milk 1/2 pint. I was losing weight so fast that it wasn't funny. Now if the doctor had of told me that I had to jog or something, I would have never done it, cause I was in a wheel chair. So any time that somebody I know would call and ask for a compendium of me, the doctor would say that I was taking the machine, and that I would have brain damage inside of 2 months. That got everybody to panicking. Everybody was freaking out. The husband and wife that gave me the benefit called to get a compendium of me. And when they found out my compendium, they told everybody. Pricilla Coolidge wrote me a letter telling me to don't kill your self, take your medicine. My girlfriend from Vancover said to me, what about me? Please don't die. Absolutely nobody would listen to me. All I wanted to do is to do what I've been doing all of my life. That is to try something new. The lawyer that I had just wouldn't hear of this. He called the girl that was going to get married to in Vancover, and told her that I was trying to kill myself.

(409)

10/18/93

By now the whole town was panicking the word had got out that I was verbally inimical even writing about that period of my life just make me shake thinking about it. This guy Carl Chico Jackson and his wife came to see me. Man was I glad to see him. I've known him for about 30 years. The last thing he says to me is don't forget to take your pills. Man my face dropped even he had heard about this thing and I hadn't seen him in 10 years. You'll never know what its like to be in that situation and not to be able to move or to talk. People that you know serving you on all the time. They would come around and wake you up at 5:00am. And they would call themselves giving you a sponge bath what they was doing was going through the motions. Man I was so molodorus that when I would scratch my head, cakes of dandruff would fall out of my head. I had scabs on my lips as big as your little finger. Cathy McBroom came out to visit me. I told her to please not to come to see me. I said to her that I didn't want her to see me like this and had some dignity. They would strap in the wheelchair and make you sit in it all day long. When I would complain about that, the male nurse would say to me you complain too much how would you like it if we would put you in the prison ward. I would say to him that the only crime that I committed was having a stroke.

(410)   **DIANE BROOKS**

10/19/93

Now this is my compendium of Diane Brooks. This is why this is not a nice environment to live in. Diane Brooks and Dionne Warwick came to Toronto in the late 50's. Dionne Warwick went back to Newark NJ and went to college. There she met up with Burt Bacharach. The rest is history. Diane Brooks stayed in Toronto and worked locally. At that time Toronto hadn't opened up. I think at that time there were about 30 thousand blacks there at the time. Nobody was doing nowhere near what Diane Brooks was doing at the time. Diane's a very very talented lady even though she's an extremely shy, layed back, withdrawn person when she opened her mouth to sing the audience stopped dead in their tracks. Now being that she was the only one at that time that was doing what she did Diane worked all the time. She could and can sing any thing R&B, jazz , Country and Western, pop you name it Diane can sing it. She was doing so much stuff up there like commercials, T.V. Shows, Radio Records and etc. So it was like that all the time I arrived in front to on Jan 17 1964 . I met and saw Diane Brooks February 22, Friday at 11:00pm on Walton and Younge St. at Al Stieneus' famed Blue Note. There she was playing with a group called The Silhouettes. Doug Riley was in that band Steve Kennedy was in that band. That's where I met Steve Kennedy. Diane and Steve were an item.

(411)

10/19/93

Steve and I hit it off right away. I was working down the street at the Flamingo Club. Later I went on the road with the Billy Martin Band, but I kept in touch with Steve Kennedy. We had this idea of putting a band together behind Diane Brooks. So we did. The third week in April of 1966 we put together a group called The Soul Searchers. The real name was Diane Brooks, Eric Mercury and the Soul Searchers. Our first job was at The Memory Lane off of Younge street in Toronto, Canada. Things were going good Diane was so busy doing other stuff, like Radio, TV and etc. at that time she got an offer to do her own record. The band was not good enough to play on her record, we at that time hadn't had the recording experience that Diane had. Man she could and can sing. Being that she was a pioneer up there she opened the door for not only a few blacks in Toronto, but she opened the door for all of the blacks in Toronto. I did a duet with her on the TV show Music Hop. The song was a Motown hit then. It was called " It Takes Two Baby". Man was I nervous to sing with Diane Brooks. That blew my mind. I remember I sang another song with her, "Everytime we say Goodbye". Now that one I messed up, I was so nervous. Anything that was anything Diane did it. We would be in a car for about an hour riding and on the radio would be commercials and out of that hour, maybe you would have about 7 or 8 commercials. Diane would be on at least 5 of them.

(412)

10/19/93

When the late great count Basie had his big band Diane Brooks was the singer at one time. I remember sitting watching Diane when she was the singer with Rob McConnells Boss Brass. When Anne Murray had out her hit Snowbird, Diane Brooks sang backgrounds on that song. By that time Diane had done all and everything in Toronto. So Brian Ahern, Anne Murrays producer on Snowbird had moved to Toronto. He married Emmy Lou

Harris. So being like everybody else, he was a Diane
Brooks fan. He suggested that he do a record on Diane
Brooks for Warner Bros. Here in L.A. Brian had a big old
mansion in Beverly Hills and he also had a portable
recording studio. At the time Diane was new here, so she
stayed at Brian's mansion, even though I had a song on
the record, "Down the Back Stairs" Diane wasn't to happy
with how it turned out. Her first love was and still to this
day is jazz. Brian Ahern is a country and western
producer. Well at least that's what his bread and butter
has been. The record didn't sell. Down in L.A. things
were different for her. A lot of people didn't understand
her shyness, her layed back with drawn way. A lot of
people in L.A. mistook her for being a stuck up person.
Like when I recommended her for the Boz Skags gig. She
did the gig then I asked Venetta how did she do. Venetta
said she sang nice. But she acted so stuck up.

(413)

10/20/93

I Remember living in Toronto I literally got a musician's
education from on and off the side streets of downtown
Younge street in Toronto Canada and Diane Brooks. The
clubs like Grannys, The Sapphire, The Town Tavern, the
Jamaican Room, The Colonial Club, The Friers Club, The
Brown Derby, The Flamingo Club, The Edison Hotel, The
Blue Note, The La Cog Dor, The Brass Rail, The Embassy,
The Concorde, the Saveren, The Wif Club. From those
places I saw people like Jimmy Smith, Miles Davis, Earl
Father Hines, The Band, Bo Didley, The Flamingos, Lional
Hampton's Band at the Casa Loma Castle. I saw the great
Count Basie, Ronnie Hawkins and The Hawks, Chick
Corea, Coleman Hawkins, Eddie Jefferson, James Moody

various Rock Steady Bands at The Wif Club and The
Jamacian Room and etc. And being in a group with
Diane Brooks gave me a musical experience I'll never
forget. Like I said before producers and people in L.A.
didn't understand Diane in L.A. They took her layed
backness for being a stuck up person. For those of you
that have been to L.A. know what this place is like. Those
people just simply said "next", which made Diane a very
bitter person. As she tried to sing jazz here in L.A. that
didn't go over to well here. The more people rejected her,
the more she sang jazz. Being that jazz didn't go over so
well she had to get a job selling clothes in a dept. store.
Even though she says that she's content, there's an
invisible chip on her shoulders. It's just human nature.

(414)

10/20/93

When you've had the kind of fame that she's had, you get
a subliminal bitterness about you. Now I met through
Cathy McBroom, these two lovely people name Ellen and
Dick Mallock. When I went to their home in Northridge
CA. to dinner, it was perfect. They had so much in their
house. Rich is a jazz buff. He's right up my alley, not only
had I played jazz, but I'm a jazz buff. He's got jazz
flowing through his house. Just him and his wife live in
this beautiful house in Northridge. Alot of his friends are
jazz buffs. He use to have jazz parties at his house. Now
Diane was singing jazz at a club called Scobys. Eric
Johnson's lady managed the club. Diane was sounding
good as usual. They, the band was making little money.
but at the club, they ate free. The food there was great. I
suggested to Rich instead of having your jazz party at
your house why don't you have your party at Scobys. I

said its right in Northridge, I said its about a mile from you. I took him down to the club the first Sunday I got out of the hospital the first time to see her. He liked her. He said good Idea. I was so excited. I called Diane Brooks to tell her about what I had done. She said she had quit. I said what !! She said she had quit cause the band didn't want to rehearse once a month. Then I simply said to her you shouldn't have quit, the band should have quit. Then I said I would have helped you. Then I said I would get you some other musicians.

(415)

10/20/93

Then I said to her that as long as I've been living in L.A. I know all kinds of musicians that would not only like that job, but they would be happy to play behind you to this day. I don't know for what reason she got mad at me for making that suggestion. The next week Eric Johnson had a party at his house. I went to the party. As I came in, I saw Diane Brooks over in the corner. I went up to Diane and said, hey Brooks, How ya doin? She looked at me all mad, and said to me that she didn't like what I said. Then I said to her, you've got to be kiddin, then I said to her, I meant you no harm. So in an innocuous way I pinched her on her breast. A couple of weeks later Eric Johnson and Eric Mercury fervently berated me for doing that to her. She had made to both of them that I was trying to fondle her or something. Man was I hurt, the second time when I was in the hospital, a mutual acquaintance of both Diane and myself called me when I was in the hospital when I was on intravenous. The Doctor was by my bed try to teach me how to walk and talk and this girl was

fervently berating me about how I was trying to fondle
Diane Brooks. Man that really got to me.

(416)

10/20/93

She was the one that introduced me to Pricilla Coolidge. I
use to have fantasies about Pricilla for 17 years. So you
know I was grateful for Mary for introducing me to
Pricilla. Now Mary is in her forties. But she has a breast
like a 20 year old girl. I always joked with her about her
breast her other writing partner. Michael O'hare jokes
with her about her breast. I call her nobs for short. She,
Mary, even calls me, and tells me breast jokes about her
breast. When her and I go to listen to somebody doing
one of our songs. She gets all dressed up. Then I'll go
over to her house to pick her up. She might ask me she'll
say to me B3 (that what she calls me) how do I look. The
I'll tweak her breast and say to her, "baby, you look
great". Well both laugh at each other. that's my partner,
like the guy said on Hunter the T.V. show. One guy was
looking at his partner, the guy said to Hunter your
partner's a pretty female. Don't you ever think about
wanting to put the make on her? Hunter then said yeah,
then he said she's my partner she always will be there for
me. And if I get intimate with her the relationship would
be different. If Diane Brooks didn't like my weird sense of
humor, I've been knowing her long enough for her to
fervently say to me don't do that, I don't feel comfortable
with that kind of humor. I would never would have done
that to her, as much as a Diane Brooks fan I was.

(417)

10/20/93

Now this lady I use to be libertine with when I got out of the hospital, she used to cook for me and bring the food over my house for me. Even though I use to be libertine with her I wasn't anymore. I was so grateful for the meals she cooked for me, I would thank her and then I would tweak her breast. She fervently said to me, please don't do that. Even then she knew I was joking with her. With both Mary and Cathy that was my humor my way of saying thanks. My way of saying you look great. Diane Brooks is a great grandmother even though she still gets ask for her I.D. when she goes to a night club. Diane should know I don't have to fondle a woman to be libertine with her. I was in a band with her. That was in 1966. I hadn't had as many women then as I've had now, back then it was small, about 300 women. With Diane Brooks, I'm not angry with her or nothing like that, I have too many fond memorys of her talent and me learning and playing with her. It's nothing I can do about that invisable chip on her shoulders. In these days you can't have your cake and eat it too! That's why I think it's better we go our separate ways. Good luck Diane, I will always think fondly of you.

Diane Brooks

Diane, I hope you can find it in your heart to forgive me. If you can't, that's all right too. I would never do anything on purpose to offend you. I have too much respect for you to do that. Besides, look at my humor, can you blame me? Look at the people I know. Hell! You know half of them yourself. I've known you since I was 19. Even though it's been years since I've seen you, I fondly think about you and your music. Say hi to your family for me. Take care.

Smitty

(418)   BEING AT RANCH LOS AMIGOS
                    10/20/93

I was lying in my bed just setting there thinking. That's all I could do. I couldn't get up or walk around or nothing like that. I was still in a wheel chair because of that, I was confined to my bed or wheelchair. So I would do nothing but sit and think or lie down and think.. I would think about what I would do when I got out of that awful place. They had a digital clock in my room on the wall. I used to stare at that clock for hours. It had the date on the clock. I would watch that clock and count the days hours and minutes until I could leave that place. My release date was March 10, 1992. When I wasn't watching the clock or thinking real hard I was thinking about patting myself on the back. Cause I was so proud of myself, cause I could go home to a brand new car that I had got and paid for with my own money. Before, I was paying $1200 a month, now I have or had a brand new car that had all kinds of features and it was mine and the banks for $469 a month. I'm not a person who's hung up on material things or nothing like that, I was so glad for once I beat the system. Instead of paying $1200 a month for rental car, I got one for $469 a month. For the first time I was proud of my self. Then I got this phone call from this person I knew. They were telling me that the wife that held the benefit for me wanted to move me in to a smaller place, like one room cause I was paying too much rent where I was and she wanted to sell my car cause I was paying such a big car note.

(419)

10/20/93

It was all I could do from going crazy. You see being that I
had had a stroke when I came to, it made me a strong
thinker. My girl calls it genius quality, I call it doing what
you have to do to survive. Even though I was like that,
my tolerance level was zero. I was really inimical with a
lot of people. I was really proud of myself once again
cause I rolled my wheelchair to the phone and ask her
fervently not to sell my car, or to put me out of the house
were I was staying. The bottom bottom line is they knew
me as a talented person, but they never took the time to
know me as a human being. I'm so grateful that they took
over my affairs, I'm glad I had somebody there for me.
But you'll never know the price with my dignity I had to
pay for that. I would have rather gone into the streets
then to have them do what they did to me. The husband
said he had heard that I accused them of stealing money
from me. If they would have known me as a person, they
would have known It was never about the money. Other
people suggested that to me, I would say no, they might
be many things but they are not thieves, It was from the
beginning about dignity. It never dawned on them till this
day that that what it was. They just know this talented
impecunious when it came to the business of music, this
lunatic person, so they acted accordingly. It started right
from the beginning. They didn't realize that having that
stroke and almost dying, that stroke

(420)

10/20/93

scared the living day lights out of me. It scared to the
point that It made me want to get my life together. When
I got sick, the ladies that I was seeing panicked, cause they

had heard through the grapevine about what had happened to me, and they read and heard on the radio about it. They called the lady that gave me the benefit. She messed things up for me so bad, that I said later for that stuff anyway. I couldn't do nothing about it no way and besides she in no way could juggle like I could. She didn't have to. So I just let it go. Anyway 2 weeks before I was released, the therapist walked me through the house I lived in. By that time I was using a walker then. I walked through the house with the walker. She said to me that I couldn't use the bedroom door to get to the bathroom cause there wasn't enough space to get the walker through. She said you have to use the hallway. I said to myself no way, I'm not going to walk around the hall, I'm going to use the bedroom entrance. And I found a way. I would lay in that hospital and think about making a million dollars a day and you know what, I'm going to do it. I use to tell people about my dream. People use to shine me on. It's not that I'm hung up on the money or nothing like that. I just want be in a position where I want never again in life have to ask nobody for nothing. Cause as you can see things get crazy when your lunatic business.

(421) LEAVING RANCHO LOS AMIGOS
10/25/93

I know the hospital scene is not chronologically in order, is just that period was so dark for me. Dealing with that hospital when I think of that period, I get the shakes. I remember I wanted to leave that place so bad, that on March 9th, I layed there in the bed wide awake all night long just staring at the clock. I was so glad to get away from that place you don't have a clue. The president says they want to do something. They should start by cleaning up that awful mess at Rancho Los Amigos. Being that I complained so much about that hospital to my ex-lawyer ex trustee of my benefit, instead of saying are you trying something or something to that matter, He said about your sleep apnea? We'll send you to UCLA. I told him that it was all right that I didn't have to go to UCLA hospital for my sleep apnea. My girlfriend is a nurse she checked me out for 6 days. Her compendium of me is, "after listening to you for 6 nights you have your sleep apnea under control". Then she said that I didn't hear you snore once. When she told him that, he said to her that I can't take your word for it. Then he said I have to hear it from a doctor. Then I said to him, who do you think tells the doctor. It's a nurse who monitors the patient at night, then she tells the doctors her compendium. At UCLA it would have cost $1200 a day to stay there.

(422) BEING AT HOME
10/25/93

I was so proud of myself. I got professional advice for nothing. When I got to UCLA, the lady at the front desk ask me when I was registering, she said what are you here for. I said to be quite honest with you, I don't know. I ended up not going that night, cause the campus was so big that I couldn't find where I was supposed to go. You see they wouldn't take my word or my girl friend's word for it after all it wasn't their money what did they care. I had this little bit of money, and I was trying to make it last. Back then I was using a walker. I didn't know when I would be able to walk. It's just human nature, when somebody does something for you, they feel a need to control you. But those people don't realize that when you have a disaster like that you get into a survivor mode of which even you, let alone them, that you never been in before. Its just like somebody cutting off your right arm you automatically get unbelievable strength in your left arm. From having that stroke, even though I had developed a inimical tolerance level verbally. I had developed a wealth of knowledge, of which nobody understood. You thought I was weird before I had the stroke, man you should see me now. It is now I understand the saying, be careful what you wish for, you just might get it. Man, what a far out way to get your wish. The lord works in mysterious ways. My girlfriend was insulted by what the ex-lawyer said. She's been a nurse for 25 years, a head nurse at that.

(423)   THE GIRL FROM VANCOUVER
10/27/93

Now this girl that I was going with at the time, she was from Vancouver. She's a jocund person. The tickets at my benefit was a hundred dollars apiece. The girl from Vancouver bought $1,000 worth of tickets. Her friend chipped in even though I didn't know some of the people and some of the people couldn't make the benefit. They gave money anyway. I was so grateful for what she and her friend did for me . I ask her could I do anything for her. She said if they made a tape or a video of the show, I would like to have a copy so I could show it to the people that couldn't make it to your benefit, I said to her you got it I'll give you my word that I'll get you a copy, that's the least I could do for you, being that you were so nice to me both times that I had a stroke. the benefit was Jan 30, 1992. I started to call the wife that gave the benefit Jan 31, 1992. When I would call her, she would put me on hold for

about 15 minutes, cause she had so much going for her.
She was working out of her home at the time. Every time
I would call her I would ask her about the video. She
would say to me when she would come back to the phone
that she was so busy. Being that she lived in Malibu, and I
lived in North Hollywood, it cost me about $3.00 to call
her, cause it was a toll call most of the time I would spend
on hold. I tried so hard to get a copy, finally May of 1992 I
gave up. I felt so weird asking her for something cause
those two people had there own lives to look after.

(424)

10/27/93

I asked her about twice a week from Jan. to May of 92.
Even though the girl and I had broken up, I still wanted to
get her a copy of the benefit. I felt that that was the best
thing to do cause what she had done for me was a nice
jester. Finally I went to Malibu and I got the tape and had
a copy made, and I gave it to her. Being that she was
fractious with me for breaking up with her, she doesn't
speak to me or call or visit me when she comes to L.A., but
she's now she's best buddys with the husband and wife
who gave the benefit for me. Live and learn I always say.
For those of you that have diabetes, you know that your
sugar count is normal when its between 80 and 120, but if
your a diabetic and our sugar is higher then 120, you can
go into a diabetic shock if your sugar is below 80 you can
have a diabetic shock. Now when I got out of the hospital,
I was watching my diet, like you wouldn't believe being
that I was taking insulin, my sugar was real low, cause I
wasn't eating no sugar or salt. That's what insulin is
about when you eat a regular meal insulin destroys the
sugar and salt in your system. My sugar was real low at

the time cause I was taking or shooting insulin. It was no sugar or salt in my system for the insulin to destroy, so my sugar was low. So I kept calling the wife, the lady that gave the benefit for me. I explained my situation to her that is when I could got through to her. Being that she had a bartering co., she knew a lot of doctors. She didn't like my private doctor, Dr. Winn was his name, she would tell me that she would get me another doctor.

(425)   PROBLEMS
10/27/93

She would tell me that he was a quack. I said to her okay all I need at this point is to have somebody who's in the medical field to monitor me cause I think should have been looked at, cause I was getting low readings like 39, 50, 59 and I said to myself, I shouldn't be taking insulin. I wouldn't come off of the stuff without the doctors permission, and I couldn't do nothing without their permission, cause they controlled the money so as usual I got tired of calling her. So Michael Hormel of Hormel foods loaned me money to see a doctor. I went to see a doctor, he took my sugar, the first thing the doctor said to me was get off of insulin you don't need to take Insulin no more, your sugar is too low. I told the doctor I thought I didn't have to take insulin no more, but I haven't seen a doctor since I've been out of the hospital and I've been out of the hospital since March 10, 1992, it was May 21, 1992. He said to me do not, I repeat do not take insulin any more. He said you could go into shock. If your sugar gets any lower. Once again I felt so bad cause I had to impose on these people, cause I really thought they knew me. Sure they knew the talent that I had, but they didn't know the person. The me. To me that was the only thing that was wrong, miscommunicating. What they did was give a benefit for the talented person, not the person you see. I had the stroke, not the talent had the stroke.

(426) VISITORS WHO CAME TO SEE ME
10/28/93

When I was in the hospital with a stroke, and recovery from the stroke, at the place I lived at in North Hollywood, I had a lot of visitors. With their encouragement and my self esteem, I'm now able to walk and talk. I was talking the other day on the phone to Dr. Sperber, He said to me that I sounded like I hadn't had a stroke. I owe that to the great people who visited and supported me mentally. They are, Rita Coolidge, Laura Satterfield, Mike Post, King Cotton, Mike Finnegen, Shawn Finnegen, Marty Grebb, Brenda Russell, Bonnie Sheriden, Rock Deadrick, Cathy McBroom, JoAnn Albert, Joe Sheu, Maria Sheu, Rick Skow, Larry Williams, Jerry Williams and Yvonne Williams, Phil Chin, Bernie Larsan, Larry Fulcher, Alvino Bennett, Bill Sharpe, Frank Wilson, Priscilla Coolidge, Mary Unobsky, Michelle Hormel, Barbara Willamson, Gloria Coleman, Johnnie Mathews, Cathy Mathews, Carol Dennis, Sheri Glenn, Shiloh VonMeche, Robben Ford, Tom Bretcline, Evelyn Buriak, Christine Heffner, Jody Heffner, Geoffrey Gurd, Jimmy Dale, Jimmy Roberts, Carl Jackson, Jeanne Shaw, Amani Smith, Catfish Hurd, Sala Smith, Jeff Laine, Sigred Ravel, Ellis Hall, Lara Geddes, James Geddes, Donald Griffin, Bill Griffin '(63). Guys, thank you so much for your encouragement and just being there.

(427) THE VISITOR WHO VISITED ME
10/28/93

I had gotten out of the hospital, and I was recovering and receiving visitors. At the time I couldn't walk. People where bringing me flowers, get well cards and stuff, like that. Being that I couldn't walk to answer the door, I would tell Joe Sheu (He was taking care of me at the time) to leave the door open so if anybody came to visit, I could tell them to come in. One day I heard a Harley Davidson pull up in front of my door. It was real loud. I said to myself, that's got to be Bill Elkins. He owns the Alley rehersal studios in North Hollywood then I said good he's coming over to bring me flowers or a card. Then I said to myself, It would be good to see him anyway. I haven't seen him in a while. He knocked on the door, I told him to come in to the back of the house, that's where my bedroom was. I greeted him, I looked there were no flowers or a card, instead he had a porno magazine called Lips and two cans of chicken noodle soup. He stood there with his leather on. As he stood there I ask him, what's the chicken noodle soup for? He said that's just in case you run into a Jewish girl. You know Linda Ronstadt was right, he does wear his baseball cap a little to tight. Anyway I appreciated the gift. I'm just glad on top of the stroke I didn't go blind. If only you could have brought me flowers: By Bill, "I had 4 Jewish girlfriends, 2 of which ashtrayed me upside of the head, another stabbed me once in the arm and the last one shot me in the chest." Didn't we all say the same thing. Chicken soup and pussy will always get you well.

Renaissance Man   10/7/93

While enjoying this solitude, I was sitting at the motel one day and I said I got to call Bill at the Alley. That's the only guy that I keep in touch with from my past. He reminds me of a Renaissance man. He owns a studio or studios in North Hollywood. He's the only person I know, and I know a lot of people, that's a real person. He knows a lot about everything. He's got a lady named Shiloh, what an educated woman. The only thing about Bill is he's a very sick person. Other than that, he's all right. That's the only person that I keep in touch with from my past. I've never met no one like him. If only he would get a baseball cap to fit him, he would be cool.

(428)   MY MEETING WITH DR. SPERBER
10/28/93

By this time I was so frustrated. I use to see my therapist once a week. I would tell him about how fractious I was about the trustees handling the money and about seeing the plaque concerning my benefit that the husband gave to the wife, and it was on the counter laying in a gift basket with a basket full of teas. So he suggested to me why don't you have a meeting with them, and discuss it with them nicely about how you feel. Then I said I can have the meeting at your office, that way they'll see that I was not ungrateful, for what they did for me, but I was just frustrated. So we get to the doctors office. Dr. Sperber with his jocund self, said to me to speak my mind, what a benign man. I said to her that the benefit they gave for me was the best thing that ever or anything that ever happened to me. Then I kindly ask her why that was on the counter in your tee box. She said to me that they had moved out there about a year ago and we haven't had time to put it on the wall. Then I said to nail a plaque on the wall takes about 30 seconds besides you have a framed picture on top of your TV of your dog. But you don't have time to put the plaque on the wall. Then I kindly said to her I really really appreciate you giving me a benefit for me, however I feel a little uncomfortable interfering in your personal life bugging you for money anytime that I need something.

(429)

10/28/93

Then I said to her I would like to take the money that you raised for me at the benefit and give it to an accountant, then I said you take Ben Mier. I worked with him when I was working with Leah Kunkel in 1980, and David Lindley in 1985 to 1988. I then said to them that I would see him in 8 years all of maybe 4 times . I said to them that I don't know if he is even married, where he lives or nothing like that. All I know is when I came down with a stroke he was one of the first people to donate money to me. What do I have to lose, by asking him. Being that I only got a little bit of money, an accountant he could take that little bit of money and make it last. I figure if he could handle Jackson Browne, the guitar player with the GoGos, Danny Kortchmar, Bon Jovi's producer, Bob Glaub the bass player with Jackson Browne, and etc, he could figure out all kinds of ways to take care of my situation. She said to me yeah but I'm handleing your money for nothing, he's gonna charge you. Then I said I don't mind that if he could think of a way to make that money last. I saw right then that they didn't want to part with that money. They had the final say so and that was that.

(430)   MEETING WITH DR. SPERBER

10/28/93

Now by this time, this was around June of 1991 I was crazed with frustration. Any and everything I wanted from the people who gave the benefit for me, I had to beg. Like I wanted to get the pictures of the concert framed. It was two diagrams of the seating arrangement of my benefit. In each plaque there were peoples names, people like Henry Mancini, Mike Post and etc. That meant so much to me, Henry Mancini coming to my benefit, is something that I'll never forget as long as I live. That's why I wanted to get those pictures framed. Plus a couple more pictures that I've had under the bed for about 4 years that I wanted to get framed. I honestly thought I could do that being that I had the money. When I told the wife of the husband that gave the benefit for me, she freaked, she only paid half of the bill, being that I told the lady to send the bill to her. The lady at the frame shop rightfully complained about the money. I've not spoken or done business with that lady in a little over a year. Then I was thinking to my self, I said If I couldn't play. I'm going to use my brain and come up with a creative way to use it.

(431)

10/28/93

I would lay there at nights thinking how was I going to do this. Then it hit me, I said yeah I will write a book then I said to myself I've never written a book before, then I said to myself, If I can write a song, I could write a book. Then I said I didn't write the lyrics to the song, I wrote the music. Then I said to myself, I must have learned something from those great writers that I've worked with like, David Palmer, Harriet Schock, Mary Urobsky, Pricilla Coolidge, Cathy Wakefield and etc. So that's it I'll write a book, so I told Lonnie Sill what I was going to do. He told me to call this writer he was a ghost writer. He was working on a book by Mick Jagger and Dion, two separate books. I explained my situation to him, he said that he would help me for $7,000. Then I said to myself oh no!!! If I would tell those trustees about this, they wouldn't approve. The whole time I felt that it was their money and they would give it to me only if they felt that if it was right for them. I always felt being that they gave the benefit for me, that I was borrowing the money. Man what a sick feeling.

(432)

10/28/93

Having a stroke and being in a coma is no way worse then what I was going through with the trustee of my benefit. When I got the idea about writing the book, I was so exited to tell the wife of the trustee that I was writing the book. The first thing she said, she didn't wish me well or good luck or nothing like that she said well how are you going to get the book funded. Funded? That's the least of my problems. The main problem is writing the book, and I'm doing that. So Doctor Sperber suggested another meeting at his office. We got there I was so fractious with them I was fulminating with them. I was telling them about the doctor, that I needed to see a doctor for my diabetes, and I couldn't depend on her to get me one and I had to borrow money to see a private doctor. When I said that, the husband said to me that I was of a mendacity being. Man was I insulted I then exploded and called her a fucking flake. To this day I'm so sorry I said that to her. But I was so frustrated that I didn't know what else to do. That's what it has come to. I was crazed, after I said that they got up and left.

(433)   WRITE ON
10/28/93

By this time around May of 1992, one night it hit me, I said
to myself being that my hand is all numb, I'll write a book.
I'll write about "friends of a stroke victim". That's what
I'll call the book. Being that I can't write, I'll put it on tape.
Hell I can't write, so I'll tape the doggone thing and
Delores can type it. So that's what I did. Man I was
excited. Finally I could do something besides lay in bed
and do nothing. The first thing I did was call the lady that
gave the benefit for. I was so excited when I told her. The
first instinctively thing she said to me when I told her I
was going to write a book, was do you have it funded?
The lawyer that I knew for 20 years, we were mates, I said
the same thing to him, the first thing he said was that
great, now when are you going to start to play? Like I
have some control over this stroke or something. My
compendium of my ex-lawyer and the husband and wife
who gave the benefit for is they are nouveau riche people.
The wife in my opinion is a matriclinous person. The
reason why I say she is matriclinous

(434)   COMPENDIUM
10/28/93

for example, when my bank account was empty I got a
mate of mine to take me to their house, to clean out my
bank account cause I was evicted, I waited in the car. She
went in to get the money for me, now I hadn't seen her
father since I had the stroke. The very first thing he said
to my mate was, is Smitty keeping his weight off? Not
how is Smitty or is Smitty allright? That's why I think on
top of being a nouveau riche person, she's a matriclinous
person. I think I'm a matriclinous person for example

when I was 13 years old, I use to sit in my grandmothers
kitchen and listen to Chuck Berry, Frank Sinatra, Frankie
Lymon, and etc. I would say to her grandma, I want to
sing and play and write like those people, the first
instinctive thing she would say to me is, son, if you want
to be like those people, you've got to practice real hard,
she didn't say you can't do that, or she didn't say who's
gonna fund you, nothing like that. I think that I'm a
matriclinous person. I will never be able to tell in words
how much I appreciate them giving the benefit for me, but
I'll never be able to express upon you how glad I am that
I'll never have to deal with those people again.

(435)   DOUGIES WIFE
11/2/93

First of all Doug and I go way back. I met Dougie at the
Flamingo club, around February 15, 1964 when he was
rehearsing with the late Jack Harding then, I played with
Dougie. He took my place one time when Motherlode
opened the show at the Rock Pile, a club on Younge street
in Canada. Dougie produced Motherlode, he managed
Motherlode, so when he got married it was just apropos
that I sing at his wedding. When she came to L.A. to do
an ad for a T.V. show, I treated her like she was my sister.
I didn't even work every day I was with her. That's
Dougies wife, I not only have to but I want to do my best
to make sure she's comfortable, at that time I was and still
am with Delores. I would sit and have lunch with her lay
in bed with her talk about Dougie and his wife, and the
fact that the girl I use to go with in Vancouver comes to
L.A. all the time, she visits the people that gave me the
benefit, but doesn't call me, I don't understand. Finally
one night Delores got tired of me talking about Dougie

and his wife then she said something to me that shocked the heck out of me.

(436)

11/2/93

She said to me STOP talking about them! I said what? Delores never raised her voice at no one let alone me. I said what do you mean? That's all you talk about Dougie and his wife. His wife was in L.A. a month ago for a month. I said what? I said how do you know, she wouldn't come to L.A. without letting me know she was here. Delores said to me that she went to the club where Dougie was playing at in Toronto to give him a copy of the video, of the video of the benefit. I had a copy made and gave Doug a copy, Steve Kennedy a copy, and Donnie Troiano a copy. I wanted to let them see that I was all right. Delores ran into Dougie wife at the club. Doug's wife said to Delores what's the occasion you're here, Delores said I'm here to give Dougie and Steve a copy of Smitty's benefit they had for him in L.A. Then Doug's wife said I just got back from L.A. I was there for a month. She said I didn't want to call Smitty. He's acting verbally inimical to the people that gave the benefit for him. I said what! You mean I've known Dougie for 30 years, I just thought we were close enough for his wife

(437)

11/2/93

to at least call me, not to agree or disagree but at least listen to why I was like that. Maybe she would disagree with me, that's all right too, but I thought we were close enough, that she could at least listen to me. As far as the girl from Vancouver my ex-girlfriend, I could understand

her coming to town and not calling me, like she said, she
was still angry with me. At one time we had a personal
relationship. And like she said she didn't want to call me.
I feel with her, that was my fault, cause we were all living
together me Kenny, Marco, Wayne Stone, and I would see
her alot walking around or in bed with Wayne Stone.
Even though Wayne Stone is very much in love with his
wife Liz now and Wayne has grown children with Liz, to
me that will always be Wayne's ex-girl even though the
sex was nice and all of that and she's a pretty girl.

(438)   DOUGIES WIFE
11/2/93

To this day, I'm so shocked by Dougies wife's
compendium of me, and the girl from Vancouver cause
the girl from Vancouver, when I was sick she took care of
me. A lot of guys you see on TV, a guy with his buddies
girl or married woman or etc.., I just don't have to do that,
I've had too many women in my life for that. With the girl
from Vancouver? I'm truly sorry that it had to end this
way I never meant you any harm. I would hate to come to
Vancouver and not call you and at least say hello to you.
Anyway thank you for everything you did for me. I'll
never forget it, and please enjoy the video of the benefit
that I gave to you, and never judge a book by it's cover.

(439)   A COMPENDIUM OF DONNIE TROIANO
11/3/93

Domenic Troiano is his real and full name we call him
Donnie, short for Domenic. I first met Donnie on January
25, 1964, when he was playing with Ronnie Hawkins at
the Le Coc Dor Club on Younge street in Toronto Canada.
I was playing at a club called the Flamingo Club, 3 doors

from him, when I saw Donnie, he was showing Terry
Bush, the new guitar player the music to the show. He
was leaving the band to start his own band. That band
was to relieve Diane Brooks and Doug Riley's band two
blocks up the street. The Blue Note club, Donnie and his
group were the house band there. The group was call the
Vogues. It consisted of Penti Glen on drums, George
Oliver on organ, and Don Elliot on bass. I use to sing on
the floor show there, so did his wife to be. Later on, about
a year later, my first wife Helen moved down the street to
his wife's families house at 136 Howland Ave. They lived
at Howland, that was in Toronto Canada. Being that I was
new in Canada I would be at Donnie's wife to be's
families house almost every day.

(440)   DONNIE'S WIFE
11/3/93

Being that I never had a father, Donnie's wife to be's
father was a father figure to me. I would go to their house
and play cards with him and talk with him. Then
Donnie's wife to be would come home from school with
her pony tail and bobby sox. I would give her a lollipop
kiss she would get mad at me. I would laugh at her she
was just a teenager then. She would be coming from or
going to rehearsal with the group she was singing with,
the Taras. Everybody from that group is successful, my
ex-wife and second girlfriend Aslene Trutman who died.
Even though Donnie's fiancee to be's father was bibulous,
he was very smart. I looked up to him, as a matter of fact,
he was like that to all the young Americans who were
trying to find their way in Toronto. By this time Donnie's
group, The Roques had hit it big. They changed their
name from the Roques to Mandela. I sang some

backgrounds for Mandela on their record.   It was very successful in Canada. Then Roy Renner took George Olivers place in the group. The group moved to L. A.

(441)

11/3/93

When they moved to L.A. in 1967. They changed a couple more members in the group. Precash John (Elephant Boy) on bass, and they late Huey Sullivan on keyboards. The group had some success in L.A. but not like it had in Toronto. So Donnie changed the name of the group from Mandela to Bush. I recorded with him as well on that album that received some success. So he changed the name from Bush to nothing, cause he went on his own. We recorded his and Bush's album in Van Nuys, CA at Sound City Studios with then Keith Olsen the engineer. Now Keith is a big time producer for Fleetwood Mac, Tom Waits, Foreigner, etc... His album didn't fulfill his expectations. He did an album with his wife to be, of which myself and Eric Mercury had a song on her album. "I Apologize" it was called. We were like one big family. Things were a little slow for Donnie's own thing. So he did Diane Brooks album with me and I got Donnie on some sessions, also, I got his wife to be in on some albums. Allthough she's a good singer, her head's into the music, but her heart's not into it.

(442)

11/3/93

Anyway Donnie ended up taking Joe Walsh's place in the James Gang. He played and wrote songs for the James Gang while Roy Kenner sang lead. That lasted for a while, then he moved to Toronto where he joined The

Guess Who, he played with them awhile. Then he left the
group. Then he got his own thing together again in
Toronto. In the meantime Donnie's wife to be was doing
all kinds of jingles in Toronto. She was doing all kinds of
records in Toronto. She was very, very, very, successful in
Toronto. In the meantime, Donnie sent the producers of
Night Heat a tape of his original music. The producers
heard the songs, liked what he heard. Donnie not only
wrote the theme song for Night Heat, but has done dozens
of T.V. shows in Canada. Among the many shows he does
music for "Top Cops". I traveled alot, I've been around.
Donnie is the only man I know who's a millionaire from
scoring T.V. shows, but can't read a lick of music. Donnie
finally married the girl he met when he was a teenager.

(443)

11/3/93

Between his doing T.V. shows and his wife doing jingles
and doing bit parts in shows that he scores, it's no telling
how much they're worth. They have an indoor swimming
pool in there house. To me it's the prettiest house in
Canada. In my opinion when I had my stroke they both
sent me a get well telegram. I had them framed. I'll keep
that telegram till the day I die along with the framed
picture of Donnie's father. Then I got a call from Donnie
saying his father inlaw had terminal cancer. Man I
freaked. I told Delores that he had to change. She's a
nurse, she said to me, being that she's a nurse, why should
he change now. It's unfortunate that he has cancer, she
said but if he's been drinking and smoking cigarettes since
you've known him why should he stop now if that's what
he enjoys doing. She said let him go out with dignity
don't feel sorry or pity him. Be like you were with him

like you were when you first met him. She said, he would
like that, she said, I know, I been around thousands of
cancer patients. So that's the way I treated him.

(444)

11/3/93

So I had told Donnie when it happened to call me. Donnie
called me and told me, man even though I tried to do
what Delores told me to do I couldn't hold it back. He
was the only father figure I knew. Anyway a year later
Michelle Hormel gave me money to see a private doctor. I
got up May 21, 1992 and I drove myself to the Wilshire
district to the doctors office that's about 15 miles from my
house, I ask the doctor was I able to travel alone on a
plane. Cause I had just gotten out of the hospital March
10, 1992. He said yes, if you can drive yourself 15 miles to
my office, I don't see why you can't fly on a airplane he
said. Then I said what about the insulin I'm taking. He
said to me, don't take it no more, you don't need it. Then I
said what about these fruit and vegetable pills, should I
take them. He checked them out, he said to me, there's
nothing wrong with these pills on top of that you've lost
67 pounds. He said if all of my patients were like you, I
wouldn't be in business.

(445)

11/3/93

Man, you have no Idea how excited I was. Man, was I
excited, I could travel on a plane what makes it so good, I
could walk to the place as oppose to being in a wheelchair.
Anyway I got home from the doctors office feeling all
jocund. When I got in the house, the answering machine
light was blinking. I checked the machine, Donnie had

called, then I said oh wow! I was just thinking about him and his lovely wife. So I called him back, and his wife answered the phone. I said Hello, I was just thinking about you, as a maters of fact, I'm coming to Toronto to see my girl, and while I'm there, I wanna see you guys. Then she said to me, don't come up here, I started to laugh, then I said what do you mean? She said just what I said , don't come up here, she said I'm still grieving. My father died a year ago and if you come up here and die, I couldn't get over it. Then I said is somebody going to kill me, cause I'm in better shape then the average American. Then I said the doctor just gave me a clean bill of health.

(446)

11/3/93

Then I said I'm not asking you for nothing, all I just want to do is to see you guys. Then she said, if you're coming up here don't come to my house. Man, I didn't know what to say. When her father died, I grieved just as much as she did. The only thing was that no one in L.A. knew who he was. So I had to do my own grieving by myself when I was in the hospital, Chico came to visit me. He just got back from Chicago from Eric Mercury's play preview. Donnie's wife was there along with her mother. Chico gave her his condolences (Donnie's wife that is). When he said that to her she got verbally fervently inimical with him he said to me. Then he said in his halcyon way, that's all right, I forgive her, cause I know what she's going through. My advice to her is let go. Her father had alot of friends that loved him, I and Chico were just two people out of hundreds. If you had 100 houses with indoor swimming pools, your mind couldn't be as peaceful as his is now. I know, I was in a coma for three days so all I can say to you is get a grip.

Donnies' Wife
Shawn, if you remember I had just got out of the hospital in '92. My comportment was that of a mentally inimical person. I've known you and your family for over 30 years. You're like my little sister. I'm sorry, and I love you. Don't forget that. You're like the song I use to sing to you all the time, ("You're a Sweetheart")
Smitty

(447)   AND I THOUGHT WE WERE CLOSE
11/5/93
Like I was saying through the book, I had this 1990 Mazda Navajo 4 wheel drive, recreational vehicle. Man did I like that truck. I had it hand washed. I took good care of that truck being that this lady co-signed for me, I made sure the payments was on time. I even gave her three payments in advance. Then my health started to act up. I had to cancel gigs which made me late for one payment. I was just late, I didn't miss no payments. Then I when I was in the hospital for 2 months, I was late again, cause they hadn't given me the benefits yet, that's why I was late. Being that I was late with the payment, the financial department came down on her as you remember, the minute they gave the benefit for me I wanted to take some of the money and pay the car off for a year. But the trustees wouldn't let me do that. They said we could make your current payments, but we couldn't pay in advance. So when the finance company called her, and started to press her, she panicked.

(448)

11/5/93

When she panicked, she called me. Being that she did a
lot of coke, she was really nervous. I remember me and
Marty Grebb. Marty Grebb and I used to do a lot of coke
together in the old days when Marty was doing coke. He
weighed about 288 pounds. Now that he doesn't do that
stuff no more, and has cleaned up his life, he and his wife,
he weighs about 150 pounds. When Marty came to see
me, I didn't know who he was, he looked so good. His
wife looks like her daughter's sister. Anyway I ask Marty
if he would help me to get her off of coke Marty said yes
he would help. I remember her son tried to help, and I
tried to help as well. I was talking to her one day on the
phone, and her son had flushed her stash down the toilet.
I started to laugh when she said to me it was about an
ounce of coke. She freaked and said why couldn't he have
buried the coke? Man, did I laugh. She did coke a lot, I
don't know how old she was, but she was up there. She
was too old to be doing coke the way she was doing coke.

(449)

11/5/93

By this time, I had put about $15,000 into the car. I tried to
explain to the trustees that I was late with two car
payments, and could I please pay in advance, cause as
good as that lady was, she did do a lot of coke. And
people that did coke were capricious people. I know,
cause I use to do alot of coke. They said that they couldn't
do it. Anyway that lady called me when the car was in the
shop being repaired and told me that I would have to get
some body else to carry the loan cause the finance

company was on her case. I told her that in the condition I was in, no. The trustees was stripping me of my dignity. Bad enough, let alone other people, even though she was fervent about what she was saying. She was persistent. I was trying to concentrate on the book and trying to get well. That was the priority. After being so persistent, I threw my hands up and said, take the car. It didn't matter to me if I had already put $15,000 dollars into the truck. I gave her back the car, and thought for a moment, what am I going to do?

(450)

11/5/93

I thought real hard, then I said I'll get a bike. That way I can get around. Then I said I can't ride a two wheel because of my balance. Then I said to myself, I know, I'll get a three wheel bike, and put a basket on the back. I can get around that way. I got a bike and fixed it up, with the help of Bill Elkin. When I was living in the other house, I was riding 12 to 15 miles a day. So far I've put about 2000 miles on that bike, I have lost 67 pounds. To the lady that co-signed for me, thank you very much. The best thing you ever did was to take that truck from me. I feel so good now that I'm riding that bike. Oh and by the way, the bike is paid for cash, and not by coke money.

(451) MENDACITY

11/8/93

After I had figured out how to get an income to happen, Eric Mercury called me from Chicago, and I was telling him about the book. He had told me that the book Idea was nice, however he gave me another great idea for a book. I said wonderful I won't mention what the book was about, cause I intend to write about it, that's how great the idea was. I said great whenever you're coming to L.A., just give me a day notice and I'll set up a meeting with my therapist Dr. Sperber and that way the three of us will discuss it together. He said fine. So the first week in July of 1992 I think it was he called me on Monday night and said he was coming to L.A. I said great, I said I'll set up an appointment with Dr. Sperber for Tuesday. Monday Eric didn't call. I panicked cause as long as I've known Eric he was always on time. He didn't show up Tuesday. I really got nervous, I didn't care about the meeting anymore, I was worried about him. I called his house, and his answering service answered. Then I really got nervous.

(452)

11/8/93

I started to call his brother or sister in Canada, but he had so many mishaps in his family, that I was scared to call up there cause I didn't want to upset his brother and his sister. Then I said if I don't hear from him by tomorrow, I'm going to call them anyway. Sure enough he called me the next day or night, he told me that he was busy, could I book if for that Friday. I said yeah, so I booked the session for that Friday night. Thursday night he called me and said he couldn't make the session, man I lost it. He was trying to explain to me that being that he was doing the Michael Jordan, Coors, and Cool Whip adds, that took priority over what I was doing. In other words, what I was doing was trivial compared to what he was doing. Then, I was so mad I hung up on him. The moral of this story is a friend in need is a friend in debt. Now you know why I called this chapter mendacity.

(453)   DAVID CLAYTON THOMAS
11/9/93

My compendium of inimical persons is David Clayton
Thomas. I first met David C. Thomas February 8, 1964 at a
place called the Flamingo Club on Younge street in
Toronto Canada. I was playing organ in the house band
there. We were going to take a break when this guy came
up to the organ with a silk brown suit on with 2 women
on his arms and said to me, I want to sit in with you guys
and sing some blues with you. I said we are going on a
break, I said you're going to have to wait. He said man, I
can't wait, he said I'm good. I've got to do it now, so he
pushed his way to the stage then he said I'm David
Clayton Thomas of The Shades. Then he said, don't you
know who I am? He said we had hit records all over
Canada. He said I'm good. Then I looked at the guys I
was playing with, Eric Johnson on drums, Gene Evans on
guitar and Doug Richardson on sax, and I said who is this
guy. Then I said boy is he pushy. Anyway he sang two
songs. He finished singing then he said you see, I told you
I was good.

(454)

11/9/93

I had never met nobody that adulated about himself so
much. Anyway he then offered me a job to play with him.
I told him that I already had a job. Then he said if you
ever get tired of this job call me. Anyway I didn't see him
no more until a couple of months and when I saw him
again, the same thing happened. Then after him being
inimical with a lot of people, he left for New York. There
he bummed around until he landed a gig playing guitar

for Muddy Waters. By that time I was with the Soul Searchers then. We went to play at Steve Paul's Scene. It was there I ran into D.C.T. And again I was setting in the Village in Toronto and I ran into him again. That's when both of us ran into Rick James. The three of us had coffee. Then David went back to New York. There he ran into the leader of Blood Sweet and Tears. Al Kooper, the lead singer had left the group, so the leader of the group was looking for a lead singer to replace Al Kooper. He heard D.C.T., and liked what he heard.

(455)

11/9/93

So the leader of Blood Sweat and Tears hired David to sing lead. Now that was a strange combination of guys. The four horn players were jazz musicians. The rhythm section was rock musicians. When David joined the group he brought with him a folk song he use to do in clubs around Toronto. When he would sit in with us, the Del Five, he use to play and sing this song called Spinning Wheel. Anyway the jazz part of the group took that folk song and made a jazz song out of it. What do you know I don't know it was a hit. The song sold over 16 million copies. Man, was that song big. The only thing was that in that group, there were nine leaders. That group was the weirdest thing I've ever seen in my life. I remember I went to visit D.C.T. at his house in Cartia Medera, CA. I was playing piano in D.C.T.'s living room. There was David, he wanted me to play some blues, the horn section wanted me to play some jazz and rhythm section wanted me to play rock and roll. That group couldn't come together on nothing.

(456)

11/10/93

You see the problem was D.C.T. wrote the song
"Spinning Wheel". Before that great horn section
arranged the song, it was a folk song. But when the horn
section put an arrangement to the song, it became a hit.
D.C.T. wanted to be the leader of the band cause he felt
that he made Blood Sweat and Tears what they were. The
guys in the band felt that they made the band what they
where because of the arrangement of the song Spinning
Wheel. Boy was it a mess. Before they came along there
were people like Sly and the Family Stone, Elvis Presly,
Bing Crosby, Frank Sinatra and etc.. You knew who the
leader was, but nine leaders? My suggestion is why not
get along with each other. That way all of them can go to
the bank. Anyway, they argued so much, that broke up in
1971. D.C.T. moved to Brentwood, CA. He felt that he
was so big of a star that he wanted to go on his own.
Before he moved to L.A. I visited him in Marin County. I
had just left Toronto, and was working in Virginia, trying
to get a new life.

(457)

11/10/93

So I called D.C.T. from Norfolk Virginia and told him that
I was in transition and I told him that being that I had just
left Motherlode in Canada, I was looking for something to
do. He suggested that I fly out to San Francisco to see
him, he paid for my ticket. I flew out there to see him. I
said to myself, what a nice gesture. So I spent a week,
with him in Carta Medera, CA. Then I had to get back to
Virginia. I packed my clothes, D.C.T. was getting ready to
take me to the airport. Before he took me to the airport he

checked all of his belongings to make sure I didn't steal nothing from him. Anyway I went back to Virginia, worked a while there, moved to San Francisco for six weeks then I moved to L.A. I established myself there, met a lot of people there. Soon after D.C.T. broke up with Blood Sweat and Tears, he moved to L.A. After leaving San Francisco I moved to L.A. also. I got a call from Joel Sill, he told me that he was producing D.C.T's solo album, would I like to play on the album, then I said to him, who's playing on the album.

(458)

11/10/93

He said to me Penti Glen (also known as Whitey)on drums, and Precash John on bass, both of which were in the Alice Cooper Band. Donnie Troiano on guitar, he used to be with the James Gang. I told him yeah I'll do it, I know all those guys. They're Canadians. You see with D.C.T. being that he's so inimical, nobody to this day that I knew of liked him. The people that I knew that knew him tolerated him because of his position. He was and is so capricious. Being that everybody in the band knew him, and knew what kind of a person he was, we just put up with him. Boy was he an inimical person. Anyway I don't know if that song we did made the album or not. That was about April of 1971. After that, I moved to Laurel Canyon down the street from Danny Kortchmiar and Joel O'Brien. Danny then was playing guitar for James Taylor. Joel O'Brien was playing drums for Carol King. Both of those guys shared a house together. Joel was married to Connie then. Being that I had an apartment down the block from them we use to jam all the time.

315

(459)   A COMPENDIUM OF AN INIMICAL PERSON
11/10/93

That day, February 14, 1972 we had a jam session that
day. Danny Kortchmiar on guitar, he's on Carol King's
Tapestry album. Joel O Brian on drums, he played drums
on Carol King's Tapestry album, and Charlie Larky, Carol
King's ex-husband. He also played on Carol King's
Tapestry album. Ernie Sandy lead vocals. She holds her
own, she's a star in her own rights. We were all jamming
having a good time when D.C.T. came to my apartment.
We all stop playing D.C.T. started to talk. He was telling
us how great his place was. He was telling us that he had
a big place in Brentwood, and how his place was real big,
and how he had all the instruments in his rehearsal room.
That he had drums already there why don't you guys
come over to my house and jam he said. In other words
he was bragging. Just then Danny looked at me as if to
say who is this guy? Being that I know D.C.T. (well as
much as you can get to know him) the guys looked at me
as if to say whatever Smitty, cause we were already
having a good time at my little small apartment.

(460)
11/10/93

I had a small two bedroom apartment at 8811 Wonderland
Ave. in Laurel Canyon in Hollywood , CA. I'll reiterate
D.C.T. is a type of person you tolerate. We went over to
his house to jam. Even though the guys had a good time
they were tense, cause nobody was starving or nothing
like that, Evie had a record deal Joel was working with
Jackie De Shannon. Danny was working with James
Taylor, (and now he produces Bon Jovi), and Charlie was
working with his wife then Carol King. So none of those

guys really needed him. After the session was over,
D.C.T. ask me to stay awhile, he wanted to talk to me. He
explained to me his version of what happened with Blood
Sweat and Tears. He ended by saying to me that's why
I'm by myself. You know as inimical as he is, he has a
way of convincing you that he was right, then he ask me if
I would be his Straw Boss in other words put a band
together for him, write with him, oh and far as publishing,
he said that he would own that, then I asked why? He
said to me that he was bigger then me, he said that he had
more success then I had.

(461)
11/10/93
Then I said what's that got to do with publishing? He said
I've been around more then you have I know a lot of
people. People like Clive Davis (then president of
Columbia Records) little did he know that I knew that
Clive Davis didn't like him. So I wasn't in the same
position that Danny, Charlie or the rest of the guys were
in so I told him let me go home and think about it and talk
it over with my then wife. Then he said the first song you
write with me you'll get an advance on the publishing. So
I went home and talked it over with my then ex-wife. So
after I discussed it with her, she said to me, I think that's
bad about the publishing you've never given up your
publishing to another artist. So you could play with him,
but we need the money. Being that she was Canadian, she
knew D.C.T. and she knew that he was an inimical person.
So she said to me, work with him, I know it hurts you to
give up your publishing, but what the hell, get the money,
don't get involved in his personal business. But then I
said he's so inimical, he talks at you, not to you.

(462)

11/10/93

In spite of my feelings, I said yeah to him. He said to me
that I had to write that album, arrange the album record
the album, play on the album, sing on the album, for that,
I'll put you on retainer, and give you 7 percent of the door.
I said okay, If were going to write the album, lets take
turns writing at each others house. Then he said to me no
lets write at my house he said, cause my place is bigger
and I live in Brentwood. Once again I bit my tongue and
said okay, then I said to him you don't have a piano at
your house and I have one. Wouldn't it be better if we
write over my house? I said. Then he said if you go with
me to a piano store tomorrow, I'll buy one. Then I said
okay. The next day we got together and went a music
store he bought a baby grand piano for $3,500 that was a
lot of money in those days, anyway, I went to his house
every night and wrote songs. To give you an example of
why I say this is a nowhere place to live, I had to drive
from my house on Wonderland Ave. to Mandeville Lane
in Brentwood CA. I lived in Hollywood off Laurel
Canyon, he lived next to Beverly Hills. I had to drive my
truck every night out of Brentwood.

(463)

11/10/93

Sometimes D.C.T. and I would write until 12 or 1:00 in the
morning. Every time I would leave and drive through
Brentwood the cops would stop me for something. They
would tell me that my back light was broken, I was going
too slow or too fast. Now on my van I had my name and
where I was from on the door. The cops could have a run

a check on me that way. If they would have done that along with checking my plates, they could have seen that I was from Toronto, and I was a black man. But being that I was a black man in Brentwood driving a van at 1:00 in the morning, they stopped me every night. The humiliation I went through in those days cause I was a lunatic business man in those days is horrifying. That's why I say for a minority, this is not a nice place to be. This went on for about 2 months. Man, did I do a lot of drugs in those days that's the only way I could handle things. I remember one time I ran out of smoke then, and in my ash tray I had enough butts to roll five joints. That'll give you an idea of how many joints I was smoking. That's the only way I could feel good about myself.

(464)

11/10/93

Then after we wrote the album, we or I had to get guys to record the songs. I got Chuck Rainey on bass, he played bass on Sanford and Sons, Danny Kortchmar on guitar. He use to play with James Taylor, now he's the producer for Bon Jovi. Kenneth Rice on drums, he use to play with Aretha Franklin, Tessie Cohen on percussion. She use to play with Jackie De Shannon. At that time all of us were really close. None of the guys really liked David, but if I did the gig, it was all right. Because of me, they tolerated D.C.T. and did the gig. So we rehearsed for about 2 months (May to July 1972) Then we went into the recording studio to do the record. Mike Post was the producer, you don't know what it was like when you had Post in the studio, his lawyer, his manager, his agent, his house boy, and all of the guys in the band, and nobody liked him. It was so intense in that room that you couldn't

cut the intensity with a hack saw. That went on for about
a month, I've never been in a situation where you had all
of those people in one room) and nobody, but nobody
liked D.C.T.   Man was I nervous wreck.

(465)

11/10/93

You'll never or know what it was like writing rehearsing
and recording with D.C.T. not only was he mililate, but he
was out a benign person. You could cut the tension in that
room with a knife. To be in a room with his lawyers his
manager, the musicians, his agent and etc. Nobody liked
him, they were there for one reason, the money. That's all
it was no love lost in that room for him. It just so
happened I was producing a dope dealer. At the time I
had plenty of drugs, so I doubled my intake to about 30
joints a day. That's the only way I could work with him.
After the session was over I almost had a nervous break
down. I couldn't get affection from home, she (my ex)
didn't understand nothing about that, so I took a vacation
to Toronto. There I knew a lot of people I came up in the
music business with, some benign people. I went to
Toronto, the first person I called was Delores. We almost
got together sexually, but she rejected me cause I was
married. Little did she know the situation both with
D.C.T. and my ex. She kept telling me that I was married.
I was with somebody.

(466)

11/10/93

If Delores only knew my situation, maybe she would
have considered anyway, I saw a bunch of my cronies up
in Toronto. I felt a little warm. Being in Toronto made me

feel a little human again. I got back in L.A. around July of 1972. Then he told me that he had a tour in September of 1972 we had to go to Brazil. He told me to ask the guys in the band would they like to go, I ask the guys in the band would they like to go. Everybody agreed except Chuck Rainy and Danny Koctchmar. Chuck was busy doing a lot of sessions in town. Like The Jeffersons, Sanford and Sons, Smokey Robinson and etc. Danny was getting ready to go on tour with James Taylor. Danny told me that he didn't want to go out on tour with him anyway. He to inimical. So I had to get somebody to replace both guys. I got Kenny Marco, he use to play with me in Motherlode (that was guitar) and Willie Weeks on bass. He played bass on David Bowies record Fame. Once again we rehearsed to go to Brazil. We got to Brazil now I won't say that the people in Brazil are slow. They're just a little layed back.

Missing pages 467 – 476 (Smitty possibly just mis-numbered them)

(477)

11/10/93

I remember it was in September of 1972 we were at the local arena in Rio. The show didn't start on time. D.C.T. freaked. Being that we had portable dressing rooms, D.C.T. was so pissed, he tore down his dressing room. He completely destroyed the room, that's just to show you how inimical he is. Being that it was a international song writers festival we were playing, we, David and I won first prize with our song. First Prize was $17,000 which I got my part in February of 1973 with the help of Sam Trust, at the time he had the Beatles catalogue, (thanks

Sam) and a statue of a golden cock. I remember when we won I had to carry him over my shoulder. To this day I never touched that thing. I had to beg for my money. To this day I never understood why he didn't want to pay me. The two things I remember about Rio, they have some crazy people there and number two the dope was great.

(478)

11/10/93

I guess the only reason I'm writing so long on D.C.T. because I've never met such an inimical person in my life. And I'm from the projects of Portsmouth VA. I thought I've been around everything. Anyway, we got back from Brazil and we had some time off. Willie Weeks went and played bass for Herbie Mann. The following year we went to Mexico. Being that the D.C.T. name was still in those days linked with Blood Sweat and Tears, they wanted to hear D.C.T. with horns. Being that I didn't know how to lift the Blood Sweat and Tears arrangements off of the album, I hired Trevor Lawrence of Stevie Wonder's Wonder Love to lift the horn arrangements for me. He was and is much better at that then me. And I hired Paul Stallworth to play bass. He use to play for George Harrison. We went to Mexico to play. I remember that time it was August of 1973, I must have been very good at that time cause the climate was so weird in Mexico that when I played organ, I had to play a third down. In other words, when the band played in the key of "C" I had to play in the key of "A". Boy, when I was in Mexico, I had to think real hard.

(479)

11/10/93

We were in Mexico (remind me to never go shopping with Trevor Lawrence) and we were doing a Mexican T.V. show, and a Mexican came up to me (after we had finished playing) with broken English, he said to me when you guys play, you guys play with environment. That was twenty years ago, I've never forgotten that since. I understood what he meant. Anyway on the way back from Mexico we played Tahoe. On the Rowan and Martin show at Ceasars Palace that was September of 1973. I remember standing in line to register to stay at Ceasears Palace. I've never been in an environment like that, man, was that a big gambling casino you had one arm bandits all over the place. As I was standing there in line waiting to get my room, the one arm bandits were going off like crazy. People were winning thousands of dollars, so I said to myself, I might as well try my luck at this one arm bandit stuff. So I ask the information lady how to play the game. She said all you have to is put a quarter in the machine, and if your number comes up, you'll win. So I put a quarter in the machine and the first time I did that I won $25.00

(480)

11/10/93

Man, I won that $25.00 with one quarter. I went crazy, I put another quarter in the one arm bandit and I won another $25.00. This time I won another $25.00 by this time I ran to the line, took my bags out of the line (the bandits were all over the lobby) then the information lady said to me that if you put four quarters in at one time you'll win 4 times as much as you would when you put a quarter in the machine. I was just about to give D.C.T. my

notice. I didn't see him or I would have done that.
Instead I ran back to the machine and started to putting 4
quarters in the machine. Not only did I lose the money I
had won, but I lost $100 dollars of my money inside of ten
minutes. Which goes to show how a bird in the hand is
worth two in the bush. We came back from Lake Tahoe
and we had no more tours. D.C.T. wanted to put me on
retainer, but I didn't want that. I didn't want to be owned.
He was upset that I wouldn't go on retainer. You don't
now how glad I was to get out of that situation. Just think
I could go back to doing 15 joints a day instead of 30 joints
a day. I could have 5 girls a week instead of ten girls a
week.

(481)

11/10/93

Anyway we did the tour, and things were pretty slow for
D.C.T. then what little bit of happiness I could have, I was
happy. I couldn't get it from home being with my wife or
working with D.C.T. So I kept myself busy doing
sessions, doing drugs, running women. Don't get me
wrong, I was no saint myself, but I wasn't an inimical
person. When I left the group in 1973 Lani Hartley took
my place. He use to play with the Fifth Dimension, and
Eric Johnson on drums, he use to play with KiKi Dee.
D.C.T. was losing so much money that he had to stop
touring. So in 1974, I did one last session with him, then
he left to go back to Toronto. He was such an inimical
person, that nobody in Toronto got along with him. At the
time Bobby Fischer was singing lead for Blood Sweat and
Tears, I don't know what year it was but D.C.T. rejoined
Blood Sweat and Tears they played around the country a
while until they berated each other to smithereens.

Finally they broke up. In 1975 I did an album for Warner Bros. called A Good Feeling. On that album I did a song that D.C.T. and I wrote.

(482)

11/10/93

The name of the song was "Harmony Junction" I ask D.C.T. how did he like the song, He said that the arrangement was different. That's all he said. In the mean time he was doing some records in L.A. with Blood Sweat and Tears. When he would come to L.A. he would rent a sports car like a Porsche or a Mercedes or something like that and come over to my house pick up my kids. Take them for a spin the kids would like that. My kids would always ask me when was uncle David coming to town so we could ride in one of his sports cars. After he would take the kids for a ride, he would then take me out to dinner, lunch, or breakfast. Then he would talk at me. Then I would say to myself, for an inimical guy, he's all right, even though he does talk at you to do that to the kids? He is all right. The years went by. I remember the beginning of 1980 we did "An Evening at the Improve" together. Then around that time I was doing a duet with Lenny Castro. He was on percussion, and I was on piano. I remember I never had to rehearse with Lenny, with Lenny all you

(483)

11/10/93

had to say to Lenny was the next song was a fast or slow song. Anyway we played at a place in studio city called the Bla Bla Cafe. It was Ventura Blvd. D.C.T. came to sit in with me. I said to myself me and this guy must be all right. By that time Blood Sweat and Tears had broken up for quite a while. D.C.T. some years later got the group together again, being that they were has beens, they were making about five hundred dollars a night. Then they got together with this great guy who was a young man, and a fan of the group when he was young. His name's Larry Dorr. Larry reminded me of Elvis Presley's manager Colonel Tom Parker. He took that group from a five hundred dollar a night group and turned it into a $15,000, $20,000 and sometimes $30,000 a night group. Larry's a very very very smart man. Once again Blood Sweat and Tears was making some money. Like not what they were making when they were in their hey day but they where grossing close to a million a year.

(484)

11/10/93

Larry Dorr's from outside of Boston Mass. He was a die hard Blood Sweat and Tears fan as a teenager so in his young 30's he got a chance to meet and manage. Even though D.C.T. was of an memesis character, and he was of a brimace mien, Larry Dorr did his job. Larry personally didn't like D.C.T. but he does his job, gets his money, and goes home. Larry can do that cause he's a young man and he can handle the stress, but one day he's gonna get my age, and he won't be able to take it. Like this guy I know, his girlfriends a stewardess she recently had the Blood Sweat and Tears band and D.C.T. on a flight. Being that she wasn't in the music business, she was amazed that all of the guys in the band bad mouthed D.C.T. She couldn't get over the fact that nobody in the band liked him. She said he was verbally inimical, and he acted like a wanna be. Anyway the way that Larry was when he was around him, everybody was like that when they were around him. I remember the guys from the record co. was playing softball for the record co. David was on one team, one guy from one record co.

(485)

11/10/93

ask me, who is that guy. I said D.C.T. of Blood Sweat and Tears. He said to me that is an inimical person, he said I can tell by his face, then he said he had a brimace face. Then he said that D.C.T didn't feel right. That's the feeling everybody got when you were around him. The way I feel, everybody feels this way about him, nobody has the guts nor the time to say it. Knowing D.C.T. for 30 years, the way he is, he's not matriclinious. His father is one of the nicest people I've ever met. And his mother, when she was living ditto. His brother's a nice person as well. The only thing I can say about D.C.T. is that he's one of a kind. He sings well, but so can I so can a number of Afro Amercians I've met. Go to an Afro American church sometimes and out of 500 members in that church, 400 of them can sing. Anyway, he would come to town to do a Blood Sweat and Tears album, and come over to the house, take the kids for a ride, take me out to talk and eat, I remember one time he was in town doing a Blood Sweat and Tears album, and the leader of the band, the drummer ask me to sing and play on the album.

(486)

11/10/93

I sang, wrote and played on the album. All and all I put about 16 hours into the album, I went to the leader and gave him the bill. He got offended. He said to me that he

thought that I was just hanging out, that I was just
hanging with D.C.T. and doing him and D.C.T. a favor.
This guy's now a big executive at capital record. You see
if I was a white boy, I would have been treated differently.
I don't want to use his name. He just might be a vaxotious
litagater. I remember telling D.C.T. about the incident
D.C.T. said to me that I shouldn't offend him because he
was a big wheel in the music business. Then I said to
D.C.T. what kind of wheel, I said GoodYear or Goodrich.
Its all rubber to me. Moving on, I had my stroke and as
you can see the people gave a benefit for me. The
husband, wife and ex-lawyer was giving me a $100 a
week. That's $100 out of $55,000 that's what they told me
they made. Being that the husband and wife gave me the
benefit I never saw the money. Maybe I was too stupid
too handle my own affairs.

(487)

11/10/93

Anyway is their opinion against mine, on how a benefit
should be run. The back bills were piling up. The
landlord was freaking. I would get a call to do a $15,000
commercial. I couldn't do it cause of the stroke, I would
hang up the phone. As soon as I would do that the
landlord would rightfully so cry about how he wanted his
back money. He would tell me if I don't pay him he
would evict me. Then there was the biddy that co-signed
for my car. She wanted to put that car in somebody else's
name, for she no longer wanted the responsibility for the
car. Here I was trying to recover from the stroke. So I
said to myself, I've got to get out of this situation, what
can I do, I know, I call D.C.T. He has a 1/2 million dollars
home in Sufferin NY, a big ole swimming pool, and he

drove around in a Lotus, and he has a Ford Bronco. I said
being that we have a writing session, and one of the songs
we wrote is gonna be on the Blood Sweat and Tears
album, I'll sell the publishing to him out right. Then I said
I know I'll lose money like that,

(488)

11/10/93

but that's all right. What little bit of money I could get, I
will pay the landlord, and pay the biddy for the car.
Blood Sweat and Tears were in town at the time. (L.A.
that is) I was still recovering from the stroke. Larry Dorr
wanted to come and visit me. We had struck up a great
business relationship. He wanted to help to get
Motherlode back on their feet. He use to call and tell me
D.C.T. horror stories. I would act surprised but I had
heard them for almost 30 years, from everybody he had
worked with. Every time D.C.T. would come over to visit,
Larry would want to come over with him. But D.C.T.
would tell him I wasn't excepting visitors. To this day, I
don't understand why he would say that. I really don't
know why that guy's so inimical. Like I said before. His
parents are so benign, so is his brother. In all of my days,
I've never seen someone so possessed. Anyway, David
came over to where I was staying, I explained everything
to him slowly and carefully, the first thing he said to me as
that the people that gave the benefit for me were trying to
help me.

(489)

11/10/93

I agreed with him, I told him I know they're trying to help
me, but they really don't know me like you do. I said I

need the money to pay my back bills that piled up while I
was sick, and besides I could pay some bills, go to Toronto
to see my girlfriend. They never thought about that, after
all, I'm a human being, then I said I don't have to worry
about a place to stay, I can stay with Dougie and his wife.
Dougie said I'm welcome in his house anytime. Then
D.C.T. said to me, How do you know that Dougie and his
wife want to deal with a cripple? Then he said about the
publishing, I have to consult my lawyer. Then I said
David, this isn't about a lawyer, this about a 30 year
friendship. I'm not trying to sell you my part of the
publishing to get rich, I just need enough money to get
these people off of my back. So I can think what to do, I
need enough money so I can breath. I'll be here lying in
bed with no clothes on and the landlord would take his
key, and come right on in. I can handle the stroke, but
between the landlord and the benefit people my dignity's
being stripped.

(490)

11/10/93

I could handle anything else but not my dignity trying to
being taken from me. He reiterated to me again about the
loan. The next day he called and told me what he wanted
to do. He said to me that he would take 50% of my
publishing (which is all of my part cause he owned the
other half) for $2,000. Man I got sick to my stomach.
Here's a guy that had a Lotus, and half a million dollar
home a Ford Bronco, I know for a fact cause his manager
told me that his take from Blood, Sweat and Tears Inc. was
1/4 million dollars a year. All he had to say to me is he
couldn't or didn't want to do it because of what ever. I
would have understood, but like Rock Deadrick, the

drummer with Tracy Chapman said to me when I was explaining my situation to him, even though he didn't know D.C.T. he said to me that sounded like a person who would kick a person when he was down. Walfredo's wife at the time was handling my personal affairs, then she use to be Journey's business manager. Now she managed Neil Shawn's personal affairs. He the guitar player

(491)

11/10/93

that use to be with the group Journey. They're now dismantled. She looked at the contract, and she said to me if you sign that thing, I'll never speak to you again, you said he's your friend? With friends like that, you don't need no enemies. I told him that I couldn't sign the contract. Cause if I did, I wouldn't have no business managers. If I signed that contract, she didn't think it was right. He berated her to me something bad. All this time I thought him and I was close. At that moment I saw that I was like the rest of the people. He couldn't understand that that wasn't about business, it was about a friend in need. He just looked at it as though here's my chance to get something for nothing. The reason why I got so mad at him, cause I was so hurt. I watched him do that to other people for 30 years. Not me, I'm different. Oh yeah, I'm going to show you how different you are. It was then I realized that I was like everybody else.

(492)

11/10/93

To D.C.T's. housekeeper, his lawyer, his gardener, his manager, his accountant, the guy that owns the name Blood Sweat and Tears, the guys in the band, the secretaries, his agent, his limo driver, the girl he has for a week, and etc. My humble apologies, for I don't in no way wish to take food off of your table I just want to say I know what you're going through, for I've been there myself, for I was his writing partner ex-writing partner. I wrote all of these pages to find out one thing. Now I really,really, really, understand why behind his back the guys in the band call his estate DISGRACELAND.

(493) POETIC JUSTICE
11/10/93

It was after the D.C.T. incident around September of 1992, when I was approached by a guy name Jeff Laine. Jeff is a guy who I've known since 1977. He's a singer writer guitar player who has a group called Poetic Justice. He ask me if I would like to produce him and his group. I said first I would like to hear them, they were playing at the Whiskey a GoGo. That's now a pay to play place in Hollywood CA. First of all I was honored that he asked me to do it for him. I went to the Whiskey, I heard the band. The band was good but right off I knew they hadn't had any recording experience. It's not that the band sounded bad, its just that I knew guys that could got the job done faster and quicker. Anyway we went to Clear Lake Studios to record with his band. He wanted to use his band. The music came out okay, it's just that I knew guys that had studio experience. So we had another recording session at Clear Lake audio, that's located on Burbank Blvd. in North Hollywood, CA. This time we used some guys I knew.

(494)

11/10/93

On keyboards we had David Garfield, he's the keyboard
player that's on the Fame theme song. On guitar we had
Carl Verheyen. He's the guitar player that's on Cheers,
and on bass we had Hutch Hutchingson he plays bass
with Bonnie Raitt, and Joe Sheu on guitar, he was my
across the street neighbor. He also played guitar. Now
that came out great, because of that session, I was able to
buy me a three wheel bike, and plan a trip to Toronto. To
Jeff Laine, what you did for my ego was Poetic Justice.

(495)   YOU CAN NEVER GO BACK
11/10/93

Now all of this controversy about the benefit money, they
never considered that I was human and my girlfriend
lived in Canada. I wanted to see her real bad. Thanks to
Jeff's project, I was able to go up there to see her being
that I use to live in Toronto, I could not only see all of my
buddies but a lot of them are talented people. I'm not
Canadian, but most Americans think that I am. I lived
there for so long, that's why I take it personally about the
stigma the Americans have over the Canadians, for
example, I was telling this one person how proud I was
that my oldest daughter had sang in a movie, the very first
thing that they said was is the movie Canadian or
American? I knew what they meant you have so many
talented Canadians that you'll never know about, cause
the ones that have some money are so busy trying to keep
what little they have and the talented ones that don't have
money are trying to get to the so called top where the
talented so called rich Canadians are which by American
standards are at the bottom.

(496)

11/10/93

Because of the Americans going up there and doing cheap
productions, almost all of the Canadians I know lost the
will to fight. Nobody up there wants to try anymore.
Everybody up there is just happy the way things are. For
example a pack of cigarettes is $7.00 a pack up there.
Nobody wants to do nothing about it, they would just
bury there head in the sand and just buy the cigarettes, It
seemed like everybody up there had just plain given up.
So I thought up an idea to get all the talented people in
one place and I would take my studio experience that I
learned in L.A., and put it with theirs. I would produce
some Canadian talent, cause there's a lot talent up there. I
said to my self nobody's thought of that idea but me,
Wow!!!! I said. I got there, It was Dec 23rd. 1992. Delores
picked me up from the airport. I went with Delores to get
me a winter coat cause I didn't have one. I got all ready to
go to the club, (that was the meeting place) I got there,
nobody showed up, the reason some people gave? It was
too cold outside. I'm the one should have been cold, I'm
from L.A.

(497)

11/10/93

It's not that I was hurt for myself, I was so hurt for them.
By them not showing up, showed me that the self esteem
they had for themselves, was zero. It had been beaten out
of them. If only they could see that I was only trying to
help. One guy who was so called Canadian successful
said to me, that talented musicians were a dime a dozen.
Maybe so but the talented ones that make it, I rather listen
to them then the untalented ones that do make it. I had a
love affair with that city and the people there, but after

going there all of those years, closing my eyes to everything that it was then that I realized one thing, you can never go back.

(498)   A BROKEN PROMISE
11/10/93

Like I reiterated in the book before, I met the landlord May 31, 1986, moved in to the second bedroom. He was auditioning woman, he got married a year later. He moved to Santa Monica Ca. I took over the house in 1987. About six months later I got sick then it got a little worst around 1991, all I was doing was throwing up from this stroke I was getting. I couldn't pay my rent, cause I couldn't work, I explained to the landlord what was happening, he said okay he understands, man was I sick, finally I got a stroke November 3, 1991 then another time Jan 1, 1992 as you can see I had a benefit Jan 30 1992. It was there in my wheelchair I saw my landlord he was there taking pictures of the benefit. I said to him that I was sorry that I was behind and my trustees would not pay my back rent. He said to me that's all right, you can take care of the back rent when you get on your feet. Then I said what a relief. I said to him that all I think about is the money I owe you. Once again he said to me don't worry about the back rent, you just hurry up and recover.

(499)
11/24/93

I can't tell you the load off my mind, I was so relieved. After the benefit, I went back to the hospital they released me March 16, 1992. The day I got out of the hospital the landlord started hassling me for the back rent. What he would say to me is why don't you get it from your friends

that did the benefit for you. Half of the people there, I
didn't have no idea they would even do some thing like
that for me. Graham Nash I hadn't seen in 15 years I
didn't even know were he lived. I played behind Michael
McDonald once in 1986, I went out to dinner with him
and the rest of the band. That's what it was like with the
rest of the people. Oh Jackson Browne, I saw him
recently. It was with him and Darreyl Hannah about 5
years ago you think he was surprised. Man I was
surprised as well, that kind of people showed up for my
benefit. Boy did he put pressure on me. I would tell my
trustees about that. They would tell me he couldn't evict
you. Oh yeah.

(500)   BROKEN PROMISE
11/24/93

So March of 1993. The sheriff came up to the door. They
gave me five a day notice. Just think I would get a phone
call to do a $15,000 commercial and I couldn't do it, I
would hang up the phone frustrated as all getup. The
landlord would use his key come into the house, start
crying to me about the back rent, I was so frustrated, I
would scream at him, the trustee's didn't understand.
Anyway, I had to leave the premises in five days, I left just
under half of my stuff there. I've never been evicted in
my life. I was so humiliated people that I thought was my
friend, wasn't there for me. Jimmy Roberts took me to a
motel. To the landlord, never break a promise. Due days,
its going to come back on you.

(501)

11/24/93

It was March 22, 1993, I was evicted. I had never been
evicted before in my life. The marshall came to the door,
gave me a five day notice. The trustee called me, he said
that the landlord sent the rent check back for that months
rent, that's the first time I had spoken to him in a while, he
said to me that what did I want to do with the money? I
told him that I had five days to move. I said being that I
had 5 days to move, could I take that money and send for
my girlfriend from Canada to help me to pack and get out
of here. He said he would discuss it with the rest of the
trustees and he would get back to me. I never heard from
him again. I started calling people to help me to pack,
cause I couldn't get around fast because of this stroke.
Everybody was busy. I called Cathy McBroom, she
helped me to pack, we packed what we could, we only
had 3 days. I called her the second day. The thought of
the cops coming up to the door and moving me out was
awful. We packed what we could in three days. What we
didn't pack we left. Jimmy Roberts and his lady friend

(502)

12/6/93

Tracy helped me to find a place to live, cause I had no
place to go. Thanks guy you see it took that for that to
happen for me to find out who's in your corner. I found
this place called the Tolucan Motel I checked in that place,
in the meantime, I had sent out some of the songs I had co-
written with various writers, man, I didn't hear back from
nobody. I mean I sent the songs to some big names in the
music industry names I won't mention, to reiterate I didn't
have here from nobody. I called a lot of people this one
girl said she would help me out with my phone bills, I
never heard from her again, this one famous drummer

turned me on to this big Beverly Hills lawyer to help me
with my ex suing me, I never heard from her. Nobody
but nobody helped me, I know hundreds of people, but
soon as I needed help nobody came to my rescue. In three
days my phone bill at the motel was $37.00. I couldn't get
from none of the people I knew. Finally not knowing
what else to do,

(503)

12/6/93

I put my face in my hands and said Lord please help me
out of this situation, now I wasn't a abjure person but I
didn't pray. The only time I ever said oh lord was when I
was having sex. Anyway I don't what made me say that,
but the next day I was talking to Delores, and she was
telling me how hard it is to raise two kids alone. She said
to me you know sometimes love is not enough. I said you
know there's a song there. I said as soon as I get out of
this situation, I am going to get one of the great lyricists to
write some lyrics about that. Then she said why wait,
why don't you do it. I said me? I do music I don't do
words. She said I know. She said why can't you do
words, she said you do the music to your songs why can't
you do the lyrics to your songs. Then I said to her that
I've written with such great lyricists like David Palmer,
Harriet Schock, Cathy Wakefield and Brenda Russell.
That they have spoiled me, I never had to write lyrics. She
said nobody's calling you back anyway why don't you try
and write some lyrics.

(504)

12/6/93

I wrote my first set of lyrics, poems or anthologys, I read it
to Delores over the phone, she loved it. Then I was
watching a TV show about the color of love. When
Delores called me the next night, I wrote an anthology
called the Color of Love. Delores liked that one too! I said
wow! I couldn't believe what I was doing. As of today I
have written over 1,700 anthologies, two books. I am a
lexicon person. I now have a vocabulary like you
wouldn't believe. It use to take me about two months to
read a book now it takes me two to three days to read a
book. I'm not bragging or nothing like that, I'm so
grateful to the Lord for opening up my brain, and for him
giving me the knowledge to do what I am doing. I'm
grateful to the Lord for taking all the anger out of my
heart, instead he instilled love and understanding, and a
wealth of dignity in my heart. When I asked him for help,
I didn't hear a voice or thunder and lightning or tables
and chairs moved. I got a peace within me like you
wouldn't believe.

(505)

12/6/93

It didn't matter no more whether people called me or not,
I no longer had to prove anything to any body anymore. I
knew within my self it was going to be alright one way or
the other. Being angry at somebody is oh so stupid. And
to think I use to be that way even though I don't have
millions, and I'm still at the motel, I know within my heart
that one way or another, everything's going to be all right.
I don't ask nobody for nothing I know for the first time in
my life what true love is. Thank you again for just plain
showing me where it's at. I not only wouldn't wish a
stroke on myself, but no one else, however this stroke is

the best thing that ever happen to me. It made me get it together quick, fast and in a hurry. That's why thanks to my girlfriend this book is called "A Stroke of Luck".

(506)

12/7/93

To reiterate, I'm not angry at no one. However when I went to see Dr. Sperber, he told me that I was angry with myself for being the way I use to be. Even though I've made a drastic change, I still have dreams about the past. Mind you all wasn't bad, but a lot of it was. A lot of people perceive me as this lunatic person when it came to the business of music. I was talking to Delores, and I was telling her I said you know I've changed, why can't other people who knew me see it. She said to me cause your relationship with people has been that of crazy person business wise, so now you're crying wolf. Then I said don't bother to explain just do what you have to do. If I were to call the people I know and tell them that I have changed they would probably say to me, oh yeah, I figure why bother. Just do it, people are going to talk anyway. Like Bonnie Raitt said in her song "Let's give them something to talk about". Once again God, thank you so much for this new life you've given me.

(507)

12/7/93

It was the morning of July 4, 1993, I was having a lazy morning, sort of feeling peaceful, when the phone rang it was Delores. She had called from Canada. She had called because she wanted a spell check on my poems, she also knew that on Sundays I go and eat at this Mexican restaurant called El Toritoes. They have a buffet there. I

eat and read on Sundays, that's the way that I relax. She
called, she corrected my spelling then she said to me you
know Smitty you should be in menza, I said what! Then I
said do you know what menza is? She said yes I know
what menza is, you should be in it. After she hung up the
phone, I laid there in bed blushing. Even though I was
going to the restaurant, I was so flattered, I didn't want to
move. Just then the phone rang it was Eric Mercury, I said
how you doing? He said fine. I then complemented him
on his success on the Michael Jordan ad, and the Coors
and the Cool Whip ads and Etc.

(508)

12/7/93

Even though we had not spoke about a year, I was glad to
hear from him. We were catching up on each other.
There was so many things I wanted to tell him, first of all I
was telling that being that myself and his sister were
diabetics, they had a cure for that. I was explaining to him
how they did it. He told me that was a stupid idea, that
nobody in his family would do nothing like that. Then
reiterated about him doing TV ads. He told me yeah you
could never do nothing like that, they get you to do some
pretty stupid stuff. I've been doing ads for TV since 1967.
Then I was telling him about the misunderstanding that I
was having with my ex-wife. He said I should eat crow
and call my lawyer, the one that was the trustee for my
benefit. In the mean time he kept telling me, yeah man
I've known you for 30 years, he said I know you inside
out. If he knows me so well, he should know me well
enough to know that I had and have too much respect for
the relationship trust I had for my ex lawyer to do
anything like that.

(509)

12/7/93

My ex lawyer and I had a great working relationship. I
got as close as your could get to a lawyer. I had my faults
he had his, but that never interfered with our business
relationship. Deep down inside one day this would
happen. I wouldn't lower or stoop that low to bother him.
What's done is done. I can't see nothing in this world
that's important to call him. I knew what he wanted me to
know about him, and very well he knew the old Smitty
through and through. We wasn't that close for him to
accept me as I am now. I could never expect him to
understand me. Who's got the time. He's to busy raising
his family and trying to survive. Though I told him that I
was going to write a book. He told me that I would never
pull it off the he said that I should be over at Eric
Johnson's house. He's having a 4th of July party. That I
should not be alone. If he knew me, I was having a
wonderful time that day by myself. That if I was to go
over to that party, it would bring out in me the worst.

(510)

12/7/93

Eric Mercury didn't have a clue where I was coming from.
He went on to tell me that I never looked outside my
problems I was too wrapped up in my own problems to
look at other peoples problems. I knew then that the
relationship was a dictate like the girl said, we were old
friends but not good friends. I called Dr. Sperber and
explained my situation with Eric Mercury. He already
knew, he knows everything about me already. He knows
more about me then Delores does. I ask him to please

write me a compendium about what Eric had said and the book in general. He said no, what we talk about in his office is personal besides that's what you're in therapy for cause you look to much at other peoples problems, and I don't want to get involved.

(510)

12/7/93

I asked Delores to write a compendium for me. She said Okay. She did. Man was she on the money. This what she wrote:

Self esteem, self respect, confidence and positive thoughts some people appear to have these attributes while others do not but in an attempt to fool those around them and sometimes to fool themselves put on a false portrayal to the world. Others want to have these feelings but they just aren't there. Smith and I talk on the phone every night and more that once our conversations have focused around these aspects of one's personality. Smith has often told me that he felt the only reason he over his lifetime has had so many friends and women were do to his talent, his musical ability to express himself. He states he is aware that he has used his talents to meet people and more specifically women. When we first talked about this I felt affronted for I was one of those many women. You must understand that Smith and I did not see one another for approximately 20 years. During those years I would reminisce about things in my past. I would tell people about Smith and you know one of the last things I would mention was the fact that he was a musician. No, what I would remember vividly was the size of his heart, his ability to truly listen, his honesty, the feeling that I had a big brother to answer my many questions about men, sex, being on my own in a big city, the respect he paid my friends,

the fact that my friends liked him, the very gentle
way he helped me understand prejudice for you see
I'm white and had never seen a black person until I
was 18. I regarded Smith as a very important person
in my life at a time that was naturally difficult. I did
not hold his hand, laugh and joke with him because
he was a musician. In fact I shied away from that
part of his life. I loved to go to a club and hear him
play and listen to him sing. I didn't love the music
scene. I was never a groupie.

Smith and I have talked about these issues and
these discussions have taken place since his stroke.
I feel that the stroke has been a positive thing in
William D. Smith's life. This near fatal life event has
caused him to ask questions and face realities about
himself both good and bad that he may never have
taken the time to do if not for the stroke. We have
talked about insecurity, his utter humiliation at
having his financial affairs exposed to individual that
he would not want to know. To have his affairs of
the heart exposed. In short to be out of control of
his life. Money, what to do with it and what it
represents has been a revelation. Recognizing that
people do not view money in the same way as he
does. He spent hours beating himself up after he
completed his bio and realized the amount of money
he had held in his hand over the years and how little
he had to show for it. As we talked about his past
one could see that a pattern had developed. Survival
Mode that was the name of the game. Smitty as a
youngster felt that two of his brothers were his
responsibility. His mother had her own demons to
battle and there never was a stable male role model
in Smith's life or another consistent male figure in
his mom's life to help her with the burden of raising
seven children. Smitty learnt that money related to
the size of the ache in his belly. He didn't learn the
adages that middle America grew up on, a penny
earned is a penny saved or save a little something for

344

a rainy day. On the contrary money never did burn a hole in his pocket. Basic survival was that money was for, "I will survive today and tomorrow will take care of itself...... something will come along. Early on in his life he learned that his ability to play keyboards was a way to survival and as the years moved along the financial rewards increased. There was no respect for the value of a dollar. When he had the money he spent every cent he made and lived by the belief that tomorrow would take care of itself. There was no sense of long time future, that was an advanced step in survival and there was no one in his formative years to be an example. In short as long as Smith had his health he could survive. He lost his health and as financial planning was not as acquired skill he found himself in a position where he was seriously ill with no health insurance of any kind to cover his heath care expenses, had very few material possessions which could be considered assets and no financial investments. What he did have was a tremendous amount of people who cared enough to put on a benefit for him. On the surface it looked like Smith was right once again "tomorrow took care of itself." Smitty's "friends" respected his talent, his humor, his kindness his ability to offer a shoulder to cry on but were very concerned about his ability to manage his financial affairs. The trust fund was set up the way it was with the best intentions in the world. This was a man who from the age of eight had virtually looked out for himself and all of a sudden his ability to care for himself was gone. Smith fiercely protected himself presenting an image to the world keeping people in their place never getting too close. He, when healthy could juggle all the various components of his life. Safely shielding away all his feelings of insecurity and inadequacy. If he kept people in their place they didn't need to know that he felt the only reason people had anything to do with him was because of his talent and in certain situations he doubted even that. He didn't stoke himself for his accomplishments, stopping cigarettes before it was in vogue to do so. Giving up chemicals (drugs and alcohol) after suffering a minor heart attack and his doctor saying to him .....No, the heart attack was not serious but it was a serious warning if you don't give up your addictions you will die before your time....... Smith took a lover's advice and went to see a therapist and stopped abusing chemicals, that was over ten years ago. Smith did not see these things as accomplishments instead he felt a generalized sense of failure. Self pity was not his style and he has continued with the therapist to work on his problems. Smith is a person I admire. I am a nurse by profession and I truly respect the determination and courage Smith demonstrated in planning and implementing his own rehabilitation. At no time did Smitty roll over in his bed face the wall and say or act as if he had given up.

He arrived home from the county hospital barely able to walk even with assistance or to communicate either by written or verbal word without a great deal of effort. Once again Smitty aggravated and caused frustration for the caring people around him. He has told me that he would lay in bed when he first came home and try to figure out what he could hold on to to get to the bathroom and then he would try it out. I can't count the number of times I saw Smitty fall, in the limited time I was with him, trying to accomplish the smallest of tasks in order to regain his independence and eventually control of his life. He set goals for himself every day. He has accomplished so many tasks I couldn't begin to mention them. I have heard him described as bull headed, stubborn, unrealistic and unappreciative. I don't agree I feel he was determined and focused. I believe he was overwhelmed at times at what lay ahead of him frustrated at his rate of recovery afraid

of what was to come. He has told me many times
from the bottom of his heart just how much he
appreciates what everybody has done for him. He
didn't always agree with what was done and perhaps
his comments that expressed this disagreement were
misinterpreted but as far as being ungrateful
nothing could be farther from the truth. He can't
believe the number of people that rallied around in
his time of need. Smith was forced to move from his
rented house as he could not make the rent and in
fact he owed back rent. Smith's view of this
situation differs from the majority. The owner of the
home in my opinion was a poor business man. He
allowed Smith to stay on far too long before he had
the stroke without paying his rent and was then
caught. For it seems he was not only Smith's
landlord but a friend and he couldn't see evicting
Smith when he was down and out and in very poor
health. The other factor to be considered was that
as long as the money from the benefit was there he
would receive his monthly rent. Smith can't
understand why he was evicted because he feels that
as soon as he gets back on his feet he would pay the
landlord his debt. In short that is what a friend
would do. For the rest of the world the landlord
should have evicted Smith a long time before
friendship or no friendship. It is a perfect example of
a different set of values. Smith is now settled in a
motel and from my perspective has gone though a
wide range of feelings regarding his current living
situation. Fear, initially, how am I going to manage.
Fear of the solitude. Frustration at finding himself
reduced to this situation peppered with
embarrassment. Anger at those around him for
allowing this to happen to him and yes to the God
above. This boiling pot of emotion resulted in a
variety of behaviors. Not always understood by
those who knew him. He seemed to withdraw did
not want people to know where he was, building a

protective wall. Devoting himself most necessarily to establishing a routine that would allow him to attend to the tasks of daily living. In discussions with Smith I was to learn that it was difficult to answer the question. "When are you going to play again?" The truth is he can't play at least not to the level that he once could and secondly, if he could he does not want to go back to doing sessions and playing behind people. He wants to explore his creative abilities and do his own thing. Presently playing is not an option that he can deal with. Smith has written many tunes but always had help with the lyrics. He is now writing lyrics, poems, limericks and his thoughts and feelings about things that have in some way touched his life. It is a new horizon.....a dream.....something to be explored and lived. Surely no person should be deprived of that opportunity. Smith is happy now, enjoying the solitude, enjoying the discovery of different parts of himself. Struggling with his past, searching for a way to improve himself and the world around him. For some who have listened to his ideas they may appear to be grandiose, to others the uttering of a man who has lost touch with the realities of the world around him. To still others the demonstration of courage. A person who has refused to wallow in self pity but instead to strive for a way to regain his dignity, to gain self respect, to feel true security, to acquire confidence in himself and to reach for self actualization. Are these not values that we hold close and is it not necessary to recognize that not all people will follow the same path and is it not important for individuals in today's civilization to allow our fellow persons the latitude to choose a different course within the broad boundary that they not cause harm to themselves, to others or to the environment around us?

(511)

11/24/93

Eric hung up the phone, for the first time since I came to that motel I felt depressed. I prayed for a better understanding and strength. For here is a man that I came up with as a young man, and over the years we had drifted apart. Man were we good friends, we were like Mutt and Jeff. Then July 28th 1993 he called again. I was very calm, I explained to him that we just didn't see eye to eye on timing, I told him that I didn't expect to agree with everything I said, but expected you to repeat my wishes. Then I said to him that I had a stroke and I have high blood pressures and I had one heart attack. Then I said that I don't and you don't have to accept me the way that I am now. Then I said I'll be 49 years old next month I'm no longer a young man no more. I couldn't handle beggaring no longer. I think that we should go our separate ways. The very last thing he said to me was to have a nice life. If he knew me so well, he should know that I'm having a great great life.

(512)

11/24/93

It really hurt me to say to Eric what I said. but it would hurt me more if I didn't say it. If I would have said that a long time ago, I would found a peace within me I know I must have changed to say what I said to him. I'm so happy now with this life that I have now. Like the son says take a deep breath pick yourself up and start all over again.

(513)   COMPREHEND

12/7/93

That night July 28, 1993, I was supposed to go to the
Hollywood Bowl to see Etta James, Robin Ford and Robert
Cray. Joe Sheu called me and told me about the concert. I
got excited for he knew that I use to play with Etta, and I
use to work with Robben, I said great you get the tickets,
and I'll pay for them. Then Joe said sure but why do you
want to buy tickets when you can get in and go backstage
for free. Then I said I didn't want to do that, I just wanted
to hear the music. When I or we go backstage the first
think they would want to know is when will you be ready
to play with them. That's not what I want to hear now. I
want to play music, but I don't want to play for nobody I
wait to play my own music. I've been playing other
peoples music for 33 years now. Its time to play my own
ideas. He couldn't understand, being that he was in
college taking a music coarse. He wanted to do what I
had been doing for 33 years. Please don't get me wrong,
that's nice work if you can get it.

(514)

12/7/93

I enjoyed working with those artists, that's why I've been
in therapy all these years. I felt as though I was hiding
behind some of those artists. I'm so glad that I had the
talent enough to play with them. I'm so honored to have
done that. Now I want to do what they've done. I don't
know if I can sustain myself like they did. All I can do is
try. Joe respected the way I felt, but didn't understand
me, being that he was in college to learn what I had
already knew. That's why I stay to myself and I don't
bother nobody from the past, cause they think that I'm
trying to be stand offish or something. All I'm trying to be

is the best that and can be like the song says, " I got to be me".

(515)   THE CREW
12/7/93

People use to come up to me and ask me hey man, what's the best, who's the worst who's the greatest, who's the this. So this is what I think: The most off beat person I've ever met, Bob Dylan. The funniest person I've ever met, Bette Midler. The most perceptive person I've ever met, Linda Ronstadt. The greatest musical experience I've ever had working with somebody, Steve Kennedy. The sickest person I've met, Bill Elkins. The strangest person I've ever met, David Lindley. The most punctual person I've ever met, Rita Coolidge. The greatest as a young man that could spot something, Graham Nash. The most intelligent person I've ever met was Zanwil Sperber.

(515)   THE MUSIC BUSINESS
12/7/93

I'm talking a lot about the business of music. However being a side man in the music business is a 24 hour job. Most people think that a sideman makes a lot of money. For example, the guy that was making copies of my poems for me, I said to him, I did the tonight show with Michelle Schock how much do you think I made. He said I don't know, I said take a guess. Then he said a million dollars, I said a million dollars! I said I made $295 for this show. He looked at me like I was a lunatic.

(516)   THE BENEFIT
12/7/93

Being that there was so much controversy about the benefit, that any time I would mention it to people and people would say to me, oh they were trying to help you. I agree they were trying to help, but you don't do that by trying to strip a person of their dignity. Anyway here's a review of people or friends giving their friend a benefit for them and here's how they did it.

Los Angeles Times
February 1, 1992

POP MUSIC REVIEW

Lending a
Helping Hand
to a Friend

By STEVE HOCHMAN
SPECIAL TO THE TIMES

We're quite used to seeing Jackson Browne, Bonnie
Raitt and Graham Nash performing in support of some political
or environmental cause. So though the circumstances were
unfortunate, it was a nice twist to see them Thursday at the
Palace singing to benefit an ailing friend, keyboardist/songwriter
William (Smitty) Smith, who is recovering from a stroke he
suffered on New Year's Day. A friend in need just seems to be
a better inspiration than an issue.

As a musician, Smith, 47, is known both for his
conviviality and his command of rock, soul and gospel styles,
and has long been a favorite musical partner of such notables as
Bob Dylan, Nash, Ry Cooder and David Lindley. As a
songwriter he's known for smooth gospel-rooted soul. Both
facets were represented Thursday, the former in casual acoustic
sets by Lindley, Cooder, Browne and Nash, the latter by more
formal turns by pop-soul stalwarts Boz Scaggs, Brenda Russell
and Michael McDonald.

Thoughout the show there was a warm feeling of family
– literally in such moments as Cooder's 13 year-old son Joachim
joining his dad on percussion in the early show's opening set
and Lindley's 21 year-old daughter Roseanne impressively
belting a blues number with her dad in the second show.
Unscheduled quest Raitt joined Browne for two gorgeous songs
in the second show.

The warmth extended to the soul portions as well. In a
particularly fitting case of what goes around comes around,

drummer Dallas Taylor, himself the honoree of a concert two years ago after he had a liver transplant, backed singer Bonnie Sheridan (formerly Bramlett) on a show stopping blues.

Scaggs (looking fit and trim and comeback ready), Russell and McDonald all turned in powerful short sets of their own, backed effectively by a versatile crew, including Toto guitarist Steve Lukather and noted drummers Jeff Porcaro and Jim Keltner.

The only slightly sour note was the absence of Dylan who, though unavailable for this date, had been included in some press releases and advertisments due to a miscommunication.

But that hardly dampened the spirit of the event, which hit it's peak at the end of the first show when Smith was brought on stage in a wheelchair as singer Phil Perry raised the roof with a gospel – fired version of "I Need You", a song Smith co-wrote. Choked with emotion, Smith waved his hand across the musician – strewn stage and said simply, "My friends – give them a hand."

(517)   ACKNOWLEDGMENT
12/7/93

To Eric Mercury, Eric Johnson, David Clayton Thomas, Priscilla Coolidge, Dianne Brooks, Willie and Carol Ornelas. It was nice to have worked, met and know all of you. I will remember you fondly. You played a very important part in my life, and to the trustees that gave the benefit for me. Thank you so much for if it wasn't for you guys I would have been sitting under a freeway or walking the streets being a person of mendicity. To each and everyone of you, I'll not ever forget the part you played in my life. I would like to close my writing by saying this, Walt Disney said, "If you can dream it, you can do it".

(518)   ACKNOWLEDGMENTS
12/7/93

Wendy Spergal, Dave Thompson, Phil Chen, Jeff Peterson, Alexandria Hatans, Linda De la Rosa, Jay Stein, Doug Richardson, Vance Dorsey, the late Ronnie Parks, Cathie Oliver, Eddie Wynrick, Brenda Russell, Jim Heineman, Ken Fritz, Ricky Rouse, Erin Malone, Valerie Johnson, Jerry Moss, Bill & Shiloh Elkins, Willie Leopold, Willie Weeks, John "T" Davis, Irvin Hunt, Carloina Reyes, Lester Williams, Jimmy Roberts, Glenn McDonald, Bobby King, Sharon "Shay" Stewart, Doug Riley, Roy Kenner, Johnny Scott, Randy Barnes, Soroya Lamastra, Evelyn Arong, Steve Kennedy, Sean Bullock, Dee Dee Tucker, Rick Wilson, Chris Waller, Diana Luxem, Ronnie Fowler, Reggie Smith, Sammy Smith, Sandra Adams, Cheryl Taylor, Barbara Dudley, Thelma Jones, and last but not least, the girl that this book is dedicated to, Delores Apps.

Some of the people that I worked with when I did the Brenda Russell albums

Dave Swanson	keyboards & BG vocals
Bill Sharpe	bass
Donald Griffin	guitar
James Harrah	guitar
Alvin Bennett	drums
Rock Deadrick	drums
Larry Williams	keyboard
Diane Brooks	BG vocals
Rita Coolidge	BG vocals
Mary Wilson	BG vocals
Maxanne Lewis	BG vocals
Andre' Fischer	Producer
Patsy Powell	BG vocals
William Smith	keboards & BG vocals

I worked with the world's greatest rythum section when I worked with Jimmy Weatherspoon

Bernard Purdy	drums
Cornell Dupree	guitar
the late Richard Tee	keyboard
Chuck Rainey	bass
William Smith	keyboard

People I worked with when I worked with Jimmy Soul

Herbert Rogers	lead guitar
Sonny Boy Rogers	rythm guitar
Frank Wilson	drums
William Smith	piano
George Perkins	club owner

People I worked with when I worked with Eric Mercury

Ron Selico	drums
Melvin Wonder	guitar
William Smith	keys
Doug Richardson	sax
Keith Olsen	engineer

People I worked with when I worked with The Soul Seachers

Jackie Gabriel	singer
Dianne Brooks	singer
Eric Mercury	singer
James Clark	guitar
Bruce Yates	guitar
Terry Logan	guitar
Glenn McDonald	sax
Steve Kennedy	sax
Eric"Mouse"Johnson	drums
Matie Gavin	singer
William Smith	organ
Soda Pop	guitar

People I worked with when I worked with Donnie Troiano

Pre Cash John	bass
Willie Weeks	bass
Roy Kenner	vocals
Venette Gloud	bg vocals
Shawn Jackson	bg vocals
Carman Twillie	bg vocals
Cathie Collier	bg vocals
Penti(Whitey)Glen	
Kenneth(Spider Webb)Rice	
Kieth Olsen	engineer
David Foster	keyboards
Eric"Mouse"Johnson	drums
The Late Huey Sullivan	keys
William Smith	keyboards, bg vocals

People I worked with when I was with
David Clayton Thomas

Chuck Rainy	bass
Willie Weeks	bass
Paul Stallworth	bass
Kenny Marco	guitar
Danny Kortchmar	guitar
Donnie Trioano	guitar
Pre Cash John	bass
Penti(Whitey)Glen	bass
Tessie Cohen	percussion
Kenneth(Spider Webb)Rice	
Trevor Lawence	sax, arranger, producer
Joel Sill	producer
The Late Gabrial Meckler	producer
Mike Post	producer

David Palmer, thanks so much for letting me create with you, oh, and thanks so much for making it so comfortable for me to create with you. You're first class all the way.

William Smith	keyboards, co-writer, bg vocals,
Chaka Kahn	lead vocals on the song David and I wrote "Dreamin' as One"
Carl Osborne	lawyer
Jay Stien	lawyer
Dick Allen	agent
Gail Bracker	secretary
Guttman & Pam	public relations
Chris Houston	engineer
Larry Dorr	manager
Micheal Weinstein	harmonica

People I worked with when I worked with Bill Wyman (of The Rolling Stones)

Bill Wyman	bass
Dallas Taylor	drums
Danny Kortchmar	guitar
William Smith	keyboards

People I worked with when I worked with Gary U.S. Bonds

Frank Wilson	drums
Sonny Boy Rogers	rythm guitar
Herbert Rogers	lead guitar
William Smith	piano

People I worked with when I worked with Jerry (Swampdog) Williams

Earl Long	drums
Sonny Boy Rogers	rythm guitar
Herbert Rogers	lead guitar
Jerry (Swampdog) Williams	lead vocals
William Smith	piano

People I worked with when I worked with the great James Ingram

Willie Ornelas	drums
Buzzy Fieten	guitar
Jimmy Haslip	bass
William Smith	piano

People I worked with when I recorded with Rod Stewart

The Late Al Jackson	drums
Duck Dunn	bass
Steve Cropper	guitar
Mike Landau	guitar
Andy Taylor	guitar
Tony Thompson	drums
Bob Glaub	bass
Chas Sanford	producer
William Smith	organ

People I worked with when I was with Richie Heavens

Herman Ernest	drums
Tony Brussord	bass
Darryl Johnson	guitar
William Smith	keyboards, bg vocals
David Kershenbaum	producer
Chris Bond	producer

People I worked with when I was playing with Bob Dylan

Jim Keltner	drums
Tim Drummond	bass
Fred Tackett	guitar
Carol Dennis	bg vocals
Madlyn Quebec	bg vocals
Clydie King	bg vocals
Regina Mcreay	bg vocals
Brenda Russell	bg vocals
Eric Mercury	bg vocals
Chuck Plotkins	producer
Bob Myers	road manager
Don Williams	security
Ron Woods	guitar
Ringo Starr	drums
Jerry Wientrub	manager
William Smith	keyboards, vocals

People I worked with when I was with Ry Cooder

Chuck Rainy	bass
Chris Ethridge	bass
Herman Johnson	bg vocals
Pico Payne	bg vocals
Bobby King	bg vocals
Willie Green	bg vocals
Jim Dickerson	piano
John Hyatt	guitar
Ian Wallace	drums
George (Baboo) Piarre	percussion
Chris Rankin	guitar tech
Jim Keltner	drums
Tim Drummond	bass
Paul Weston	bass
Lee Hirshburg	enginner
Paul Brown	engineer
William Smith	keyboards, bg vocals
David Lindly	guitar
Chaka Kahn	lead vocals

People I worked with when I was with David Lindly

David Wells   sound engineer

Sadaa Ki Sugil   guitar tech

Doug Sturgis   road manager

Paul Irwin   concession stand

Reggie McBride   bass

Jorge Calderone   bass, bg vocals

Ian Wallace   drums

Walfredo Reyes   drums

Bernie Larsen   guitar, bg vocals, keyboards

William Smith   keyboard, bg vocals

Ed Cherny   engineer

Jackson Browne   producer

Linda Ronstadt   producer

Val Garay   engineer

The Late Roger Bethelmy   drums

Ray Woodbury   guitar, bg vocals, tour manager

Rock Deadriek   drums

Roseanne Lindly   vocals

Harry Dean Stanton   lead vocals

Jim Napier   recording engineer

Ross Hogarth   road sound engineer

George (Baboo) Piarre   percussion

People I worked with when I was with Nell Carter

Betsy Fels	secretary
D'Vaugh Pershing	conductor, piano
Willam Smith	organ, DX7
Dave Collins	road manager
Kimberly Evens	bg vocals
Siobhan O'Carroll	bg vocals
Denise Swanson	bg vocals
Reggie McBride	bass
Bob Parr	bass
Walfredo Reyes	drums
Mitchito Sanchez	percussion
Carl Verheyen	guitar

Reggie, thanks for getting me the gig.

People I worked with when I was playing with Robben Ford

Tom Brechtlein	drums
Roscoe Beck	bass
Vince Denim	sax
William Smith	organ, DX7
Robben Ford	guitar
Micheal McDonald	lead vocals

These are some of the people I worked with when I was with Etta James off and on from 1972 to 1986

Chuck Rainy	bass
Freddy Breckmier	bass
Reggie McBride	bass
Buzzy Fieten	guitar
Leo Nocentelliguitar	
Brian Wray	guitar
Larry Carlton	guitar
Greg Thompson	drums
Kenneth (Spider Webb) Rice	
Jimmy Roberts	sax
Marty Grebb	sax
Bobby Keys	sax
Trevor Lawence	sax, arranger, producer
Steve Madio	trumpet
The Late Gabrial Meckler	producer
Val Garay	engineer
Andre Fischer	drums
Donto James	drums
Phil Kaufman	road manager
William Smith	piano, DX7, bg vocals

People I worked with when I was with Chuck Berry

Willie Ornelas	drums
Jim Horn	sax
Richie Zito	guitar
Eric"Mouse"Johnson	drums
Jim Marsalis	bass
Ingram Berry	vocals
Tina Turner	vocals
Ian Wallace	drums
William Smith	piano

When I worked on Neal Sadaka's record "Laughter in the Rain" I worked with people like;

Danny Kortchmar	guitar
Russ Kunkel	drums
Lee Sklar	bass
Jim Horn	sax
Brenda Russell	bg vocals
Abigail Hyness	bg vocals
Brian Russel	bg vocals
William Smith	bg vocals, organ
Robert Appere	producer

People I worked with when I was with
Jackie DeShannon

Joel Obrien	drums
Collin Lameron	bass
William Smith	organ
Randy Edelman	piano
Tessie Cohen	percussion
Randy Myers	writer
Sam Russell	producer on "Put a little love in your heart"
Irving Hunt	producer on "Put a little love in your heart"
Steve Ferguson	guitar on "Put a little love in your heart"
Ron Silco	drums on "Put a little love in your heart"

People I worked with when I was with Mike Finnegen

Bob Gluab	bass
Reggie McBride	bass
Rick Jagger	drums
William Smith	keyboards, bg vocals
Marty Grebb	sax, bg vocals
Tommy Yuill	road manager
Kenny Wiess	TV show producer
Danny Kortchmar	guitar

When I had my 8 track home recording studio, these are some of the people that worked and visited with me;

Chuck Rainy	bass
Robert Popwell	bass
Reggie McBride	bass
Paul Stallworth	bass
Kenny Lewis	bass
William Smith	bass
Willie Ornelas	drums
Mike Baird	drums
The Late Roger Bethelmy	drums
The Late Jeff Pocaro	drums
James Gadson	drums
William Smith	drums
David Piach	fender rhodes
William Smith	keyboards
Venetta Fields	bg vocals
Carman Twillie	bg vocals
Leon Ware	bg vocals
David Palmerantz	bg vocals
Richie Zito	guitar
William Smith	bg vocals, lead vocals
Rick Wilson	engineer
Jerry Moss	visitor
Robert Appere	visitor
Jim Horn	sax, flute
Jimmy Roberts	sax
Jim Keltner	drums

Larry Carlton	guitar
Steve Lukather	guitar
Greg Poree	guitar

When I sold my 8 track home studio to Eric "Mouse" Johnson these are some of the people I worked with;

Paulette Brown	bg vocals
Teresa James	bg vocals
Bobby King	bg vocals
Carl Graves	bg vocals
Donny Gerrard	bg vocals
Arnold Mcollough	bg vocals
Laura Satterfield	lead vocals
Priscilla Coolidge	lead vocals
Phillis Brown	lead vocals
Loreli McBroom	lead vocals
Laura McBroom	lead vocals
Bernie Larsen	guitar
Jerome Lopez	bg vocals
Lenny Castro	percussion
Walfredo Reyes	percussion
B.J. Cooke	lead vocals
William Smith	keyboards, bg vocals, lead vocals
Rick Wilson	engineer
Eric"Mouse"Johnson	engineer
Carl Verheyen	guitar
Danny Wiess	guitar
Willie Ornelas	drums

Reggie McBride	bass
Larry Wiess	visitor
Cathy McBroom	visitor
Cathie Oliver	visitor
Cathy Wakefield	visitor

Wow! Do I know some great people or what!

Now, upon reading this book, you would think that I was a born again Christian, a Jesus freak, or I have found God. On the contrary, I didn't know God was lost. The only thing that I ever thought about that it took a higher power to create the sun, moon, stars, clouds, water, the earth, humans, animals. Some people believe that being is God. I also believe that this being too is God. However most people show their gratitude by practicing organized religion. I see those preachers on T.V., they remind me of used car salesman. Me, I believe that if you get on your knees and ask god for what you want, (providing that you believe in him) it will happen. Presto! It happened. I asked Him for peace of mind. Even though I had a good time living the life I was living, I paid a price for that. I've not seen my kids in years. I've grand kids I've never seen. My youngest daughter told me that she hoped that I would burn in hell. Now the only thing that can make me deal with that is having this peace of mind that God has bestowed on me. Also I read the bible, man, what brilliant people. God, thank you for this new life.

Acknowledgments

No wonder my phone bill was so expensive every month.
My brain hurts, I can't remember anymore names. I've
been doing names for a year and a half. If I didn't
mention your name, I'm sorry. Just remember what Bill
Cosby said, I don't know the formula for success, but I do
know the formula for failure, that's trying to satisfy
everybody.

Smitty

Acknowledgments

If you're wondering why I'm thanking so many people?
Cause over time I've seen hundreds of big time celebrities
write their autobiography's, not once my name was
mentioned. Please don't get me wrong, at no time was I
looking for fame, cause my name's been all over the
media. It's just that I spent 25 years contributing off and
on to their music. You think they would say, thanks dog.
Then I said to myself if I ever wrote a book, I'm going to
try to mention everybody that played an important part in
my life. Well (I'll try to anyway) for example Miss
Martha, (can't remember her last name) from 14 to 19 I
would go to her apartment in the same building in the
projects where I lived and eat her home made rolls. Man
they were good. I looked forward to that every Sunday.
She treated me like family. To Shirley her daughter,
Barbara her granddaughter, thanks so much for being nice
to me. Okay, here goes.

NAMES THAT I DIDN'T MENTION

If I would write about some of these people, the book would be about as big as three dictionaries:

Kenny Cleveland	crony
Ronnie Cleveland	crony
Eddie Beaty	crony
Tyler Groson	crony
Dave Autist	Chiropractor
Brandy	acquaintance
Aubray Kelly	crony
Jay Troutman	crony
The late Arlene Troutman	acquaintance
Bobby & Bill Blackburn	Music Colleagues
Guido Basso	Music Colleague
Jr. Kelgo	crony
Billy Boy	crony
Milley Jackson	mentor
Jackie Richardson	Music Colleague
Ray Kenner	Music Colleague
Ann Murray	Music Colleague
Kevin McKenzie	Music Colleague
Sherry McKenzie	Music Colleague
Precash John	Music Colleague
Moe Koffman	Music Colleague

TORONTO

Mister & Miss Weber	Colleague
Dianne Penny	Colleague
B.J. Reed	Music Colleague

Terry Logan	Music Colleague
Sharon Evin	Colleague
Sascha Evin	Colleague
Sarah Evin	Colleague
Jim Henniman	Music Colleague
Erin Henniman	Music Colleague
George Oliver	Music Colleague
Jackie Gabriel	Music Colleague
June Gabriel	Music Colleague
Bob Ashston	Colleague
John Anderson	Music Colleague
Karen Kennedy	Colleague
Doc Fingers	Music Colleague
Larry Green	Colleague
Ashew Horowitz	Music Colleague
Bob Mitchell	Colleague
Donna McDonald	Colleague
Carol Knox	Colleague
A. Haley	Nudist Colleague
Earl Seymour	Music Colleague
Wayne St. John	Music Colleague
Lenny Soloman	Music Colleague

Misc.

Mark Ibobsky	San Francisco Colleague
David Thompson	Riverside CA Colleague
Todd Wagner	Park City UT Colleague
Danny Weiss	LA Music Colleague
Pat Vegas	LA Music Colleague
Roberto	Vally LA Music Colleague
Tony Warren	LA Music Colleague

Joe Wheeler   Vegas Music Colleague
Willie Wheaton   LA Music Colleague
Raphael Washington   San Francisco
                         Music Colleague
Marty T Bone Wehner   San Francisco
                         Music Colleague
Penny Belfied   LA Music Colleague
Kimberly Evans   LA Music Colleague
Siobham O'Carroll   LA Music Colleague
Dave Callens   LA Colleague
Mitchito Sanchez   LA Music Colleague
John Mucei   LA Colleague
John Aerias   LA Colleague
Joel Bennett   LA Colleague
Scott Bradman   LA Music Colleague
Tom & Molly Broder   Minn.   Colleague
Kenny Arnoff   Indiana Music Colleague
Steve & Franny Ackmann   LA Colleague
Walter Brecker   Hawaii Music Colleague
Elaine Blackwell   Oakland CA Colleague
Nadine Bagnarol   Redwood City CA Colleague
Deabra Daniels   LA Colleague
George Bohanon   A Music Colleague
Ruth Chawssal   Dewpoint CA Colleague
Eric Davis   Atlanta GA Cousin
Diane Drolet   Sherbrook Quebec Colleague
Paulino DeCosta   LA Music Colleague
Jamie Cohen   LA Colleague
Deborah Evans   LA Colleague
Jim Fielder   LA Music Colleague

Morris Fink	LA My Dentist
Steve Ferguson	LA Music Colleague
Brenda Lee Eager	LA Music Colleague
Groce Eisenstein	LA Colleague
Tune Hamada	Las Vegas Colleague
Brian & Robbin Elios	Redway CA Colleague
Terry Garthwaite	San Garonimo CA Music Colleague
Ascher & Alen Gellman	Garberville CA Colleagues
Terry Nusyna Gordon	Toronto Ont. Colleague
Sam Harris	LA Music Colleague
Paulette Hawkins	LA Colleague
Rick Hannah	LA Music Colleague
Jeff Inber	LA Colleague
Art McNow	LA Colleague
Chico Jackson	LA Colleague
Sill Words	LA Colleague
Rick James	Buffalo Music Colleague
Marlene Berry	Toronto Colleague
Marilyn Schneeh	Toronto Colleague
Randy Secord	Toronto Colleague
Shawn Wilson	Toronto Colleague
Terry Theaton	Toronto Colleague
Leo James	Toronto Colleague
Hang Out	Toronto Crony
Rosie Evans	Toronto Crony
Dianne Green	Toronto Crony
Jack Shaw	Toronto Crony
Clarence Campbell	Crony

Rocky   Toronto Crony

Vance Dorcey Toronto Crony

Larry Dukane   Vancouver Crony

Sue Conifat   Vancouver Crony

Nelson Simon Montreal Music Colleague

Clayton Johnson   Toronto Music Colleague

Leonard Johnson   Toronto Colleague

Howie Matthews   Toronto Colleague

Salomi Bay   Toronto Music Colleague

Kalvin Kennedy   Toronto Colleague

Debbie Ingram   Toronto Colleague

James "Jamo" Jameson   L.A. Colleague

Marcy Levy   LA Music Colleague

Mike Joseph   LA Music Colleague

Kendal Lutz   Vancouver Colleague

Tammi Klammer   Boulder Creek CA Colleague

Tex Joseph   LA Music Colleague

David Kemper   LA Music Colleague

Pat Lucas   LA Business Colleague

Robbie King   Vancouver Music Colleague

Craig Karp   Nashville Music Colleague

Kip Krones   St. Albuns Herts England Colleague

Alex Kazanegras   LA Colleague

Tim McCavlley   Toronto Colleague

Robert Kraft   LA Colleague

David Kessner   San Francisco Music Colleague

Pamela B. Landern   New Orleans Colleague

Bobby Martin   LA Music Colleague

Joe Medwick   Sacramento CA Colleague

Peter McCulloch   Toronto Colleague

Molly Maniquis	LA Colleague
Peter Newman	LA Colleague
Leslie Morris	LA Colleague
Michelle Marx	LA Colleague
Donald Miller	LA Colleague
Lee Morin	Vancouver Colleague
Karen Murphy	LA Colleague
Danny McBride	Toronto Colleague
Peter McGraw	Toronto Colleague
Brad Mitchell	Willowdale Ont. Canada
Jack Price	LA Music Colleague
Gene Page	LA Music Colleague
Dan Navarro	LA Colleague
Greg Poree	LA Music Colleague
Ty Purr	LA Music Colleague
David Pomerantz	LA Music Colleague
Dianne Quander	LA Music Colleague
Bill Quatman	LA Music Colleague
Larry Rolando	Austin TX Music Colleague
Sponer Oldham	LA Music Colleague
Ray O'Hara	Redondo Beach CA Music Colleague
Dean & Carol Parks	LA Music Colleague
Bob Parr	LA Music Colleague
Mary Griffin Reagen	Portsmouth VA Colleague
Lara Steinburg	LA Colleague
Louis Pugliese	LA Music Colleague
Richard Reicheg	LA Music Colleague
Tony Ray	Carlsbad CA Colleague
Howard Rosen	Eureka CA Colleague

Meribeth Soleman	Toronto Colleague
Mickey Eube	Toronto Colleague
Katey Sagel	LA Colleague
Al Schlesinger	LA Colleague
Sigrid Ravel	Carmichael CA Colleague
Paul Shiki	LA Colleague
Carlos Santana	San Francisco Colleague
Ivy Skoff	LA Colleague
Lester Sill	LA Colleague
Silvia St. James	LA Colleague
Peggy Sanwig	LA Music Colleague
Chas Sanford	LA Music Colleague
Bruce Robb	LA Music Colleague
Lucille Seals	Norfolk VA Colleague
Steve Siegfried	Hawaii Colleague
Diane Steinberg	LA Music Colleague
Larry Satterfield	LA Music Colleague
Roger Safien	Petrolia CA Colleague
Paul & Suzane Stallworth	Petrolia CA Colleague
Sadaaki Sugii	San Luis Obispo Colleague
Doug Sturgis	Claremont CA Colleague
Robert Shipley	LA Music Colleague
Lester Williams	Los Angeles
Ronald Willams	Los Angeles
Jenetta Johnson	Los Angeles
Simon Quarterbaum	New Jersey
Eugene Dudley	New York
Clyde Bates	Los Angeles

(there are 46 more pages of names Smitty wrote down
that still need to be typed)

www.ingramcontent.com/pod-product-compliance
Lightning Source LLC
Chambersburg PA
CBHW030936150426
42812CB00064B/2930/J